Becoming a Professional Leader

Edited by

Johanna K. Lemlech

SCHOLASTIC
LEADERSHIP
POLICY
RESEARCH™

New York • Toronto • London • Auckland • Sydney

This text is dedicated to the memory of my aunt,
Jennie Stamell, who inspired me to become a teacher
and who was named an outstanding middle-school
teacher in the public schools of Detroit, Michigan.

Copyright © 1995 by Scholastic Inc.

No part of this publication may be reproduced in whole or in
part, or stored in a retrieval system, or transmitted in any form
or by any means, electronic, mechanical, photocopy, recording
or otherwise, without permission of the publisher. For
information regarding permission, write to Scholastic Inc.,
555 Broadway, New York, NY 10012

ISBN 0-590-49334-5

12   11   10   9   8   7   6   5   4   3   2   1   5/9

Printed in the U.S.A.

Library of Congress Cataloging-in-Publication Data
Becoming a professional leader/
   edited by Johanna K. Lemlech.
         p.   cm. — (Scholastic leadership policy research)
   Includes bibliographical references and index.
   ISBN 0-590-49334-5
   1. School supervision.   2. Educational leadership.   3. Teacher—
principal relationships.   4. Teachers—In-service training.
5. School improvement programs.   I. Lemlech, Johanna Kasin.
II. Series.
LB2806.4T43   1995
371.1′00973—dc20
                                                        94-29653
                                                          CIP

Acknowledgments

I am indebted to the many reviewers who provided substantive feedback and suggestions for refining the manuscript. I would like to thank Margo Pensavalle for her careful reading of the chapters in this text. I am most grateful to Lloyd Chilton for his encouragement and support.

Contents

THE ROAD TO PROFESSIONALISM   1

Introduction   3
Johanna K. Lemlech

CHAPTER 1
Leadership and Professionalism   7
Johanna K. Lemlech

CHAPTER 2
Issues Affecting Leadership and Professionalism   34
Johanna K. Lemlech

CHAPTER 3
Putting It Together: A Constructivist Perspective on
    School Leadership   52
Peter Hodges

CHAPTER 4
Taking the Lead from Teachers: Seeking a New Model of
    Staff Development   76
Mitzi Lewison

MEANS TO ACTUALIZE PROFESSIONAL ROLES   115

CHAPTER 5
Teacher Research   117
Laurie MacGillivray

CHAPTER 6
The Professional Teacher in a School-University Partnership   141
Hillary S. Hertzog

CHAPTER 7

The Staff Development Course Leader: A New Professional Role
   for the Classroom Teacher   172
   Scott M. Mandel

CHAPTER 8

Building New Professional Roles   195
   Johanna K. Lemlech

Appendix   221

About the Authors   227

Author Index   229

Subject Index   232

The Road to Professionalism

Introduction

JOHANNA K. LEMLECH

This book is about *teacher-leaders* who work in schools, universities, district and county offices, and other educational institutions and who serve as consultants, mentors, principals, project leaders, and teacher educators. The book is written by individuals who believe strongly in the professionalization of teaching. The professional model of teaching emphasizes the role of teachers as informed, responsible decision makers, grounded in the intellectual knowledge of teaching, who interact with colleagues ethically and respectfully.

Each author draws upon his or her own work experience as project director, classroom teacher, school administrator, staff development leader, researcher, and teacher educator to dramatize the professional behaviors of teacher leaders. The examples provided are based on our real-life work roles. The characters in the stories are fictitious, but the leadership tasks, role conceptualizations, and professional issues are candid, factual, and represent school and university cultures.

In Chapter 1 I provide a historical background of the societal issues and forces that have inhibited teacher leadership and examine contemporary concepts of how to develop teacher leadership and professionalism. Midway through the chapter is a case study of a young teacher who begins her career scared and uncertain about the appropriateness of her choice of occupation. As she begins to study teaching earnestly, she becomes reflective about her experiences. The process of reflection, which includes *mulling* and *pondering* the "what," "how," and "purpose" of teaching, is also linked to participation in collegial relationships and professionalism, as is shown using examples from both preservice teacher education and experienced educators.

In Chapter 2 I identify current issues affecting both school improvement and teacher leadership. Constraints include bureaucratic, hierarchical decision making, rigid schedules and time limitations, and the problem of teacher evaluation and professional accountability. The chapter concludes with suggestions for changing habits and leadership styles to improve school culture and develop a learning community.

Peter Hodges, in Chapter 3, provides a principal's perspective of school leadership. He discusses collaboration, collective action, and community building. He emphasizes the need for a shared commitment to school improvement goals and how these can be pursued in a climate that encourages disclosure and the acknowledgment of imperfection in a community of trust and mutual support. Hodges points out that schools are not creating products with unitary functions but, instead, are in the complicated business of working in the social realm and developing multifaceted individuals through complex learning processes. School improvement models, he says, are constructed through people and their imaginations, creativity, and commitment; rather than isolated systems, institutions must be communities and focus on persons.

In Chapter 4 Mitzi Lewison explores the changes that took place at an elementary school as a result of implementing a Collegial Study Group model of professional development. Participation in the project was voluntary and the teachers decided on the topics for each monthly study group session. Issues discussed in the chapter include the advantages of combining professional reading and study group sessions, the role of the principal in an informal staff development program, and the changes that took place at the school that spread beyond the teachers involved in the project.

Laurie MacGillivray, in Chapter 5, defines teacher research and then describes various ways to go about collecting data, including interviews and questionnaires, samples of children's written products and daily work, anecdotal records from observations, informal assessments, and journals. Addressing the different ways to go about teacher research, such as interpretive studies, she examines the hurdles to such research and to its dissemination and makes suggestions about how to overcome them. Stressed throughout the chapter are the importance of professional interactions as well as the positive impact on teachers who choose to conduct their own studies.

In Chapter 6, Hillary S. Hertzog, a teacher educator, examines the role of teachers in school-university partnerships. Her own experience working as the university liaison for a professional development school enriches her examples and helps us to understand the roles and responsibilities of master teachers working with preservice teachers. Dr. Hertzog discusses the needs of the professional teacher and the emerging opportunities for leadership in professional development schools.

In Chapter 7, Scott M. Mandel, a middle-school teacher and frequent in-service leader, expresses what teachers want and expect in staff development classes. He discusses the teacher's need to have classes conducted in a professional mode with attention to adult content and appropriate methodology. He emphasizes that classes focused on the implementation of new content and methodology must provide opportunity for teachers to discuss adaptation issues, problems, and options.

In Chapter 8 I provide what is intended as an upbeat conclusion to the book by identifying the means to build new professional roles. Some of the strategies include cross-role teams, educational networks, collegial relations, action teams, peer coaching, a broadening of staff development, changing teacher and principal roles and relationships, and the implementation of a "flat" school organization. Believing that leadership and professionalism do not happen casually or by chance, the chapter describes the "steps" in new-teacher preparation to reshape the apprenticeship experience, link the university and clinical school experience, and describe what new teachers need to learn in their methods class. Included in this section is a learning-to-teach sequence of development juxtaposed with the feedback needed by the novice teacher. The chapter concludes with a discussion of how to help support first- and second-year teachers in their initial teaching experience and how the beginning teacher can contribute to experienced teachers in the school community.

1 Leadership and Professionalism

JOHANNA K. LEMLECH

In the closing years of the twentieth century, school- and university-based educators are striving to create a new reality by inventing new educational environments, experimenting with new instructional practices, and communicating new understandings. These individuals are teacher-leaders who think deeply about the work of teaching. The teacher-leader combines and applies knowledge of teaching with human relationship skills to make judgments about teaching, school-related problems, human resource needs, and collegial support. **Teacher-leaders are creative and reflective decision makers who thrive on sharing their work with others in order to gain different perspectives and ideas and improve their own and others' professional practice.** The *search* for ideas and applications, whether it is for classroom teaching or school and self-improvement, is what fuels and provides incentive and intellectual stimulation. However, most teacher-leaders have difficulty defining teacher leadership and tend to do it by characterizing their own work and relationships (Wasley, 1991).

LEADERSHIP ROLES

There are different forms of teacher leadership. Some teacher-leaders innovate pedagogically. Some work with students in creating and chang-

---

Chapter 1 HIGHLIGHTS

- Teacher-Leaders, Roles and Definition
- Historical Perspective of Teachers and Teaching
- Components of Professionalism
- Collaborative Teacher Relationships
- Collegial Behaviors
- Collegial Stage Development
- Cultivating Leadership and Professionalism

---

ing curriculum and classroom life. Others work with colleagues to improve teaching and the school and classroom milieu. While some teacher-leaders focus on teaching, others study school organization and collegial support systems. The creation of professional development schools offers another means for teachers to work together to change school culture, set professional standards, and assume role model responsibilities for new teachers.

Teacher-leaders may be classroom teachers, mentors, consultants, grade-level chairs, department chairs, supervisors, principals, and university educators. Teacher-leaders are not necessarily administrators of schools, programs, or school districts. Pajak (1993) in a discussion of the changing roles of educational leaders identifies four ways teacher-leaders can influence learning in schools:

1. Empowering self and others through cooperative work and dialogue.

2. Examining systemic problems in depth; looking at causes, not just symptoms.

3. Employing multiple perspectives (multifaceted knowledge) to study and solve problems.

4. Accepting responsibility to accomplish purposeful change.

Current interest in teacher leadership was fueled by the Carnegie Forum (1986) task force report *A Nation Prepared: Teachers for the 21st Century.* The report called for restructuring schools to create a professional environment for teachers and for developing leadership positions enabling teachers to engage in the redesign of schools and help colleagues build high standards for teaching and learning. The report recommended graduate preparation leading to a Master in Teaching degree.

Another significant influence was the report by the Holmes Group (1990), *Tomorrow's Schools*. This report recommended the creation of professional development schools that link university- and school-based educators. The design for these schools called for:

- innovation and flexibility in the teacher's job definition;

- new ways of organizing and allocating responsibility among teachers, administrators, and university educators;

- more efficient use of existing resources, including administrative overhead, to support instruction;

- more time for reflective professional conversation;

- new formats for assessing students and evaluating teachers;

- encouragement, resources, and collaboration with school and university colleagues to think through, work out, test, and revise teachers' own best ideas about teaching and to solve their most frustrating problems. (p. 94)

These reports emphasized the need for teachers to assume professional responsibilities to break down the traditional isolation and passivity of teachers, to become involved not only in professional education for oneself and for new teachers but in the redesign of schools. The reports had far-reaching implications for preservice and in-service education and led to the development of professional development schools, school-based management that encouraged teachers to work collaboratively to solve school problems, and new thinking about teacher leadership.

This book will highlight the professionalism and behavior of teacher- and principal-leaders working to improve practice in schools, county offices, and at universities. Each of the authors provides a special lens with which to view the work of teaching professionals.

To promote insight about why it has been so difficult for teachers to develop leadership and consider themselves professionals, this introductory chapter will begin by describing some traditional ways of perceiving teachers that have had radical consequences. Then short vignettes that depict teachers in different stages of their careers and performing a variety of roles will demonstrate how contemporary leaders are influencing teaching, learning, and professional behaviors.

WHAT HAS INHIBITED TEACHER LEADERSHIP AND PROFESSIONALISM?

Historical Roots

The concept of teacher as hired worker has plagued the professional education and development of teachers and stripped teachers of decision-making capabilities. Beginning during the Colonial period of American history, teaching was male dominated and teachers were perceived as occasional workers contracted by the selectmen of the community to teach during the winter months. Often the schoolmaster was compensated with room and board in the homes of the children he taught. Johnson (1963) relates the story of a diary entry kept by a schoolmaster who protested that the family fed him baked gander, hot or cold, every day for a week until he was too ill to teach.

Obviously, teachers were not held in high esteem during our early educational history. However, the connection between formal education for teachers and success of the common school was first recognized by education leaders in the 1830s who seriously objected to learning on the job without formal preparation for teaching. Horace Mann, who opened the first normal school for teachers in 1839; Cyrus Peirce, who initiated role-playing to help prepare teachers; John Abbott, who wrote *The Teacher*; and David Page, whose *Theory and Practice of Teaching* appeared in 1847, were among the first to advocate professional education for teachers. But their vision of teaching was not to be realized quickly.

Efficiency Ethic

The industrial revolution glamorized the factory system, and most Americans responded to the notion of "efficiency" it spawned. Though United States citizens always cherished their neighborhood schools, they have at the same time resented the cost of a quality education. School efficiency became a national ethic as a consequence of the influx of immigrants and the growth of urban populations in cities. Business people, who predominated on most school boards, embraced scientific management. In Gary, Indiana, teachers were expected to perform their work chores at school and go home without papers and books "like other classes of workers." However, the efficiency ethic did not end in the nineteenth century; we see it in action today when school critics suggest that schools should be run like businesses without regard for the social aspects of schooling.

A contemporary version of the school efficiency ethic is the Edison Project, whose goal is an outcome-based curriculum characterized by the following features: (1) Students are expected to attend school from 7 A.M. to 6 P.M., and the school year is set for 210 days. (2) Teachers are to receive specialized training. (3) Time is to be provided for professional development and to prepare lessons. (4) Teachers are expected to provide tutorials and to lecture. It would appear that teachers' work is very narrowly defined and constrained by traditional views of teaching. The Edison Project seeks private funding to run public schools (*Education Week*, September 9, 1993). The major sponsor for the Edison Project also is responsible for the Channel One programs that deliver news to public school classrooms willing to endure commercial advertising during the news telecasts.

> **Historical Perceptions of Teachers**
>
> - As occasional workers
> - As factory workers
> - As mindless robotic implementors

Remediation of Skills

Further evidence that teachers have been perceived as unthinking drones, is found in the history of in-service education. The word *in-service* is an adjective, yet in most school districts one hears about the "in-servicing" of teachers as if it were a verb and process. Definitions of in-service education reveal that it was conceived as something done to and for teachers instead of a professional program controlled by them. In the past in-service classes were frequently taught by principals and district supervisors and in the main were characterized by atheoretical methodologies. In-service education until recent years was regarded as a means to remediate teachers' technical skills. Howey, Yarger, and Joyce (1978) called in-service education a "mindless experience."

Teacherproof Curriculum

Curriculum materials and texts in the 1950s through the 1970s were described frequently as "teacherproof" because the author-developers strived to implement curriculum without the benefit of teacher judgment. Even when they enlisted teachers in in-service classes to introduce those materials, they expected robotic implementation, not discussion of concepts and pedagogy. The concept of teacherproof curriculum demonstrates the mind-set of curriculum designers. Teachers could not be trusted to develop and implement curriculum on their own; they needed to be "trained." Eisner (1994) had this to say about "teacher-proofing" curriculum materials:

> The aspiration to create teacherproof materials rests on a mistake. Teachers need materials that stimulate their ingenuity rather than materials to which they are to be subservient. (p. 372)

Research on Teaching

Though educators welcomed effective teaching research as evidence of the knowledge base of teaching and as a support for professionalism, in fact even the research on teaching worked as an obstacle to teacher leadership and professionalism. The research was greeted by policymakers as a means to make teachers accountable to the public. School districts used the research as a rubric for designing evaluation forms and asked principals to evaluate teaching effectiveness using the forms that served to standardize teaching procedures. Teacher education institutions also jumped on the bandwagon, and instead of helping teacher candidates exercise judgment concerning when and under what circumstances to implement specific teaching strategies consonant with goals, the institutions limited teacher preparation to prescribed teaching functions.

Centralized Management

Another deterrent to the development of teacher leadership and professionalism has been the idea that teachers are on a lower rung of the career ladder than supervisors and administrators, particularly those in central office management positions. Many decisions made away from the school site by central office personnel and district administrators result in dysfunctional school procedures that affect teachers and the community. In large school districts, sometimes it is months before teachers can rectify bureaucratic rules. For example, in Los Angeles teachers at a professional practice school site wanted to "bank" time for staff development purposes. By beginning school fifteen minutes early the teachers would accumulate enough time for a planning and discussion meeting once a week. However, they had to submit their proposal to a hierarchy of decision makers—a requirement resulting in a time lapse of six months. The inability to make key decisions to improve school life and working conditions certainly has had a detrimental effect on teacher leadership.

Teacher Shortages

We frequently hear about the shortage of family doctors, particularly in rural areas of the United States. Yet we never consider emergency licenses for individuals to practice medicine without formal medical education. None of us would be willing to be treated by an unlicensed doctor, but we allow our children to be taught by individuals lacking proper certification. We allow ourselves to discount the professional education of teachers and validate pseudo equivalencies. For example, Peace Corps members are allowed in most states to obtain a teaching credential even though they may have never had experience teaching an entire class of children and know little about learning theory, research on teaching, and pedagogy. Serving in a rural village in Africa somehow qualifies them to become teachers in urban schools.

At yet another extreme, Teach for America is a vision of nonteachers for selecting the "brightest and finest" college graduates to become classroom teachers. These graduates receive summer preparation for teaching and then enter the classroom as emergency credentialed teachers. Though it responds to teacher shortages, how demoralizing this program must be for individuals who conscientiously prepare for the teaching profession, and what does this say about professional education?

Teacher shortages are in fact used by school districts, entrepreneurial individuals, and sometimes teacher educators to design what is euphemistically called alternate routes to credentialing. Darling-Hammond and Goodwin (1993) note that quick-entry programs fail to ground individuals in curriculum development, pedagogical content knowledge, learner characteristics, classroom management, and student

> ### Alternative Credential Programs
>
> Individuals prepared through alternative (compressed) credential programs are typically shortchanged through inadequate preparation in curriculum, pedagogy, knowledge of students' growth and development, classroom management concepts, and knowledge of appropriate motivation techniques.

motivation. These quickie programs serve to dissipate the energy and commitment of other teachers and maintain the bureaucratic structure of schools.

Thus the following factors have worked against the autonomy of teachers as thinking professionals and served to limit their creativity and skills: (1) historical conceptions of teachers as occasional workers, (2) bureaucratic views of teaching as an occupation, (3) policy mandates requiring uniformity, and (4) status barriers that have inhibited interaction among teachers performing a variety of roles, (5) teacherproof curriculum materials, and (6) prescribed teaching functions. Even more significant is what these obstacles have accomplished by destroying teachers' willingness to redesign their profession, and engage in risk-taking pedagogical and leadership behaviors. The consequence has been *socialized passivity*—the most powerful obstacle to teacher leadership and professionalism. The socialization process in schools has caused teachers to accept organizational decisions without thought and to conform without question to what are sometimes unwritten rules.

SOCIALIZED PASSIVITY

Since Lortie's (1975) sociologic study of teachers, educators have accepted that teacher isolation in "egg-crate" classrooms results in teacher privatism, which in turn affects teacher leadership and professionalism. The following case study describes the professionalization and leadership journey of a typical teacher. Perhaps you will see glimpses of yourself and even your associates in this episode. As you read the case study, consider the following questions:

1. What academic and school-related problems should the principal have explored with the novice teachers?

2. In Peggy's first school, how did the experienced teachers socialize Peggy? What was valued?

3. Should teachers be allowed to put their classes together in order to share teaching expertise?

4. How do teachers' professional needs change as they gain confidence and experience?

Peggy Greensom began her teaching career in a very traditional school environment. Her teacher associates responded to what Patterson (1993) calls "bossing" and "managing." Though Greensom is presently a very dynamic sixth-grade teacher, a grade-level chair, and a "coach" of partner student teachers for a university, she almost quit teaching because of lack of stimulation.

Greensom began her teaching career in a multiethnic urban elementary school of 900 students, twenty-five teachers, two custodians, and a single administrator. The school did not have a cafeteria, auditorium, or teachers' lounge. Both students and teachers had to bring their lunches and snacks. Yard duty on most days prevented teachers from leaving the campus.

Three other teachers were new that same year, and the principal chose to meet with the four new teachers bimonthly on Monday afternoons after dismissal. The principal began these meetings the same way, each time. "What would you like to talk about today? How can I help you?"

Because none of the teachers wanted to admit an area of weakness, the principal's questions were met with silence. This led to the principal choosing a school problem to highlight, and the ensuing discussion was somewhat irrelevant since novice teacher problems were survival related.

Ultimately the four teachers made a deal with each other. Each would take a turn identifying a topic for discussion, framing it in general terms so as not to encourage the principal to think that the initiator was "weak" in this area. To support each other they agreed to talk about what they were doing in their own classrooms that was related to the selected topic. This required that the four teachers communicate with each other prior to the meeting.

A friendship of sorts took root, and the four teachers began to socialize outside the school. Their planning for the sessions with the principal became more deliberate, and they became more trusting of each other.

Peggy's first year concluded abruptly when she caught the mumps. During the summer break, she reconsidered what went well and what didn't. She touched bases with her three cohorts and was surprised to learn that her male teacher friend had decided to go into the insurance business and that her fourth-grade teacher friend had gotten a job as an airline hostess. During the second year, there would be just two of the four novices returning, and they would be teaching at opposite ends of the school so they wouldn't see each other very often.

The principal assumed Peggy no longer needed tutorials as a second-year teacher. She felt somewhat at the mercy of the more experienced faculty members, who would peek into her classroom as though they were checking it out but never invite her to their rooms to talk.

At times Peggy felt conscience ridden for not being more proficient, and at the same time she was fearful of asking other teachers or the principal for advice. She was unsure of how much direction to give students or how much independence they needed. Her pattern of instruction was erratic.

The classroom never appeared quiet. To make matters worse, when another teacher popped her head in the room, the children suddenly quieted. Peggy rued her inability to elicit a similar reaction from the students.

Midway through the second year she became acquainted with a new first-year teacher who had transferred to the school. Mata Henry taught first grade at the end of the corridor near Peggy's classroom. Since Mata was the only new teacher, the principal abandoned the tutorial idea and told Mata that her door was always open. "Just come in anytime you need some help!"

Though Mata's needs were great, she wasn't about to admit it to the principal. Mata and Peggy became instant friends and began to share teaching problems with each other. Mata's strength was teaching language arts. Peggy was more comfortable teaching social studies. They began to share their teaching problems and advise each other.

On one occasion, they put their classes together and teamed instruction to take advantage of each other's strengths. After school the teacher across the hall confronted them and commented: "You know it really isn't a good idea to put two classes of children together. You'd better get permission from Ms. Young (the principal) before you do it again."

They were embarrassed and lacked the confidence to assert themselves. As a consequence, they confined their collaboration to out-of-school tasks and telephone conversations. They began to create classroom teaching materials together. They checked out lesson ideas on each other and hotly contested teaching strategies. They questioned each other about typical teaching dilemmas: (1) What should be done with disruptive students? (2) Since there were usually about three new students transferring to the school each month (and three students departing), how should these students be integrated into classroom activities? (3) Should students always select the groups they work in, or should the teacher arrange the groups? What criteria should be used? (4) How do you know if students understand abstract concepts like systems or energy? (5) How can you keep in touch with single parents who have no time to come to school? (6) For students speaking limited English, is it okay to repeat their questions and/or responses? (If you do not repeat them, how do you model language and provide appropriate repetition?)

Beginning her third year of teaching, Peggy felt confident and comfortable about her career choice. Her expertise in teaching social studies was acknowledged by her principal and she was asked to lead an in-service class on social studies activities for primary grades. However, she still felt that most of her interactions with other teachers had to do with scheduling the use of equipment, deciding on playground rules, selecting dates for schoolwide testing, presenting Back to School night, and complaining about supplies and custodial services.

During a child care leave, Greensom went back to the university for a master's degree in teaching. She continued to talk to Mata frequently about teaching methods. She was an active member of the state social studies organization and a comprehensive member of the National Council for the Social Studies. She joined a state committee to study guidelines for teaching social studies and was proactive in asking to teach another in-service class.

Returning from child care leave, she was assigned to a school where there were student teachers. The faculty of this school were vitally interested in professional challenges. Recess and noon times were consumed by talk with other teachers; they debated content, testing, parent involvement, grouping, and teaching methods. The intellectual discussions challenged her to try out new ideas and develop new skills. She realized she had been literally starved for professional interaction. Unlike her prior school experience, everyone was on first-name basis, including the principal, and the principal was as anxious to join in the frequent debates as were the teachers. In fact, often the debates concerned possible implementation of school policies formulated as a result of questions from the principal requesting teacher guidance.

Peggy Greensom's experiences reveal much about the problems of new teachers, the social realities of urban teaching, and the socialization process still intact in many schools. Her first teaching assignment was typical of what most beginning teachers endure. Her principal met with her once every two weeks and expected Peggy to "self-report" her problems—something no new teacher is likely to do. In essence the message Peggy, Mata, and their new teacher cohorts received was, "You are on your own, good luck." The veteran teachers at Peggy's school ignored their new colleagues. Their message to the novices was, "Don't try anything new; we'll watch; let's see if you can make it to June."

Ms. Young, the principal of Peggy's school had not set up any system for having experienced teachers help the inexperienced, nor a system to allow new teachers to contribute current knowledge and research to more experienced teachers. The veteran teachers were socializing the novices to "go it alone." When Peggy and Mata tried to team-teach and share their expertise in the classroom, they received advice stemming from (unwritten rules) in the form of a warning: "You'd better not. . . ."

Leading the in-service class encouraged Peggy to share her expertise in social studies and gave her a sense of accomplishment. Her relationship with Mata relieved the isolation of the classroom and provided intellectual stimulation and incentive to study teaching. Mata and Peggy were peers and did not feel competitive.

The environment of Peggy's second school was totally different. Teachers were supportive of each other; they shared ideas about practice and about understandings and applications of research, and they engaged in collective reflection. Their principal was equally involved and appealed to them for mutual decisions concerning school policies.

Peggy's story exemplifies the process of learning to be a professional. (1) We see a novice teacher seeking help and intellectual stimulation from peers. (2) She works to "master" and apply disciplinary knowledge and pedagogy. (3) She seeks additional university course work and becomes active in a professional association. (4) She begins to share her own expertise with others through leadership activities. (5) In her second school assignment she engages in team learning, which generates new applications of knowledge and mutual decision making.

In the next section several specific aspects of professionalism will be highlighted. The vignettes will describe (a) shared reflections, (b) shared expertise, (c) support for experimentation, and (d) linking knowledge through a collaborative relationship.

HOW DOES PROFESSIONALISM BEGIN?

Shared Reflections

By expressing thoughts and teaching frustrations to others, teachers are beginning to create an environment that supports the application of professional knowledge *and* ensures a psychological safety net in which it is "okay" to make mistakes.

Jean Lui, a fourth-year veteran teacher, smiled to herself as she recognized the frustration of her teacher friend Cynthia Brown. Cynthia, a second-year teacher, had just related an incident that had happened in her classroom:

> **CYNTHIA:** I was helping the students read a story about a mother's responsibility to care for her children, yet at the same time maintain a job outside the home. As we discussed the story, we focused on the traditional roles of women, and suddenly Billy (a fifth grader) became argumentative and finally shouted out, "This is dumb story."
>
> **JEAN:** What do you think was bothering him?
>
> **CYNTHIA:** I don't know; sometimes Billy is a bit aggressive and talks out, but not like this!

> JEAN: Does Billy have a working mom? Did you speak to him away from the group?
>
> CYNTHIA: I was so disgusted that I just told him to quiet down and let the rest of us work.
>
> JEAN: Why don't you try to talk to him alone. Why do you think that particular story might have bothered Billy?
>
> CYNTHIA: Gee, it never occurred to me to think about the content of the story and Billy's reaction to it. I wonder if Billy has problems at home with his mother. Matter of fact, I don't know much about Billy's home life.

Jean Lui's willingness to think with Cynthia about her problem demonstrates the ability to attend to the needs of a colleague. She immediately questioned and communicated to Cynthia the need to speak to the offending student privately. In addition, she prodded Cynthia to think more reflectively about the situation through her questioning stance instead of responding to Cynthia, "I think you should have. . . ." Jean Lui demonstrates both reflective thinking and how to communicate with a colleague. Cynthia Brown demonstrates openness in her ability to share a teaching problem and respond to her friend's questioning. It appears that the two teachers have established trust and rapport in their relationship.

Teacher-leaders care about fostering inquiry about teaching. Working with others sensitizes them to thinking about teaching; they prize engaging in dialogue about teaching because it exposes them to different values, beliefs, and opinions about teaching. Teaching professionalism begins with the premise that knowledge must be thoughtfully shared. The next vignette demonstrates how teacher-leaders can share their skills.

Shared Expertise

Derrick Smith, a ten-year veteran teacher, works for a county office of education. His job is to help other teachers integrate technology into their teaching plans. He is invited frequently to observe in classrooms and give teachers suggestions about computer integration. Bob Kelly, a fifth-year experienced teacher, invited Derrick to his classroom to help him solve a teaching problem. As Derrick observed Bob Kelly in his seventh-grade social science classroom, he realized that the computer was causing Bob some classroom management problems. He asked Bob Kelly if it would be all right for him to demonstrate a social studies research lesson in which the computer would be used by a group of students.

Bob agreed, and Derrick suggested he take notes on how he (Derrick) organizes the class for a research lesson.

Derrick introduced his lesson to the students, calling attention to the use of multiple sources of data for research purposes. Next he gave a short synopsis of each source available for the students to use (a film strip, texts, video, computer program). He and the students talked about how to use each of the inquiry procedures so as not to disturb classmates and what each group would be responsible for doing.

After school Derrick said to Bob, "Let's look at your notes and see how well I did." Together the two teachers analyzed the lesson and decided what went well and what alternative approaches could be used.

Derrick Smith is expert in the use of technology in the classroom, but his real contribution to professionalism is his ability to serve as a consultant and demonstrate planning and actions. He did not put Bob down and cause Bob to feel humiliated. Instead he empowered Bob by asking him to take notes while he (Derrick) taught the class. This helped to build Bob's confidence. Then the two teachers, as peers, analyzed the lesson. In this way Derrick was telling Bob that he, too, makes mistakes while teaching. He demonstrates that teachers need to appraise their own teaching behaviors, evaluate their own work, and talk about it with colleagues.

In the next example we see a school principal who works to develop professionalism by empowering teachers to make instructional decisions based on students' learning needs instead of preconceived ideas about what principals want to see.

Supporting Experimentation

Marjorie Crown is an elementary principal; she has just observed a creative writing lesson in a third-grade classroom. The lesson was well planned but too teacher controlled to permit student creativity. She recognized that the teacher taught the lesson so that nothing would go wrong while she was watching—and that bothered her.

She asked the teacher, "How else might you have taught this lesson?" The teacher's responses verified that the teacher recognized other instructional means for accomplishing the objective but did not want to risk using them.

At the next faculty meeting, Marjorie conducted the meeting using the group investigation teaching model. The faculty appeared to enjoy the interaction and the change in the style of the meeting. Informally, Marjorie asked several of the experienced teachers if they would like to team with and coach each other using the model she had demonstrated.

Several or the teachers agreed to form a collaborative team to learn the model and practice it. Marjorie agreed to take turns teaching their classes in order to release them to engage in peer coaching.

Marjorie Crown is a "leader of leaders" because she rejects passivity and recognizes why sometimes teachers assume "safe" teaching is better than risk taking. She demonstrates her own willingness to take a risk by conducting her staff meeting using a model of teaching. Then she encourages the teachers to engage in a working relationship with others to improve their teaching skills.

Collaborative Relationships

The separation of teacher education in universities and the practice of teaching in schools has created a chasm inhibiting the exchange of knowledge between university- and school-based educators and suppressing the link between theory and practice. The next vignette demonstrates how each supports the other and how educators in universities and schools can work together to build professional ties.

David Henry works at a university in teacher education. He believes that upper-elementary students are quite accurate in their perceptions of their own strengths and weaknesses. He shared his interest in testing the accuracy of students' perceptions with Agnes Thomas, a sixth-grade teacher who was using a portfolio system with her students.

Together they designed a study in which students would lead a three-way conference between parent, teacher, and student, using their portfolios to discuss with their parents their personal strengths and weaknesses. The conferences would be audiotaped. They decided, also, to maintain narrative notes on each student during a ten-week period and that the notes, as well as the students' grades on several tests, would be matched with the student's own perception. They decided on particular times of the school day to take notes, and David agreed to be in the classroom several hours each week.

Both David Henry and Agnes Thomas demonstrate leadership and professionalism. They appreciate the value of clinical research and the value of colleagueship between a university-based educator and a school-based educator. (In an interview Agnes said she felt "honored, challenged, and valued" to be involved collecting data and participating as a researcher.) David recognized Agnes's expertness and the privilege she granted him to conduct research in the clinical classroom. Collaboration between individuals working at the same school is not an easy process, and it certainly is not effortless if it is to occur between individuals working in different institutions with different value systems.

Signs of Professionalism

The vignettes presented in the previous section describe some key elements of professionalism and the behavior of teacher leaders. It is clear that leadership and professionalism begin in different ways for different individuals. For some individuals it may be the satisfaction of exchanging ideas with an associate; for someone else the entry point may be involvement in case study research. Though professionalism appears to begin with a teaching identity and self-confidence, working with others collegially underlies career satisfaction. (See McLaughlin and Yee, 1988.) Signs of professionalism include:

1. Recognizing and purposefully focusing your own thoughtfulness through advance thought, active thought, and afterthought.

2. Trusting others with personal insights, ideas, perplexities, successes, and miscalculations.

3. Acknowledging your own and others' expertise; sharing expertise with others.

4. Taking a chance to experiment with and extend pedagogical skills and content knowledge.

5. Risking commitment beyond the classroom to school and colleagues.

6. Appreciating professional rights and responsibilities.

7. Daring to be different in thought and actions.

8. Connecting with other educators to construct knowledge and strengthen the ties between theory and practice.

The two reports cited earlier (*A Nation Prepared: Teachers for the 21st Century* and *Tomorrow's Schools*) view collaborative and collegial behaviors among teachers as well as between school faculties and university-based educators as critical factors to improve curriculum, instruction, and the environment of schools. However, since teacher isolation has prevailed in most school settings, it is not surprising that collegial and collaborative behaviors among teachers are somewhat rare. Where these behaviors have existed there have been remarkable changes in teacher satisfaction, productivity, leadership, and school improvement.

The nineteenth-century factory model that helped to inhibit teacher professionalism by treating teachers like factory workers and reserving decision making for management also served to standardize and routinize the conditions and organization of schools (Shedd and Bacharach, 1991). When teachers have addressed the conditions of schools and made the critical decisions that affected teaching and learning, uncommon changes have occurred. Two examples follow that demonstrate collaboration and decision making motivated by dissatisfaction with the use of *space* and *time*.

Collaboration and Decision Making in an Elementary School

Three female kindergarten teachers with similar background experiences were assigned to a burgeoning suburban elementary school in Sherman Oaks, California. Each believed strongly in the need to have manipulative materials and hands-on experiences for children. The teachers were accustomed to independent management of their own program and had no previous experience working closely with peers. But the school they were assigned to was originally designed for one kindergarten class and as a consequence it had only one play area for the three classrooms; thus it was necessary for the teachers to work out a cooperative schedule. Initial conversation among the three revealed that each liked to use a variety of work stations in the classroom for the students to use. Each had developed a system to rotate their students using the learning-center approach.

The teachers realized that they had a great deal in common and that they could be much more creative if they could develop a system whereby all three classes rotated among the various centers and each teacher was responsible for developing one-third of the work stations. The outside play area could be included as one of the centers.

As the system evolved, the three teachers decided to meet together on Friday afternoons to plan the next week's work centers. It soon became obvious to them that the students needed to be treated like a large family because in order to design effective work stations, they needed to be cognizant of students' special needs. Part of their planning time was spent discussing students' differential interests, communication needs, and readiness levels. The teachers pooled all of their materials, including realia, favorite story books, science exhibits, and animals.

By the end of the semester they were working as a team and had resolved organizational problems. They were accustomed to assisting each other, and they had developed an ad hoc means of dealing with everyday problems. They had developed a format for their planning sessions. First they would begin with a discussion of the students' progress and needs; they would consider the curriculum and the students' work stations. Each classroom would be designed for a special purpose, either for academic (subject field) development, skill needs, or the arts. The planning session would culminate in designation of each teacher's work tasks.

The other teachers at the school became curious about what was happening in the kindergarten. The kindergarten team, as they began to call themselves, sanctioned visits from other teachers at the school. It was soon obvious to the entire faculty that these teachers were putting into place a remarkable program that demonstrated not only their understanding of the developmental needs of and teaching skills for kindergarten children, but teaming and leadership.

Fame spreads, and soon teachers with a variety of role responsibilities from around the school district came to observe. Ultimately it became necessary to designate specific days for teachers in their own district and other districts to come to visit. On these visitation days, the team would conduct an after-school seminar for the visitors to ask questions and attain ideas for their own classrooms.

On-Site Observations   I visited the school site on several occasions and sat in on both teacher planning sessions and a seminar for visitors. During the planning sessions it was clear that the teachers did not always agree on the content and organization of the learning centers, but they resolved these differences by talking about their observations of the children, about readiness levels, and about their own educational beliefs. Clearly their collaboration was time intensive, but despite the time commitment, the teachers were involved and believed their collaborative and collegial planning improved the program for children and gave them each considerable satisfaction. In attending the seminar for visiting teachers and administrators, I was particularly interested in the questions and comments of the visitors.

What surprised me was that the bulk of the questions dealt with the implicit curriculum and what I considered to be the team's collegial relationships. These questions came from practicing teachers, consultants, and principals and were related to collaborative work behaviors and processes, parent relations, classroom management, and curriculum decisions.

Had there not been an organizational problem involving the scheduling of the kindergarten yard for these three kindergarten teachers, it is likely each would have continued to manage her own program. No one would want to "wish" these problems on teachers; however, their collaborative problem solving resulted in a better education for children, professional education for other teachers, and a satisfying collegial relationship for the involved teachers.

> The collaborative efforts of teachers involve intensive time commitments and planning decisions that affect curriculum, classroom management, parent relations, and relationships between and among teachers.

Another incidence of teacher decision making used to resolve the age-old teaching problem of a fragmented curriculum versus curriculum integration and the organizational problem of time, occurred in a private middle school.

Collaboration and Decision Making at a Middle School

Tired of the traditional bell-controlled curriculum, a ninth-grade social studies teacher, Scott, and an English teacher, JoAnn, decided to combine their classes—forty-five students and 110 minutes—and develop a team approach. They selected a curriculum theme, "Change and Conflict," and developed a common syllabus. They integrated content and skills and their work assignments. They decided on one research project to be graded by both teachers using criteria appropriate for each subject field.

These teachers requested that the students be considered a self-contained group so that the two class periods would be back-to-back and they asked to be assigned to two classrooms separated by a moveable partition. They met with an art teacher and music teacher and asked for theme-related support. Again, they requested that the students be kept together as a self-contained group for music and art. Now the project consumed four class periods and four teachers. Early on, the art and music teachers honored the curriculum integration defined by the social studies and English teacher, but as the experiment progressed they, too, became interested in working together and experimenting with integrating their teaching.

Midway through the first semester Scott and JoAnn became interested in team teaching. They began to experiment with several models of teaching and initiated peer coaching. Their working relationship affected the school at large, students, other teachers, and the curriculum. Organizational problems had the greatest impact. The teachers had to convince others to allow them to "lock-in" the students to their two classrooms. Once that was achieved, curriculum planning was natural but required a great deal of time to talk about the students and curriculum strategies.

It was much harder for the teachers to integrate their teaching methodologies. JoAnn, the English teacher, tended to be more structured; Scott, the social studies teacher, preferred group work—but the common curriculum necessitated adaptations and common assessments. The teachers denied that they ever felt threatened by each other but were sometimes exhausted from their interactions.

Because both Scott and JoAnn had responsibilities in their respective departments, they began to share what they were doing with others. As a consequence, each became more of a leader in the English and social studies departments. Communication with other teachers helped them clarify their own goals and recognize the significance of what they were doing, and provided incentive to strengthen their collaboration.

Reflecting on the accomplishments of the kindergarten team and the middle-school teachers, one is impressed by their courage, the complexity of the decisions they made, and their contributions to others. In both cases, the organizational constraints alone have deterred most teachers from experimentation. These teachers overcame environmental handicaps (classroom walls), schedules, time barriers, and grouping constraints. The teachers began by altering routine classroom practices, a step that triggered changes in curriculum, instructional processes, and professional interactions.

It is clear that both students and teachers profit from the teachers' collegial relationships. Students gain through enriched curriculum, enhanced teaching strategies, and their teachers' mental health. The teachers gain from a working relationship that encourages professional reflection and supports collegial interactions, mutual decision making, problem solving, and shared responsibility.

COLLABORATIVE BEHAVIORS AND COLLEGIAL RELATIONSHIPS

All school improvement problems will not be solved by helping teachers interact collaboratively and/or collegially. However, collegial relationships have much to do with teacher leadership, administrator leadership, professionalism, and school culture. In Rosenholtz's (1989) study of school culture, she found that principals who supported and encouraged collaborative goals achieved "learning enriched" environments and in schools where teachers taught in isolated environments, she characterized the school culture as "learning impoverished." Collaborative goals and behavior, however, do not necessarily mean that teachers related to each other *collegially.*

Collegiality has been defined by Lemlech and Kaplan (1990) as "the establishment of a professional relationship for the purpose of service and accommodation through the mutual exchange of perceptions and expertise." Collegial relationships subsume collaborative behaviors.

In most schools, teachers lend materials to each other; they get together to decide on what books will be used for specific grade levels; they work together to plan the science fair, Back to School night, and the May Day Festival; they decide on schoolwide citizenship goals; they decide whose turn it is to bring cookies and ice tea to the faculty meeting. None of these things add up to a "satisfying" career, commitment to teaching, leadership, or professionalism. But each of these activities may require working jointly with others and require a certain amount of mutual decision making. Though working together collaboratively may be a difficult process and require experience, collaboration does not require that individuals interact collegially. Consider the following questions:

What are collegial behaviors?

How are collegial behaviors developed?

Do the "signs" of professionalism lead to collegial relationships?

To shape professional interaction among new teachers, an experimental preservice program at the University of Southern California was designed to prepare student teachers to accept role responsibilities and work in a collaborative, professional culture. The student teachers were voluntarily paired during their student teaching experience for the express purpose of creating a bond between the student teachers in order to foster a collegial relationship. Key aspects of the program and the Lemlech, Kaplan study of it are reported here to uncover the differences between collaborative endeavors and collegial interactions.

To encourage partner interaction the team of professors and student teaching coordinators suggested to the student teachers that they engage both in planning lessons and arranging the classroom environment together and, in consultation with their master teacher, teaming up to construct a thematic, integrated teaching unit. They were given, in addition, some mutual-support responsibilities, which included taking notes when their partner was teaching and providing feedback to the partner. They were also to videotape their partner's teaching, and then the partners were to view the videotape jointly and record on audiotape their evaluative discussion of the lesson.

Through the use of guided interviews, questionnaires, reading the student teachers' journals and feedback notes, listening to their audiotapes while viewing their lessons, and conducting weekly direct observation while they student-taught, the progress of the student teachers' interactions and the challenges and obstructions to colleagueship were studied over a period of five years.

First Impressions

The partners sought and accepted emotional support from each other instead of their master teacher. In the first couple of weeks after viewing each other teach, their feedback conversations were unsophisticated in use of the language of teaching, yet it was accurate and often insightful. In addition, their responses to each other were tender, and careful of feelings; intuitively they understood the responsibility of professional feedback.

Though the intent of the "collegial preparation program" was the development of collegial relationships, it was recognized that we could require specific partner behaviors, but collegial relationships mature through mutual intensive study of teaching. The helping (collaborative) behaviors such as "gopher" activities, ideas, suggestions, and lending materials, were not necessarily reflective or collegial.

As the study of partner relationships progressed, we noted six distinct interactive stages with defining behaviors and characteristics (see Table 1.1).

Stages of Collegial Development

- *Stage 1*   Peer Interaction
- *Stage 2*   Partnering
- *Stage 3*   Competition
- *Stage 4*   Study of Teaching
- *Stage 5*   Integration of Skills
- *Stage 6*   Collegiality

TABLE 1.1 Collegial Development Stages and Characteristics

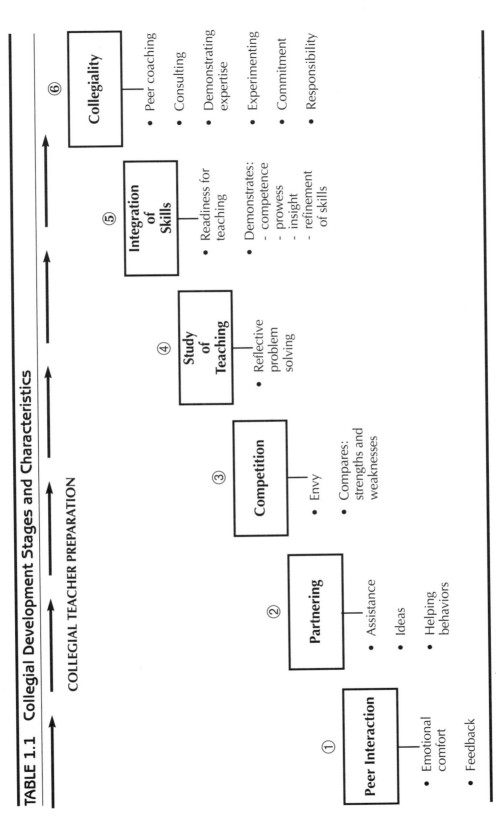

COLLEGIAL TEACHER PREPARATION

① **Peer Interaction**
- Emotional comfort
- Feedback

② **Partnering**
- Assistance
- Ideas
- Helping behaviors

③ **Competition**
- Envy
- Compares: strengths and weaknesses

④ **Study of Teaching**
- Reflective problem solving

⑤ **Integration of Skills**
- Readiness for teaching
- Demonstrates:
  - competence
  - prowess
  - insight
  - refinement of skills

⑥ **Collegiality**
- Peer coaching
- Consulting
- Demonstrating expertise
- Experimenting
- Commitment
- Responsibility

Source: Lemlech and Kaplan, 1991.

Stage Development

Stages 1 and 2 of collegial development were characterized by *tacit* learning and mutual dependence. *Contrived collegiality,* a term described by Hargreaves and Dawe (1990) was sometimes typical of partner interactions during the first two stages. Proximity, mutual dependence, and methods class assignments worked to propel the partners to help each other and to furnish informative feedback. Course requirements served to socialize them—to make them collaborate.

The first two stages are critical to the development of professional behaviors because (1) the partners begin to learn from their own experiences; (2) they depend on a peer for insight into their own teaching behaviors (not a "master," nor someone who is evaluating them), and (3) they begin to explore what works and what does not in specific classroom contexts. The partners have begun to *share reflections.*

Learning to teach is a developmental process. As a consequence individual growth in teaching ability and partner temperament affect the partners' interactions. Stages 3 and 4 are characterized by *metamorphic relationships.* The partners are alternately confident, jealous, fearful, and in search of understanding of the role of teacher. Some partner teams become competitive with each other, but most begin to link up and apply what they are learning in the methods seminar to the clinical classroom. Conversations between the partners become more focused and reflective. Though proximity alone does not make the partners colleagues, it appears to stimulate reflective thinking. The middle stages are significant because partners attend more meaningfully to each other's needs as co-learners.

In the last two stages the partners become *interdependent* colleagues. They seem to enjoy sparring with each other about ideas and techniques; they delight in demonstrating for each other their skills and creativity. They seek each other's respect. They experiment teaching together; they try out interactive teaching patterns, sometimes teaching consecutively with closely related content; sometimes they act as teacher and assistant teacher. Their conversations about teaching are technically appropriate. They are not just better problem solvers about teaching, but more critically involved in thinking about teaching.

For those partners who achieved a collegial relationship, there was evidence of *trust, sharing of expertise, shared reflection,* and *experimentation.* We concluded that collegial relationships are fostered by:

1. Investing time with one or more others to listen and puzzle together, to critically discuss beliefs and theories, and to engage in goal-oriented learning together. (Collaborative efforts do not require co-reflection of beliefs and theories.)

2. Assuming responsibility to contribute and demonstrate as an expert to one or more peers—individuals considered equals, not someone appointed as a mentor, or someone considered inferior in talent.

3. Trusting a peer to deliver advice, feedback, encouragement, and ideas. Allowing another person to coach, help, demonstrate, and guide.

4. Challenging self and others by engaging in trial-and-error learning together, experimenting with instructional methods and organizational designs.

5. Participating in shared decision making affecting the school program, student achievement, and community relations.

6. Committing to purposeful learning to enrich one's own knowledge and contribute to colleagues'.

Conclusion

The signs of professionalism are consonant with and do lead to collegial relationships, and collegiality among members of a profession creates shared norms and stimulates standards of performance. Within schools teacher leadership roles and positions vary. From designing curriculum; to arranging schedules; to serving as community liaison, grade-level and department chair, or team leader, teachers have many vital and significant leadership roles to enact. Each of these roles requires wise use of authority, influence, and control.

All teachers, principals, consultants, and teacher educators have a stake in teacher professionalism, and all the stake holders must collaborate in sharing power. By sharing school power with teachers, the principal encourages commitment, involvement, and leadership. When all the members of the profession recognize the significant roles of others, a vision of school reform can emerge, one that is collaboratively created.

Conceived as a training program for prospective teachers to learn to imitate a master, the apprenticeship model did not intend that teachers would lead, act as colleagues, share expertise, or collaborate to create a vision of new schools.

However, preparation for leadership begins in preservice education. We need to forget the idea that teachers must be *trained;* instead we must recognize that for teaches to play leadership roles, they need to experience a *professional education.*

> ### Recap Notes: Nurturing Leadership and Professionalism
>
> Leadership and professionalism are cultivated through
> - Intellectual stimulation of peers talking about teaching.
> - Sharing of insights and expertise between/among peers.
> - Team learning based on team interests.
> - Participation in decision making related to the school and classroom milieu, and student learning.
> - Responsibility in implementing decisions.

REFERENCES

Darling-Hammond, L., and Goodwin, A. L. 1993. Progress toward professionalism in teaching. In *Challenges and achievements of American education*, ed. G. Cawelti. Alexandria, Va.: ASCD.

Eisner, E. 1994. *The educational imagination.* 3rd ed. New York: Macmillan.

Hargreaves, A., and Dawe, R. 1990. Paths of professional development: Contrived collegiality, collaborative cultures and the case of peer coaching. In *Teaching and Teacher Education*, 4(3).

Howey, K. R., Yarger, S. J., and Joyce, B. R. 1978. *Improving teacher education.* Washington, D.C.: ATE.

Johnson, C. 1963. *Old-time schools and school-books.* New York: Dover.

Hertzog-Foliart, H., and Lemlech, J. K. 1993. Collegial teacher preparation: Impact on the supervising teacher's role. Paper presented at the Annual Meeting of the Association of Teacher Educators. Los Angeles.

The Holmes Group. 1990. *Tomorrow's schools: Principles for the design of professional development schools. East Lansing, Mi.: The Holmes Group.*

Lemlech, J. K., and Kaplan, S. N. 1990. Learning to talk about teaching: Collegiality in clinical teacher education. *Action in Teacher Education* 12(1): 13–19.

Lemlech, J. K., and Hertzog-Foliart, H. 1992. Restructuring to become a professional practice school: Stages of collegiality and the development of professionalism. Paper presented at American Educational Research Association Annual Meeting. San Francisco.

Lemlech, J. K., and Kaplan, S. N. 1991. Collegiality in teacher education. Paper presented at the Annual Meeting of the National Council for the Social Studies. Washington, DC.

Little, J. W. 1988. Assessing the prospects for teacher leadership. In *Building a professional culture in schools*, ed. A. Lieberman. New York: Teachers College Press.

Carnegie Forum on Education and the Economy. 1986. *A Nation Prepared: Teachers for the 21st century.* New York: The Carnegie Forum.

Lortie, D. C. 1975. *School teacher: A sociological study.* Chicago: University of Chicago Press.

McLaughlin, M. W., and Yee, S. M. 1988. School as a place to have a career. In *Building a professional culture in schools*, ed. A. Lieberman. New York: Teachers College Press.

Pajak, E. 1993. Change and continuity in supervision and leadership. In *Challenges and achievements of American education*, ed. G. Cawelti. Alexandria, Va.: ASCD.

Patterson, J. L. 1993. *Leadership for tomorrow's schools.* Alexandria, Va.: Association for Supervision and Curriculum Development.

Pensavalle, M. 1993. Helping teachers prepare for effective participation in restructuring. Unpublished dissertation. Los Angeles: University of Southern California.

Shedd, J. B., and Bacharach, S. B. 1991. *Tangled hierarchies.* San Francisco: Jossey-Bass.

Sykes, G. 1990. Fostering teacher professionalism in schools. In *Restructuring schools: The next generation of educational reform*, ed. R. F. Elmore and Associates. San Francisco: Jossey-Bass, 59–96.

Wasley, P. A. 1991. *Teachers who lead the rhetoric of reform and the realities of practice.* New York: Teachers College Press.

2 Issues Affecting Leadership and Professionalism

JOHANNA K. LEMLECH

Traditionally, school-based leadership has been delimited to the school principal, assistant principal, and perhaps the school counselor. The principal served as the boss and manager of the school enterprise. Teachers were the workers and the objects of the principal's technical and managerial efforts. If a new program was mandated by a school district, principals were often responsible for "inservicing" the teachers. (And if the program failed, it was the teachers' fault!)

In the 1990s, still somewhat bound by old customs and traditions, both principals and teachers are attempting new roles and engaging in efforts to change school cultures. For principals this means using "power" to create collegial learning communities. For teachers, it means accepting responsibility for collaborative decision making. New attitudes and behaviors are required for both principals and teachers to be successful. Some of the issues and events that have an impact on teacher leadership and professionalism are discussed in this chapter. For most of the issues identified in this chapter, I will begin with how the problem has impeded teaching and professionalism, then suggest means to alleviate the problem. The chapter concludes with a discussion of how leaders can help to change habits to improve school culture and develop a learning community.

```
┌─────────────────────────────────────────────────────────┐
│  Chapter 2 HIGHLIGHTS                                     │
│                                                          │
│  • Creating a Vision                                     │
│  • Support Systems                                       │
│  • External Accountability                               │
│  • Bureaucratic Decision Making                          │
│  • Time Constraints                                      │
│  • Teacher Evaluation                                    │
│  • Professional Accountability                           │
│  • Recognizing Leadership and Professionalism            │
│  • Changing Leadership Styles                            │
│  • The Facilitator-Leader                                │
└─────────────────────────────────────────────────────────┘
```

VISION

When one describes a person with "vision" it typically means that the individual perceives what ordinary folk have failed to see. In past years school faculties had limited opportunities to contemplate or share school goals. In the school-restructuring literature, vision has to do with setting goals that are mutually shared and help to focus the energies of the school faculty. Vision is meant to be the overarching concept—the glue that holds everyone together. School faculties are not accustomed to expressing their vision to one another. Learning to share insight about one's work with others and learning to express one's vision of good schools with others requires courage, confidence, clarity, and commitment.

The importance of shared and expressed school goals was evident to school- and university-based educators at a Professional Development School meeting in Los Angeles. After a long intensive session in which all the participants talked about what was important to them as individuals, a vision statement emerged in the form of what a "good" school looks like. It was then that those educators realized they had much in common. During that shared moment, they gained excitement and unity. They were then able to turn their vision into a backward problem-solving, planning session that helped to generate paths toward the improvement of curriculum and instruction for children (Lemlech, Hertzog-Foliart, and Hackl, 1993).

New leadership roles for teachers are a vision that many educators share. The act of empowering teachers to assume leadership roles requires redesigning governance systems, building collaborative networks and fostering leadership behaviors through staff development activities. The first step is to define and communicate the vision, then develop the plan inch by inch.

SUPPORT SYSTEMS AND A SUPPORTIVE ENVIRONMENT

Observers of athletic contests, are (usually) biased cheerleaders. By cheering they try to communicate support for a team or individual effort. Leaders who are cheerleaders may provide moral support, but real tangible help is missing unless facilitative behaviors accompany the cheerleading. Barnes (1993) studied a large comprehensive high school involved in restructuring and noted that the principal engaged in a variety of facilitative behaviors to support change. For example, instead of presenting a "plan" to the faculty, the principal shared an "idea" with department chairs and encouraged them to refine the idea—to clothe it. The idea generated several versions until what emerged was a bona fide "plan." During the ensuing planning stage each department chair shared the idea with faculty, who in turn helped to map the final version. The work environment of this school was supportive of collaborative behaviors, and teachers were encouraged to function professionally. However, it is not known whether this work environment will survive under the leadership of a different administrator.

Structures that are not supported by daily routines and/or accepted by affected personnel do not survive. At the university level African Americans and Mexican Americans have frequently sought to create ethnic studies departments. Sometimes university administrators have agreed to such departments but neglected to implement curriculum mechanisms that would change undergraduate program requirements enabling students to obtain degree credit for ethnic study classes. The result of course is very short-lived programs and disillusioned students and faculty.

Teachers involved in restructuring efforts at the elementary level anticipate participation in organizational decisions for assigning students to classrooms, scheduling decisions affecting the school day, and calendar decisions affecting teacher assignments in year-round schools. If structures are not implemented to involve teachers in these decisions, disillusionment occurs. Similar examples exist at the high school level.

A school-within-a-school structure for the development of a professional development school at an elementary site achieved verbal support from the school administrator, but subsequent actions did not support the new structure. Faculty not involved in the development of the professional development school felt left out and labeled the effort elitist. As a consequence the involved faculty were ostracized, lost courage, and began to doubt their vision. Had the principal explained the need to begin the restructuring effort with a small group of experienced teachers first, the ire of uninvolved teachers would have been avoided. Enabling mechanisms and a supportive work environment are needed to encourage change processes.

The Peggy Greensom case study in Chapter 1 demonstrated a work environment that failed to provide a support system for new teachers or even for experienced teachers wanting to share knowledge. Unless Peggy and her new teacher cohorts were willing to admit areas of weakness to their principal, they had no one to turn to for assistance. The creation of a corps of mentor teachers in many school districts is a response to this need; however, the success of mentor teacher programs depends on the degree to which mentors offer systemic help and respond to the mentee's requests for assistance. When mentors report to administrators and evaluate performance, they "beg" the value of mentoring and earn distrust from new teachers.

School study groups, such as the one described by Lewison in Chapter 4, can serve as a support system for both new and experienced teachers. Local and state professional associations also contribute to professionalism and perform as a support mechanism.

FORMAL STRUCTURES, VALUES, AND "OLD BOY" NETWORKS

In many high schools the department chair position is awarded to teachers with seniority, not teacher-leaders and teachers with exceptional knowledge and capabilities. Paterson (1993) describes a high school in which teachers with seniority coveted the chair's position in order to control class schedules, favored courses, more desirable classrooms, and decision making. Teacher-coaches received priority treatment from the administrator based on their athletic status. New teachers entering this system were confronted with a rigid value system that honored old ties and the status quo.

Valued in this system is adhering to the rules. Administrators set the rules and department chairs reward obedience and passivity. In this environment the teacher who suggests changing the curriculum, altering the evaluation system, or participating in decision making is rocking the boat and considered a troublemaker.

In such a system department chairs do not consider it their responsibility to improve instructional practices, help implement new curriculum, or assist other teachers to grow professionally. At the elementary school level, similar problems can arise when positions (grade-level chairs, subject-field specialists) are used as rewards for seniority and congeniality, instead of thoughtful decision making, competence in subject field(s), and leadership capability.

Still another problem in "formally" constructed schools occurs when "leaders" are asked to obtain faculty consensus about meaningless issues. Instead of asking teachers whether funds should be used to hire a specialist teacher in a relatively new discipline, or means to improve the work place, teachers are asked to decide whether to buy a new duplicating machine and how much colored paper to purchase. Instead of involving faculty in significant issues to obtain varied perspectives, or asking faculty to participate in collaborative projects, in the traditional school teachers frequently are asked to rubber-stamp decisions and respond compatibly. In such environments, teachers learn to avoid the system; meetings are considered irrelevant by them and participation unnecessary. Still more important, however, is the fact that teacher-leaders in these situations assume foolish positions in the eyes of their colleagues.

In collegial, collaborative structures teachers are empowered because their opinions are sought in order to respond to the needs of all members of the school community and to *make better decisions*. In a collaborative climate individuals are comfortable with expressing their ideas and enjoy the challenge of thinking about curriculum, instruction, and organizational problems. This environment rewards reflection and participation.

BUREAUCRATIC, HIERARCHICAL DECISION MAKING

Bureaucratic and hierarchical decision making affects the autonomy of teachers. School systems communicate teachers' responsibilities sometimes through specific directives, interpreted and communicated by the school principal, sometimes through established routines or through written policies. Shedd and Bacharach (1991, p. 61–62) identify the typical decision points often controlled by school district policy and procedures:

- Curriculum and textbook selection.

- Student placement and ability grouping.

- Securing special help for students with special needs.

- Grading students and communicating grades to parents.

- Student conduct and discipline.

- Standardized testing.

- Requisitioning equipment and supplies.

- School calendars and class schedules.

Add to this list, the following:

- Hiring policies affecting specializations and leadership positions.

- Philosophical orientations affecting curriculum and instruction.

- Research priorities, opportunities.

- Planning, staff development time, professional growth opportunities.

The extent of rigidity or flexibility in these areas define teachers' tasks, responsibilities, goal setting, and opportunities for decision making and leadership. Some examples follow:

The teachers at a professional development school (PDS) were expected to have special capabilities to work with student teachers. Because it was anticipated that in the future there would be a need for additional teachers at a particular PDS, the members established criteria for selecting other teachers to engage in the work of the PDS and to coach student teachers. Establishment of the criteria had been sanctioned by the union, the school district, and the administrator of the school. However, when a vacancy occurred, the personnel office of the school district assigned a teacher to the PDS with the administrator's concurrence and without regard for the new structure and participatory decision making. When the teachers protested they were told that nothing could be done; the teacher assigned to the PDS had returned from leave, and the personnel office routinely made placement decision. The principal had not supported the teachers' right to use the criteria as a basis for teacher selection and assignment to the professional development school. The teachers were frustrated and angry.

When teacher-researcher MacGillivray wanted to engage in research using her own classroom, she sought university approval. In her words, "it took much explanation and repeated phone calls to get through the process." MacGillivray was undaunted by the delay, but others would be impatient with the layer-upon-layer means of decision making.

Teachers at an inner-city school that served a large limited-English-speaking population wanted to use informal (and authentic) means of assessment to identify gifted children for special placement. Their own judgment was not considered "good enough"; they were told to use the district-approved tests though the tests were not appropriate for the limited-English population.

After working with a group of teachers who had studied the whole-language approach to teaching reading and writing, one of the teachers asked how could the approach be used with a developmental reading skill–based program. The consultant responded: "It can't; philosophically, the two approaches conflict. Why do you want to do that?" The teacher answered that she didn't, but she was required to turn in lesson plans each week identifying the skills she would be teaching, and her administrator expected her to use the skill-based program to define the skills.

The examples demonstrate the consequences of school procedures and leadership styles that conflict with curriculum goals, instructional processes, and professional judgment. When teachers are constantly frustrated because of their inability to make defining, substantive decisions about their work, they tend to give up and behave as technicians, not professionals. Contrast these examples with the decisions made by the kindergarten teachers and the middle-school teachers described in Chapter 1.

Removing the constraints that affect teacher decision making generally results in moving areas of decision making to the schools (and teachers) instead of uninvolved central-office and supervisory personnel. For example, suppose the teachers involved in the whole language staff development really had decision-making powers, these are some of the decisions they might make:

■ Set goals for creating a literate school environment.

■ Select recreational books, fiction and nonfiction at varied levels and for varied interests.

■ Review school policies affecting language arts programs (grading, testing, and articulation between grade levels).

■ Plan to communicate the rationale of program to parents.

■ Plan staff development program for interested teachers.

The teachers frustrated by the placement of a returning teacher without examination of credentials for assignment to a professional development school, would have preferred the following decision-making procedures:

■ Revise school district policy regarding the assignment of returning teachers to schools.

■ Publicize competencies needed for professional development school leadership.

■ Require teachers to develop professional portfolios.

■ Create a faculty group to examine prospective teachers' portfolios, handle the interview process, and hire experienced teachers for the PDS.

■ Recognize teacher leadership and expertise through a districtwide honor program.

It is clear that teacher participation in decision making is critical to improving school organizations. If teachers do not participate in real and vital decisions affecting their work in the schools, then authority structures will not change and schools will continue to be inefficient in meeting the needs of students and wasteful of human expertise. Problems should be managed by those affected and closest to the need and impact. Problems are to be considered "friends" because they provide direction, focus work efforts, and help to assess progress.

TIME CONSTRAINTS

The concept of time affects teachers' curriculum and instructional decisions, interaction with students and other faculty, and opportunity for professional development. Time is another aspect of decision making that is controlled by state policies, school district regulations, and site administrators.

States and legislative bodies may decide the number of minutes for teaching required subjects, the number of days required for schooling, state holidays, tenure-related time decisions, and continuing education time–related requirements.

School districts affect time-related decisions through the school calendar, testing requirements, number of "student-free" days, school hours, teacher hours, planning periods, and required subjects.

At the school site, teachers may be additionally affected by the bell schedule, special programs, supervisory requirements, non-teaching assignments (mentoring, curriculum development committees), clerical tasks, advisement schedules, resource scheduling, grade-level and/or department meetings, and all-school faculty meetings.

All of these factors affect teachers' ability to plan instruction, evaluate students' work, confer with students and parents, select appropriate resources, address school problems, collaborate with other teachers, and engage in professional growth activities. Decisions made by higher levels of authority limit decision making at lower levels of authority (Barr & Dreeban, 1985).

Teachers are affected both by the *rigidity of time schedules* and the *limitation of time*. Professional Development School teachers in Los Angeles received funding for substitute teachers to enable PDS teachers to attend all-day project meetings, but frequently the teachers were reluctant to leave their classrooms to substitutes because of the discontinuity it created.

To counteract this problem the teachers decided to try the concept of "banked" time. Their intent was to teach fifteen minutes longer four days per week in order to "save" an hour each week for a group meeting. However, to accomplish this they needed permission from their school-site administrator, their region administrator, and district-level supervisor. The process consumed six months, and by that time the teachers no longer cared.

Most school districts do not budget for staff development time or the means to release teachers for special committee assignments. Districts sometimes give principals some discretionary funds that may be used for purposes such as staff development or teachers helping teachers. Without direct allocation of funds for professional growth activities, in general, they do not occur. Teachers' evening hours are consumed with grading papers, planning instruction, and trying to lead a normal home life.

> **Inhibitors to Professional Development**
>
> 1. Time constraints
> 2. External accountability
> 3. Bureaucratic Decision Making
> 4. Privacy Norms

What Can Be Done?   A close look at some of the less meaningful activities teachers perform reveals that time is used for clerical tasks that could be performed by clerical personnel. Time is also used for supervision of students on playgrounds, at lunch and recess time, in study halls, and before and after school. Elementary teachers spend time "moving" students to and from special programs; they supervise special auditorium programs, YMCA swims, Policeman Paul's DARE presentations. These activities require trusteeship care, but not the time of a certificated teacher. By week's end most teachers have spent the equivalent of two to three hours on a combination of low-level clerical and guardianship tasks. By releasing teachers from these nonteaching chores and often demeaning tasks, there would be opportunity for teachers to assume significant school governance responsibilities and time for professional growth. (In some Los Angeles area schools, principals have begun to assume playground supervision chores. Perhaps the thinking is that a principal's time is less valuable than a teacher's.) Better use of time is essential if teachers are to attend to leadership and professional responsibilities. By restructuring how special programs are delivered and to the number of students served, great time savings can accrue.

TEACHER EVALUATION

Who should evaluate teachers? What purpose(s) should evaluation serve? For what should teachers be held responsible? These are but a few of the questions asked when teacher evaluation is considered. In Colonial days schoolmasters had contracts that specified how many students were to be taught, for what period of time, and that each child must be taught as much as he or she was capable of learning. We have no clue how schoolmasters assessed the child's capacity for learning.

According to Buffalo, New York, superintendent Alfred Hartwell in 1924 (as described by Cuban, 1984) supervision and inspection became indistinguishable processes. Teachers were rated on "personality, control of class, self-control, discipline, and scholarship" (p. 54). Kimball Wiles (1950) in what is considered a classic book on supervision described the supervisor's role in the 1920s as directing and judging, in the 1930s he characterized it as "democratic"; and in the 1940s as a cooperative enterprise. He advocated supervision that was supporting, assisting, and sharing. Wiles was concerned that supervisors not play the evaluator's role.

In the 1960s and 1970s supervision responded to the "scientific" movement embracing the research on teaching related to active learning time. Teachers were expected to increase allocated time to basic skill instruction and monitor student engagement. Many supervisors used observation instruments developed by Madeline Hunter to observe teachers. Teachers were expected to adhere closely to seven procedures in a direct instruction plan. The instruments were used to identify teachers considered "inadequate" or deficient in teaching skills.

Instead of holding teachers responsible for student engagement and professional decision making, teachers were held responsible for learning outcomes. School districts developed closed and structured evaluation systems. The consequence of this was that teachers set perfunctory, unimaginative objectives, and became averse to risk taking. (See Fenstermacher, 1985 and Shedd and Bacharach, 1991, p. 95.)

Fueling the evaluation/accountability movement were policy enactments in state legislatures that set standards for teacher evaluation. With the layperson's inadequate understanding of significant teaching goals and teaching methodologies, teachers were forced to adhere to one teaching method to accomplish all purposes—a one-size-fits-all philosophy.

Darling-Hammond and Goodwin (1993) cite collective bargaining as still another inhibiting factor to the achievement of professional evaluation. Collective bargaining, they believe, tends to increase bureaucratic approaches to evaluation by specifying procedures to ensure the connection between evaluation and a district's personnel decisions. These agreements are focused on equal treatment for teachers, job specifications, and minimum performance standards.

Instead of evaluation in the 1960s to 1980s leading to professional growth activities, teachers refused to admit inadequacies and declined to experiment with new ideas and methods. In contrast, the new movement encouraging leadership and professionalism, urges personal growth activities, peer assessment, and peer-set standards.

Such standards include expectations that teachers make significant professional decisions related to planning, instruction, subject matter, classroom management, the learning environment, and assessment. Professional evaluation includes the following components and processes:

- Teachers design the evaluation process.

- Both the context and content of teaching are assessed. The observer attends to the students' assignments, the teacher's choice of learning materials, the learning environment, the cultural milieu of the classroom, student involvement, and overall goals.

- The use of a variety of teaching methodologies matched to learning outcomes is assessed.

■ Teaching should be directed to the needs and interests of students by attending to learning modalities, language differences, and conceptual development.

The process, intent, and outcomes of professional evaluation are different from evaluations that are policy- and district-driven and only seek to identify teacher inadequacies. However, the process of professional accountability and evaluation by and for teachers is far from refined and is dependent on collegial leadership.

PROFESSIONAL ACCOUNTABILITY

Underlying the concept of professional accountability are understandings about the nature of a profession and the behavior of its members. Some of these underlying precepts are:

■ Professionals have specialized knowledge and make decisions based on that knowledge.

■ Consideration of the well-being of the public (client) served is integral to decision making.

■ Members of a profession do not shirk responsibility for setting standards of practice that are ethical and serve to both define actions and improve practice.

The problem with professional accountability for teachers is that many current, and routinized practices in school districts will need to be changed so that decision making occurs profession-wide and at local schools by involved teachers.

Many of these practices that need to be revitalized or "restructured" have been discussed in this chapter and in other chapters of the text. Briefly reviewed, these are:

1. Peer review of competence as an ongoing activity instead of administrative evaluation of effective or ineffective service.

2. Personnel decisions to be made at the school site instead of at the district level when filling positions for specialized practice.

3. Staff development decisions as a professional concern and area of decision making for involved teachers, not an administrative decision.

4. Daily decisions affected by the use of "time" as a concern of the school site, independent of district level considerations.

5. Experimentation and research as a subject for professional, parental, and faculty school site deliberation and sanction.

6. A faculty review committee (augmented by parents) to evaluate professional practice at the school site with consideration of the community served and provider service to that community.

Professional accountability also must ensure that some decisions are made professionwide and not at the local school site. These decisions have to do with the knowledge base for teaching. Access to *what's new* does not abound at the local school site. Therefore, there needs to be a professional vehicle for communicating knowledge to practitioners. Linkages to universities need to be developed and nurtured to ensure the generation of knowledge and problem solving.

Professional standard setting must occur in the profession as a whole. Again, this is apart from the school district and the local school site. Standards need to be reevaluated regularly as they affect class size, teacher certification, teachers' assignments to courses, testing of students, grading, teacher responsibilities, team teaching, and collegial structures.

RECOGNITION OF LEADERSHIP AND PROFESSIONALISM

Two of the most important decisions that will have to be made by the teaching profession are how to involve members in the committee structure to make judgments affecting professional practice and how to *recognize* teachers for their service to the profession. Teachers will need to have time away from their daily responsibilities to serve on professional committees. Such involvement will need to be recognized and sanctioned by school districts and school site leadership. Both district-wide and school site involvement will be critical.

Contributions to the profession through committee work, consulting activities, public relations, and participation in research may need to be rewarded in new ways. Presently teachers receive credit (remuneration) for continuing education and/or university course work and inservice course work. Professional development in the future will take many new directions; much of it may be self-directed. Teachers may work in study groups as Lewison described or on professional committees. Just as school governance needs to be realigned, so too does the way teachers are rewarded and recognized for professional service.

CHANGING HABITS AND LEADERSHIP STYLES TO IMPROVE SCHOOL CULTURE AND DEVELOP A LEARNING COMMUNITY

It should be apparent from the discussion of problems affecting schools and teachers, that change processes affect and are affected by everyone in the school community. Changing the way we work and relate to others sometimes requires almost superhuman effort. For individuals making the effort, it does little good to recognize that there are research-based "stages"

> **Changing Habits and Leadership Styles**
>
> 1. Build community through participatory goal setting.
> 2. Involve faculty in authentic decisions.
> 3. Utilize teacher expertise.
> 4. Develop a collegial leadership style.

that the individual undergoes during the change process (see *Taking Charge of Change* by Hord, Rutherford, Huling-Austin and Hall, 1987). What is important is the implementation of *facilitating behaviors* to generate success.

What Can Facilitator-Leaders Do?

The first issue discussed in this chapter was the significance of a *vision*. The *facilitator-leader,* by seeing to it that vision is *shared, builds community.* The principal's vision means little if teachers have not helped to shape it and recognize their role in accomplishing it. Everyone must see the significance of the goal. At the professional development school in Los Angeles, it was the shared vision that brought participants together; however, unless everyone stays on task and continues to press to accomplish the shared vision, then nothing happens.

If the shared vision is a learner-centered curriculum, learner participation, and learner self-control, then there must be enabling mechanisms to assist teachers, such as staff development focused on:

1. How to develop students' decision-making and choice experiences in the classroom.

2. How to use different teaching strategies.

3. How to develop intrinsic motivation.

These enabling strategies also suggest other processes that need to come into play, such as peer coaching and teacher collaborative activities. Each task may lead to the need for additional changes in behaviors, use of resources, goal setting, and planning of time. When people get off-track, it is the leader's task to keep the mission focus and bring in the necessary resources. The facilitator leader may be the school principal, a teacher, or an on-site consultant.

The facilitator *uses participant expertise* both to help build community and to provide role models. Participant role models help to develop morale and allies for change. The more people involved in working toward the goal, the greater the concentration on concrete changes, such as change in curriculum, teaching style, and assessment.

By *involving faculty* in decisions that affect their work in the classroom, the facilitator-leader encourages social participation. Asking the right questions to motivate interest and encouraging group process skills is as important for adults as it is for children. Empowering teachers is just a catch-phrase, unless school faculties see the value of participation in significant decisions. For example, if learner self-control is a schoolwide goal, then teachers need to recognize that rewarding student behavior through "treats" will have a negative impact. Significant decisions need to be made concerning how the goal can be accomplished in classrooms and on the school grounds. These decisions cannot be made by the facilitator-leader or principal alone. Not only must the teachers decide on how to accomplish this goal within the classroom, but they *must decide what strategies impede the accomplishment of the goal.*

The facilitator-leader should *suggest strategies* for accomplishing goals. In the aforementioned example, it may be apparent that teachers need to widen their range of instructional skills to include information-processing and inquiry-oriented teaching models. Using other teacher experts and allies, the leader may suggest in-service study and team coaching to be led by faculty members or outside consultants.

The challenge for the facilitator-leader is that there are often many facets to every change effort. Not only must faculty be encouraged to work together (and this by itself is a change) but there is a need for pedagogical change, a need to implement faculty coaching and devise a new system of assessment. Each change is linked to a variety of other professional, social, and emotional factors.

Throughout the process the facilitator-leader demonstrates risk taking, passion in beliefs, and patience. It is important to know when to encourage, when to suggest ideas, when to listen, and when to wait and see.

School life is influenced by traditional school culture, antecedent experiences by teachers both as teachers and as young learners themselves, school district regulations and routines, and societal and community values. Each of these factors affects habits and responses to problems and efforts to change. The successful school leader recognizes these influencing factors both in and out of the school environment. Both change and learning must be ongoing.

Leadership Styles That Enhance or Inhibit Change

Certain leadership styles enhance or inhibit change. The *prodder*-leader "pushes," and in general tries to keep others on task by constant monitoring of progress. The prodder may anticipate needs before they emerge and attempt to provide support services before teacher leadership takes hold. Within appropriate judgmental boundaries, the prodder may be successful in achieving change within the school culture, but there is real danger that the prodder may be too control oriented and internal leadership (by others) will not develop. If the prodder leaves the school, it is likely that all efforts toward change will cease.

The *role model* chooses to lead by setting examples. Using this leadership style, the leader may actively demonstrate means to accomplish goals by accepting school responsibilities. The role model–leader may demonstrate desired values through classroom experimentation and linking with other professionals. But if the role model is perceived as "too good" or unaccessible, the perception counteracts the leader image. As with the prodder-leader, if the role model departs, a leadership void may occur.

The *collegial leader* accepts leadership responsibilities, recognizes peer expertise, and is committed to improving the school program. Commitment takes the form of working collaboratively on real problems with others, engaging in peer coaching, and being willing to demonstrate curriculum and instructional expertise.

The collegial leader recognizes the danger of group compatibility (or groupthink) and values diverse perspectives as a means to inquire into varied processes and tentative solutions to school-based problems. Because the collegial leader helps to empower others, there is less of a void if the leader is transferred or chooses to leave.

The collegial leader *likes* working with others and as a consequence does it well. This leadership style is more natural and appears to be the "wave" of the future. New principals are embracing this style as a means to stimulate teacher learning and ownership of school improvement strategies.

CONTRASTING THE FACILITATOR-LEADER WITH THE TRADITIONAL LEADER

The facilitator-leader as principal or teacher strives to engage others in setting schoolwide goals. Goal setting becomes a means to build a learning community, and the goals are then used as a means to determine the next steps in the improvement process. By engaging others in school and classroom improvement processes, leadership is embraced by many instead of reserved for a few.

Unlike the traditional leader, management and control are not coveted; instead there is commitment to staff development, schoolwide participation in planning, and implementation efforts. Faculty expertise is recognized and used to assist the new and/or struggling teacher. Since change efforts are ongoing, goals become tentative targets as new needs emerge. Problems and challenges are not owned by the principal; they belong to the faculty-at-large. The facilitator-leader provides access to knowledge, to expertise, to resources. Actions are the province of the school faculty.

CONCLUSION

This chapter has focused on some of the inhibitors to teacher (and principal) leadership and suggested means to affect the likelihood of leadership and professionalism. It is clear that great effort is needed to change traditional roles, routines, and hierarchical decision making in school organizations. People are the answer: principals, teachers, consultants, teacher educators. Perhaps the biggest obstacle, not discussed in this chapter, is motivation. Great strides have been made; many schools are changing, and many individuals are assuming new professional roles, but the momentum must continue or school systems will revolve (indeed devolve) back into their old accustomed channels and methods of operation.

> **Recap Notes: Teacher Participation in School-Site Decision Making**
>
> Teacher leadership is enhanced when teachers
>
> - Set school and classroom goals (a shared vision).
> - Review school-site policies.
> - Communicate the rationale of plans to parents.
> - Select instructional materials.
> - Plan own professional development program.
> - Manage time pressures for school and professional study.
> - Engage in peer review of competence.
> - Engage in experimentation and research.

REFERENCES

Barnes, V. D. 1993. California high school restructuring: A case study of inland empire high school. Unpublished doctoral dissertation. Los Angeles: University Southern California.

Barr, R., and Dreeben, R. 1985. A sociological perspective on time. In *Perspectives on instructional time,* ed. C. W. Fisher and D. C. Berliner. New York: Longman.

Cuban, L. 1984. *How teachers taught.* New York: Longman.

Darling-Hammond, L., and Goodwin, A. L. 1993. Progress toward professionalism in teaching. In *Challenges and achievements of American education,* ed. G. Cawelti. Alexandria, Va.: ASCD.

Fernstermacher, G. D. 1985. Time as the terminus of teaching: A philosophical perspective. In *Perspectives on instructional time,* C. W. Fisher and D. C. Berliner. New York: Longman.

Hord, S. M., Rutherford, W. L., Huling-Austin, L., and Hall, G. E. 1987. *Taking charge of change.* Alexandria, Va.: Association for Supervision and Curriculum Development.

Lemlech, J. K., Hertzog-Foliart, H., and Hackl, A. 1993. The Los Angeles professional practice school: Impact of teacher education on staff development. In *Professional development schools—Schools for developing a profession,* ed. L. Darling-Hammond. New York: Teachers College Press.

Paterson, B. 1993. Contrastive roles of department chairs and mentor teachers in a traditional high school culture. Unpublished doctoral dissertation. Los Angeles: University Southern California.

Shedd, J. B., and Bacharach, S. B. 1991. *Tangled hierarchies.* San Francisco: Jossey-Bass.

Wiles, K. 1950. *Supervision for better schools.* 2nd ed. Englewood Cliffs, N.J.: Prentice-Hall.

Putting It Together
A Constructivist Perspective on School Leadership

PETER HODGES

Having just a vision's no solution
Everything depends on execution.
The art of making art,
is putting it together.

> Stephen Sondheim
> "Putting It Together"
> From the musical *Sunday in the Park with George,* 1984

Alicia Reyes School is located in the heart of California's Central Valley. The rural, agrarian roads passing through Merced County to the city of Merced suggest pastoral retreat. More than ninety crops are grown in commercial quantity, dairies being the largest agricultural industry. The shade of our almond orchards and our fields of green alfalfa conceal a more sobering profile.

According to federal census data, Merced has the highest poverty rate in California (20 percent), with the rate for minority group members twice that of the Anglo population. Thirty percent (30%) of county children live in poverty. Employment Development Department data indicate an unemployment rate of 19 percent. The area is distinguished by its large and extremely diverse ethnic/cultural population, and a significant number of residents are poor and undereducated. Current census data identify Merced as the seventh most ethnically diverse community in America, with one of the largest per capita refugee populations in the United States.

Alicia Reyes School is in the part of our city most impacted by poverty. A December 1992 Department of Health study indicates this neighborhood is the most medically underserved in the entire state. Government housing surrounds the school on two sides. School data indicate 81 percent

---

Chapter 3 HIGHLIGHTS

- Faculty Collaboration
- Curriculum Leadership Teams
- Participatory Decision Making
- The Principal's Collaborative Role
- Empowering Teachers Through Collective Action
- Building Community
- Principal's Role in Building Community

---

of our students are children of a minority group, and 63 percent are limited-English-proficient (LEP) children. Eighty percent (80%) of our students receive a free or reduced-cost meal. Sixty-seven percent (67%) are participants in the Chapter 1 compensatory-education program. Clearly, this is a population with a myriad of social concerns and needs.

Reyes is a year-round-education (YRE) school serving more than nine hundred K-5 students on a four-track calendar. YRE adds to our challenge; one-fourth of our children and teachers are always on vacation, complicating efforts toward communication and continuity.

Spanish bilingual students are served on one track with an articulated K-5 maintenance bilingual program. Biliterate teachers and aides serve these children. On the other three tracks, LEP Southeast Asian students are clustered, representing the Hmong, Mien, and Laotian languages and cultures. Instructional aides are employed on those tracks to meet primary language needs. Most certificated staff on these tracks have completed or are completing the state's criteria for Language Development Specialist certification.

As experienced in many schools, the realities just described, coupled with the daily routines of school, the competing demands of a diverse and often distracted public, and the red tape of institutional requirements seem a counterweight to idealism and commitment. Nonetheless, without visions of the possible, we would accomplish very little. It is through our commitment to collaboration, collective action, and community building that we nourish our pursuit of personal, professional, and school improvement. Those three imperatives—collaboration, collective action, and community building—comprise the focus of this paper and the elements that, when well orchestrated, lead to school improvement and continuous renewal.

Attempting to create such a transforming environment is an ongoing journey. Central to our concept of reconceptualizing the school is our recognition that a transformative school is a reflective environment, one in which we continuously envision a next step forward, never satisfied to rest in the comfort of routine. Imperfection is recognized as a constant. It is a constant with the capacity to energize—and to destabilize. The tightrope challenge of a commitment to ongoing improvement is to celebrate the small victories along the way while identifying and responding to the new puzzles and challenges that come into focus as we move further on down the road. In this environment, we are not solely creative *problem solvers;* we must be inventive in *problem identification* and *problem posing,* if we are to extend our thinking and realize new structures and strategies for meeting the needs of our changing student population and contemporary society. Change is never easy, but it is inevitable. We choose to move forward.

COLLABORATION

Traditionally, the workplace of the school has been one in which the physical structure of the building mirrors the social norms that shape teacher behavior and expectations. Physically separated from one another, teachers become psychologically isolated from one another. Isolation breeds doubts about personal efficacy as a teacher, and a survivor mentality develops (Lieberman and Miller, 1984). Ultimately, a distorted view of reality emerges in which the "good teacher" is seen as the Lone Ranger, cultivating a personal mystique of routine practices, rituals, and habits that define that teacher's style. Rather than expectations of continuous learning, growth, and change, the institution of education has historically rewarded the stability of routinization and predictability (Sarason 1971). At Reyes, we work to challenge those norms from the first day of a teacher's work in our school.

New teachers at Reyes School are assigned a "buddy teacher." The role of the buddy teacher is to provide the entering teacher with support and companionship. Consciously, the potentially patronizing term of "mentor" is avoided. The relationship is not about status. Rather, it is a signal that, at Reyes School, teachers are expected to reach beyond the boundaries of the classroom and interact in substantive ways with peer teachers outside of prescribed hierarchies. Buddy teachers are there to answer all of those emergent questions that even the best orientation program will miss and to let teachers know that we truly believe their growth within our school is a developmental process in which everyone is invested. The measure of their success as new teachers is not found in the established expertise that they bring with them but in their commitment to the process of an *evolving* professional practice.

As the principal of the school, I meet with new teachers every Friday during their first month and a half of school. Sessions begin with each of us sharing the impressions and experiences that stand out amidst the whirl of activity that each new week brings. What I hope to model in this activity is the norm of reflectivity—that we must periodically stop and take stock of who we are, where we have been, and what it all means to us before we attempt to move forward. I believe that teaching is a learning activity and, as learning, it is constructivist in nature. Each of us constructs personal meaning out of our world of experiences. For us as educators, reflection on professional practice and experience is a central feature of that learning process.

In our weekly meetings, we go on to look at curriculum subject matter and pragmatic activities such as addressing parent concerns, organizing a Back to School Night presentation, and structuring scheduled parent conferences. In these discussions, the message is presented that our school is focused on ideas and that we hold shared expectations about the way we pursue our core purposes. Clearly, the new teacher is learning about these shared expectations, but there is a subtext: teachers will receive support and guidance in a collaborative environment. At Reyes School, teacher practice is not a private enterprise.

Classroom management and discipline are the concerns of both new and continuing teachers. Collaboration is vital in this area of the teacher's work. The usual experience of schoolwide rules to define conduct outside of the classroom in public areas and education-code-governed procedures, are certainly a part of our work. Of greater importance, however, is the issue of collaboration as it affects central beliefs about the function of discipline and the values implicitly taught in disciplinary structures.

In the decade of the seventies, a move toward "assertive discipline" was common (Canter and Canter, 1976). At Reyes School, in the nineties, we have moved toward discipline that is focused on *teaching* social norms and problem-solving skills, rather than solely punishing transgressors. Our goal is that control move from the authority-based actions of a teacher to the self-control of the student. To achieve that end, we recognize that students must experience the rigors of life in community and learn the problem-solving skills to negotiate conflict without doing harm. Our disciplinary structures provide modeling and instruction in those domains. As appropriate to the age group, teachers and students discuss the typical issues in a classroom community that interfere with harmonious interpersonal relationships and then generate rules or norms that will govern those situations. They discuss consequences that are logically related to infractions, as opposed to punishments that may be remote and censoring.

The view in our school is that *consequences* are instructional, not punitive. For example, if a child loses or damages a schoolbook, a logical consequence of that action might be that the child would perform restitution work, perhaps in the library, to compensate the school community for the text. Students who were fighting or arguing might spend a recess playing checkers to learn how to cooperate in shared activity. In such classroom activities, several important things occur. Students learn to see the world through the eyes of other people, becoming less egocentric in their development. Students learn that rules are not solely the impositions of authority figures but are contracts among community members to facilitate their mutual needs. Students develop a stronger internal locus of control, discovering that they can effect changes in their environment through personal action and communication. Such an approach to discipline requires new learning and new ways of thinking for teachers.

At Reyes, knowing that time is a precious commodity for everyone, teachers meet for short "brown bag" lunches to discuss how discipline affects students. In these discussions, we have investigated how authority-centered strategies ultimately serve to make students less responsible; control mechanisms are vested in the teacher. We have discussed how approaches that make students responsible for conduct ultimately empower the student and cultivate self-regulation of behavior. Teachers at Reyes have learned from one another how to conduct regular class meetings, teaching students problem-solving and communication skills and the concept of the *logical consequences* of behavioral choices (Driekurs, 1964; Nelsen, 1981). The brown-bag lunch has been a forum for peer support.

Meeting once or twice a week during their lunch for the first month of school, teachers have been able to share their experiences in implementing this innovation and learn from one another's efforts. Each teacher has a copy of *Positive Discipline* (Nelsen, 1981). Meetings provide teachers a chance to discuss the central concepts of that book, developing shared meanings about its approach to classroom management and discipline. Videotapes of actual class meetings have been made in the classrooms of teachers willing to volunteer, and used as reality-based scenes, these videotapes have helped focus discussion. Again, the message conveyed through such collaboration is that innovation is valued and collegial support is central to professional growth. No one is expected to stand alone, judged solely on the merits of their personal survival skills and facility.

Recognizing that every teacher will face challenging students and find, at times, children not progressing in the instructional program, Reyes has developed a collaborative structure to support the classroom teacher at these moments. A core team has been organized on each track to assist teachers and the students they serve who are experiencing difficulty. This team involves the school's assistant principal, a track teacher representative, the track's special-education resource specialist, and the referring classroom teacher. Their discussions may lead to special-education assessment. More often, contributing causes for a child's difficulty are identified during the case study review, which results in referrals to support services in health, guidance, and parenting areas. We are now implementing a special grant that will extend this collaborative approach to include medical, social, and adult education agencies in our community in a unified system of service delivery to families in our school, with the core team as the bridge to such family support.

Since our inception, we have explored shared governance structures to extend the roster of players who influence the direction of our programs and practices. Teacher collaboration in structuring the workplace, the content of the curriculum, and the allocation of resources toward mutually valued priorities is a true measure of the central role teachers at Reyes play in creating a transformative school environment.

The Curriculum Leadership Team

A teacher representative is elected by each YRE track, and they, along with the library/media teacher, the state and federal projects resource teacher, the assistant principal, and the principal meet at least once a month as the curriculum leadership team (CLT). Their role is to guide the school in its improvement and renewal efforts. In addition, this group makes budgetary decisions supporting such efforts.

In general, the CLT takes proposals back to the staff at general meetings for their approval in general matters of organization and with respect to the annual budget. Additionally, budget and curriculum decisions made by the CLT are subject to the review and approval of the School Site Council and school advisory committees, as determined by the California education code.

The educators on this leadership team work to keep curriculum development, curriculum implementation, staff development, school climate, and general operations purposeful and progressive. Teacher professionalism and the attendant expanded leadership roles for teachers are central to school improvement. Representative governance requires trust and a willingness to empower others. We are learning with each decision how that process requires us to grow and change as individuals and as educators. No longer is there an authority figure to blame when conditions are not as one would like. Instead, it is a shared responsibility to identify problems and explore their resolution. Once these have been resolved through consensual decision making, each staff member must commit his or her support to the group's direction, even when that decision may not have taken the direction that the individual teacher or administrator might have desired. The efforts of our team represent a significant exploration of new directions in the governance of educational organizations. It is a learning experience for everyone.

Grade Levels and Tracks

Grade-level meetings, led by a peer-selected grade-level leader, occur twice each month. The purpose of this meeting is to build curricular articulation and to enable teachers collegial support in developing and implementing curriculum innovations to meet the needs of our students. Focusing on issues relevant to their grade, teachers exchange ideas, share promising practices, forecast issues that will require their attention, and attend to simple organizational tasks that facilitate their personal and shared work.

Within their grade level, teachers work to develop common lenses for assessment and shared expectations for student performance. For example, three times a year, teachers collectively score writing samples from one another's classrooms using a holistic rubric. In this process, over time, teachers have developed shared standards and, in their conversations, exchanged ideas for practice that have contributed to the writing program in every classroom.

Tracks are led by elected teacher-leaders and meet twice each month as a "school within a school" in the YRE structure. Recognizing that, in a YRE school, teachers serve the same families and promote children in a fairly predictable pattern, collaborative activity enhances their efforts. The problems one teacher faces with a child may be reflective of family issues, revealed in another teacher's experience in her work with a child in the same family on the YRE track. In a collaborative approach through multiple perspectives, the teachers and support staff on the track may more effectively serve both child and family. Recently, a child in a fourth-grade class reported family conflict. His teacher observed that he was disruptive, and not completing homework. At the track meeting that week, she discovered that his third-grade brother was demonstrating similar behavior. Together, the teachers quickly arranged a parent conference and developed an intervention plan that included parental monitoring of homework, counseling, and scheduled home-school communication. Working collaboratively with the child and the family as a focus, the teachers were able to construct a more complete picture of the dynamics involved in each child's situation and to respond with effective intervention.

Track meetings also promote articulation and continuity among the grades. Meeting on a regular basis with the teachers who precede and follow a teacher's grade reduces curricular overlap and helps teachers talk about the observed strengths and needs in the preparation of students. Further, teachers have an opportunity to discuss and negotiate the expectations they hold for students beginning a year in their class. With greater certainty than in a traditional setting as to who the preceding teacher was, teachers experience a very pointed accountability with their peers. By planning together, sharing expectations, and joining in a sense of mutual responsibility for the students they serve, the work of our school is improved.

Too often, in the desire to establish participatory decision making, schools have given roles to teachers but have not supported them in developing the skills and awareness that those new roles require. With that in mind, grade and track leaders have participated in team-building in-service education and practiced strategies that will enhance their work as peer leaders in the organization. Developing a sense of trust and support in realizing this goal of extended leadership has been one purpose of that activity, but, on a more practical level, learning how to organize and run a meeting, learning strategies to include each participant in group activity, learning to deal with obstructive behaviors, and learning to be assertive and effective in the communication skills demanded of a leader have been among the pragmatic skills our in-service program for teacher-leaders has sought to develop.

Operations

General operational decisions are developed through consensus at regular staff meetings. An open agenda is constantly posted in the staff lounge; any employee may sign up to discuss an item. At monthly certificated and classified staff meetings, the agenda's items are brought to the floor for discussion. Certificated staff meetings are chaired by a member of the teaching staff. Relevant issues emerging from this process are referred to the CLT and/or School Site Council for consideration.

Curriculum Development

Standing committees of teachers work with the principal and the Curriculum Leadership Team (CLT) in the areas of the curriculum undergoing study, development, and implementation. These curricular areas are aligned with our state's established curriculum cycle. Based on our state curriculum frameworks, relevant educational research, and informed practice, staff-identified teacher experts define for their peers what direction a well-developed curriculum in each subject area should take. They develop effective instructional practices to support the realization of that curriculum in the classroom. These committee members provide staff development and in-class modeling for peers and help identify outside consultants to support staff development effort, as needed.

Exemplifying this approach has been our work in implementing new curricula in the history social sciences. Prevailing over traditional social studies programs, which separate social science disciplines and focus on rote knowledge and the recall of isolated factoids, this curriculum correlates disciplines within the social sciences such as history and economics and integrates related disciplines such as the arts and literature studies. Higher-order, relational thinking is paramount.

A cadre of teacher-leaders, including classroom teachers and the library media teacher, have turned to resources such as the state framework, professional articles, and their own effective past practices to develop a detailed description of the content of this new curriculum in its ideal form.

Focusing on improving teaching, this cadre has developed grade-specific model units of teaching that operationalize this curriculum through varied models of teaching (Joyce and Weil, 1986). Central to this work in developing exemplary learning activities is the incorporation of technologies that support the central principles of the desired curriculum and its teaching strategies, including the laser disc, CD-ROM, video, and computer. These inquiry-based models lead students to develop a rich repertoire of accessing, processing, and presenting strategies.

All staff members have participated in these peer-led staff development sessions. With the support of the leadership cadre, teachers have developed the initial scaffold of an additional innovative unit of their own. Working as a track group and utilizing the model with expert guidance, teachers have been able to transfer the specific contours of the in-service program to generalizable models for future practice, applicable across the curriculum.

An example of this work is a unit that was designed to serve as a prototype for the third-, fourth-, and fifth-grade curriculum, focusing on the railroad. Integrating technology resources, population distributions, and settlement patterns were examined at the county, state, and national level. From these, using inquiry-based models of teaching, teacher and student learners drew inferences on the impact of the railroad on economies, settlement, and immigration. For example, the route of the railroad caused the seat of government of our county to be moved from one town to another. Today, the formal capital is a town of two or three stores and a ranchers' restaurant, while the new city of Merced is a bustling community of 50,000 people. This unit integrated the visual and performing arts, language arts, and several social science disciplines.

Extending the work, the *National Council for History Education* presented a three-day colloquium at Reyes that taught additional teaching strategies, including the use of primary source documents and museum archives. This colloquium enabled teachers the opportunity to work with an exemplary elementary classroom practitioner, a university professor, and a staff development specialist.

Concluding this year-long effort, teachers had several days of release time with substitute coverage to work in grade-level teams, continuing to create units of history social science that synthesized the presentational models of the local and national staff development efforts in the context of their classrooms and the real-life learning needs of our diverse student population. A curriculum of this design requires new approaches to teaching. Implicitly, it is recognized at Reyes School that authentic changes in the teaching/learning paradigm require *time:* time for planning, time for trying, and time for learning. Explicitly, that process of change is supported by setting aside such time for teachers as they take these steps in their professional growth. In our new school year, we are setting aside time each Wednesday for this kind of instructional development. Students leave school early on that day (making up the minutes on the remaining four days), allowing teachers uninterrupted time for professional development activities.

Extending curriculum implementation work, the teacher leadership of our subject-matter teams continue to monitor program development. Epitomizing this is the work of our Language Arts Committee. Each year, they collect a random stratified sample of language arts portfolios from each teacher. Reviewing these, they make determinations about program effectiveness on a schoolwide basis and recommend what steps to take to facilitate the continued growth of our curriculum effort in this domain. Their annual reports and accompanying in-service programs have done much to keep the momentum going as we move on to work in new areas, such as history social science. Transforming performance-based assessment and portfolio work from mere data gathering, this effort sets a standard for moving new approaches to assessment from the sole individual-student evaluation to a vital program-improvement data source.

Our site-based curriculum work and staff development not only enhance the specific abilities of teachers within the subject matter of the discipline, they build the capacity of our school over time to work collaboratively and to recognize the power of shared endeavor. Truly, two heads are better than one. In such shared enterprise, teachers are empowered through the experience of their own creativity and efficacy.

We believe that the professionalization of teaching is a key pillar in the effort to improve our schools. Teachers must increase their decision-making authority—and responsibility—in curricular matters central to their professional role. They must be curriculum builders, not curriculum consumers. The philosophy of "teachers teaching teachers" has well served our state's subject-matter projects and the curriculum development process at Reyes. Coupled with regular discussions of current research, collaborative planning, and cooperative teaching, we believe we are reconceptualizing traditional norms of the schoolplace to respond to the concern voiced by Seymour Sarason, a leader in school development:

> The assumption that teachers can create and maintain those conditions which make school living and learning stimulating for children without those same conditions existing for teachers, has no warrant in the history of mankind.

The Principal's Role in Collaboration

At the onset of my career as a principal, the role was in transition. No longer was success defined by one's competence in the *efficient management* of the plant, employees, and students; now the literature indicated that a successful principal was first and foremost an "instructional leader." Images of the ship's captain facing into the wind with one hand grasping the wheel while the other navigated by the charts of clinical teaching seemed somehow the metaphor of the times. Within this construct was a traditional linear and hierarchical construct of how educational organizations operate. Somehow, by fiat or inspiration, principals were to set the course, charge the crew, and navigate the shoals to the port of school improvement. Working within that construct, I was effective by many measures, but marginal by others. Those who operated outside of the construct had a difficult time with the established leadership style of that era.

Some of those who had difficulty with the reigning management model resisted, because they were marginal in their performance and resented specified standards for their work. The emphasis on clinical supervision (Goldhammer, 1969; Acheson and Gall, 1987), effective school formulas (Edmonds, 1979; Purkey and Smith, 1982), and objectives-based instruction (Hunter and Russell, 1981) was defining a new cultural experience for many. Such teachers had not been accountable for their work and its impact on children and found scrutiny threatening when those practices were illuminated. These were teachers who found the isolation and privacy of teaching (Lieberman & Miller, 1984) a safe haven. For those practitioners, the clinical environment of the eighties was an improvement over past practice in that it introduced those teachers to a more public conversation about teaching and learning.

However, another cadre of teachers also took umbrage with the instructional leader/clinical practice map. These were highly creative, self-directing, and effective practitioners, teachers with a strong professional ethos about their instructional practices. Excluded from charting the established course, even if only symbolically in the shadow of the designated instructional leader, and able to present truly viable routes of their own, these teachers found the reigning organizational model to be an encumbrance and often a constraint to excellence in their teaching.

Collaborative models strike a middle ground, everyone is invited to the table and all are able to participate in the conversation about the school's purposes and practices. I remain at that table, but I am joined by a large cadre of very talented teacher-leaders with strong voices of their own and equally compelling visions of the possible. A constructivist view of learning suggests that our background experiences structure our learning, opening some vistas while obscuring others. If school improvement and change are indeed processes of learning, then extending participation in the conversation brings a wider breadth of learning potential to the endeavor. I believe that our planning and development activities are strengthened as a result of that true collaboration.

In my work as an educator, I have witnessed false collaboration. Groups are brought together to "collaborate" and share in participatory decision making, but, in fact, the sum total of that collaboration is to

react to a previously sculpted decision or to affirm the "politically correct" viewpoint dominating the organizational culture. This pretense of
collaboration demeans and marginalizes the diversity of perspectives
inherent in a truly professional educational organization.

That is not the case at Reyes. Dissent is critical in our work and, there
has to be a process that allows such dissent. As the principal, I have to live
out the credo of collaboration in my willingness to be overruled or modified in my proposals, just as others at the table are in theirs., Engaged as
learners, we must each be willing to accommodate the data of experience
and insight brought to the conversation. In the experience of dissent, I
find that one of two things happen. Either the decision is affirmed and
our commitment to it deepened because we have examined the founda-
tions of that dissent, or the decision is modified and improved because of
the rigors of criticism. Unless I am willing as a school leader to be a part
of that process, I can not ask it of others. I believe we are better for the
experience.

As the principal of the school I have the unique opportunity to construct a synthetic view of our environment. Through my observations
and interactions with such a variety of classrooms, teachers, and other
players, I am privy to an expanded view of the school. In that I have the
unique opportunity to facilitate collaborations. When I see a teacher trying to reach new ground in math, I know someone I can link them with
for peer support and dialogues. If a teacher expresses concern about a
child's social behavior, I know someone that can offer insight. If a group
of teachers recognize a school need, I help them to negotiate the process
that will enable them to bring that idea to a larger audience. Helping to
build bridges and forging connections among the different constituents
of our school is a signal feature of my role in promoting collaboration as
a foundational norm at Reyes School.

The question arises, "Does everything have to have group input or go
to a committee? Isn't that terribly inefficient?" Sorting and processing
issues is vital aspect of my role. Many things are appropriately handled
by me as the principal. Just as a classroom teacher has his or her area of
responsibility and expertise, I have mine. Experience suggests that teachers do not want to have involvement in every decision and certainly not
in the minutiae of school operations. The institutionalized decision-
making processes, our CLT, and our grade-level planning structures,
offer the checks and balances that give me confidence that the sorting
and processing is properly conducted. When I err, somewhere in our system a voice will be raised to suggest that the issue needs to be revisited

and processed through the CLT, a staff meeting, or grade-level meetings rather that being dispatched by my action. In a climate of collaboration there first must be a foundation of trust. In that basic trust, hopefully we each find grace when what we believed were positive intentions are perceived as contrary to the point of view of others. Working to develop trust and confidence in each other's honorable intentions is an agenda as important as curriculum development or our work on teaching strategies as we seek to rethink schooling. Ultimately, this work reminds us that ours is a human enterprise and that it is in that arena that we must apply ourselves if we are to see true institutional improvement.

COLLECTIVE ACTION

In many schools, the classrooms of teachers, too often, seem to function as disconnected entities, each teacher an autonomous player in an idiosyncratic world of personal invention. Such free-fall classrooms, disconnected from any unifying sense of the whole, typify the norm of discontinuity in the schoolplace (Weick, 1982).

At the same time, the rational view of school improvement as a linear process shaped by a compelling central vision and strategic, sequential planning may be equally dysfunctional. Such a view of the school ignores the reality of the school as a human social organization. While linear models of organizational development may have utility in produce-oriented industries, teaching and learning occur in a social context. The ambiguous, the unpredictable, and the nonrational are inescapable dimensions of our social world.

Vision-centered models of school reform may serve to restrict and control, masking insights and possibilities not originally conceived or discovered along the way. Indeed, some organizational theorists characterize schools as "organized anarchies" in which a loose aggregate of players churn their way through a tumultuous world of problems, competing preferences, and emerging opportunities. Meanings and intentions are constructed to explain experience after the fact, rather than to direct its course (Cohen, March, and Olsen, 1972).

At Reyes School, we are attempting to find some middle ground, a place with ties that bind but do not constrain. Collective action on schoolwide issues and needs that still permits divergence and creative invention, characterizes that sensibility.

For example, in examining our compensatory-education approaches, we found that we were operating like many schools, remediating with little impact, too long after children had entered a cycle of school failure and its tailspin effects (Anderson and Pellicer, 1990). In our effort to improve, staff read related research, discussed possible program directions, and visited a variety of schools. Collective action on our identified problem was required, a schoolwide commitment to improving our work in compensatory education. At the same time, the direction of that action was a process of shared learning and developing commitment, rather than a confining initial prescription.

We were influenced by the work of Marie Clay in New Zealand (Clay, 1979; Pinnell, 1990) and a successful early-intervention program in a neighboring district in Fresno County (California Department of Education, 1993), to develop a Reading intervention program. This program involved one-to-one support for first-grade children experiencing difficulty in reading acquisition, based on the realization that the prevention of school failure is more effective than its remediation. A credentialed teacher meets with each child for a half an hour a day over a twelve- to fourteen-week period, providing a highly personalized reading program based on current theory and an integration of program elements from New Zealand and Fresno. To make this program possible, school resources had to be redistributed. Upper-grade classrooms received less compensatory-education focus as we shifted to a preventative model: collective action on a schoolwide issue. Upper-grade teachers, through the study and the visitations which had occurred, endorsed the shift to a preventative model and the accompanying redistribution of resources which that entailed because they recognized that such a shift would result in more students achieving grade-level competence. Understanding that the traditional remedial work of the upper-grade Chapter 1 program was less productive than intensive preventative intervention in the primary grades, these teachers focused on student needs and the long-term gain. Our school philosophy shifted and all levels of the organization supported that new focus.

Once consensus developed around the desired program response, that action was left to assume form over time. Working within the general contours of the early-intervention program in our region, our actions and intentions only later came into focus. Built into our process was ongoing reflection, collaboration, and the construction of shared meanings. When we began, we never would have imagined where we would be by the year's end. The reading teachers and first-grade classroom teachers involved in the Reading intervention effort met weekly.

Their discussions refined our process for identifying potential program candidates. Their work enabled us to serve students learning in Spanish, expanding the English-based program model we had adopted. In weekly case study discussions and review of professional literature, the reading teachers refined their approaches to assist students in strategic reading and developed an expanded base of authentic assessment tools to better inform their teaching decisions. Finally, a sophisticated component of parent education and involvement emerged that became one of the pillars of program success.

Throughout the process, fidelity to the adopted model was a mandate. We had to have a baseline "program" to assess. Any change, modification, or deviation from that model was allowed only when supported by case study or program evaluation data and, that decision was made collectively in the collaborative discussions of involving the Reading intervention teachers, the classroom teachers, the program leader, and the principal.

None of the directions our program ultimately took could have been anticipated when we began. Had we narrowly defined an implementation strategy and rigidly aligned accompanying activities, we would never have discovered the lessons we learned about instruction, assessment, and parent support. Collective action directed our mutual commitment, but the path of that journey was an exploration that took its own course.

The Principal's Role in Collective Action

In my role as the principal, I have from time to time had to assume a role as the protector of such collective action. Given the tradition of autonomy and idiosyncratic practice that accompanies the norms of teacher isolation, collective action may, at first glance, seem to disempower teachers. I disagree. As educators working within the same environment, we are part of an ecology, part of a greater whole. With the needs of children at the center of our work, we have a responsibility to strive for a degree of coherence and continuity in what we propose for their education. Teacher-leaders are the central players in the construction of those school directions. We have lost teachers from our school who preferred to operate as autonomous practitioners, separate in their private practice. So be it. Collective action is required if a school is to become more than a gathering of private enterprises.

This is not to say that individuality, personal interests, and unique creative activity have no place. Rather than an "either/or" construct, a "both/and" approach is necessary. Alongside our common activities, teachers are encouraged to pursue a range of independent work. Individual staff members are deeply involved in professional associations in particular curricular areas, provide leadership in professional-development institutes at the state and regional level, and, certainly, invest in creative exploration in their daily teaching. We depend on that individual initiative. In such activity, our teachers return with provocative questions and insights that enrich and energize the conversation within our school. They contribute their personal perspective and talents to deepen our collective work in developing curriculum and instruction at Reyes School. Without their individual growth and absent their leadership as exemplary teachers, our collective commitments would be impoverished.

Collective action does not require the abandonment of individuality. At the same time, individuality can not absolve each teacher from the responsibility of a commitment toward organizational development. The principal must protect that fundamental value. *School improvement is not a voluntary activity.*

COMMUNITY BUILDING

Ultimately, a school must seek to be more than a task-oriented environment to move forward. Underlying the instructional program, sustaining our efforts to meet the social and developmental needs of our children, and buttressing the work we do to educate our students as citizens and leaders of a democratic society, is the attempt to create a sense of community.

Webster's Third New International Dictionary defines community, thus:

> Com•mu•ni•ty *n.*   People living in a particular place and usually linked by common interests.

It is relatively easy to recognize a vision of ourselves as "living in the same locality" or as "a social group." Far more challenging has been the elusive "Similarity: *a community of interest.*"

Left to our own devices, we are no doubt a group of fairly disparate interests and identities. This teacher is interested in science, this one in language arts. This teacher sees her work as a calling and works oblivious to time, while another sees her teaching as secondary to family interests and is accordingly concerned about the hour. This teacher sees the needs of bilingual students as preeminent, while another worries about the inevitable separatism of such discrete linguistic and cultural groupings. There are no right answers, and countless research has underscored teachers' varied levels of concern and commitment.

Beyond surface issues, our school is a group of people with all of our imperfections, frailties, and moments of nobility intact. We are only human, attempting to do a job in a climate that, at times, seems to demand superhuman qualities. How do we attempt the impossible each day as simple individuals? It seems to me that, ultimately, if this is ever to be doable, it is only possible in the context of a sustaining community of shared concern. In the final measure, what we achieve becomes not a matter of competence but of character. *In community, we find our better selves.*

We have had some incredible battles in our time! In a YRE school, four teachers are roommates, sharing three rooms over the course of a year. People, perhaps especially teachers, are territorial beings. The demands of sharing space and materials have fomented some terrific conflicts and pitched battles.

Turmoil can still rear its head over whole language, writing as a process, and traditional skill-driven models of teaching. Finding a common course of action among these particular controversies and contentions occupied us all for several years. We have reached an uneasy detente in the realization that an embrace of multiple models of teaching is perhaps of greater service to students than educational orthodoxies and dogmas.

The budget crisis in our state's schools has been something of a blessing in that the lack of funds has quieted the annual posturing and fighting attendant to contract negotiations. These can always be counted on to elicit months of passion that distract us from instruction and intrude on relationships and school activities.

Through all of this, we have been slowly moving toward a greater sense of community. In small steps and quiet ways, we come closer. Structured team-building activities help. Using activities like the Keirsey/Bates Inventory (Keirsey and Bates, 1984), staff learn about their own personality type and those of other people. These explorations help us both to build personal awareness about how we structure our own life experience and approaches to our world and to develop both empathy and understanding for those who structure them differently. Simple activities like role playing, values clarification exercises, and art creation express personal goals and beliefs and help us to function with greater cohesion.

Of more import, getting to a place where we had a foundation of trust strong enough to allow us to make our conflicts public and confront them together was a milestone in our school history. The evolving strength of our CLT was a significant aspect of that process. As long as school climate rested in the domain of administrative responsibility, we did not move forward. Holding climate as an administrator's responsibility was much easier, if not productive. It could be the administrator's fault if things were not going well or decisions were unwelcome. It was the administrator's job to hear disputes among teachers and render judgments. Solomon-like resolution was rare. As the administrator, I have never liked the role. Ultimately, I think it reinforces patriarchal authority norms and serves to disempower teachers as mature people. Traditional structures obstruct personal growth and responsibility.

As our CLT evolved, teacher leadership assumed more definition and clarity. In leadership team discussions, it became apparent that each of us at Reyes School had to take responsibility for our own actions—and our own problems. Further, the CLT declared that they would no longer accept conduct that was damaging to the greater good and, if necessary, would intervene to protect the integrity of the school community from the damaging actions of individuals or interest groups. For example, responding to an ongoing dispute among several teachers over perceived YRE room-sharing transgressions that was beginning to factionalize staff, CLT teacher-leaders made a clear declaration that conduct was occurring that was unacceptable within the norms of our school. As peer leaders, they let it be known that if these staff members could not agree or at least observe a truce of civility, they, the teacher leadership, would intervene and, if necessary, suggest to colleagues that it was time to consider a transfer to a new work environment. The power of that looming possibility was sufficient to help people reestablish appropriate conduct parameters.

In rounding that corner, we were able to have several frank discussions in the CLT and as a staff about our concept of personal responsibility and commitment. As an outcome, we arrived at a governing statement of principles. That statement made explicit the parameters for interpersonal and professional conduct. It was important to move them from unspoken and assumed norms to overt, explicit standards. Added to the norms we had previously established for staff meetings, we now established a foundation of common belief that has since helped to guide us as we work to build community within our school.

ALICIA REYES SCHOOL

Staff Meeting Norms

1. *Use "I" statements.*
2. *Really listen.*
3. *Acknowledge the speaker.*
4. *Business will be done here, not later or elsewhere.*
5. *Engage in one-to-one communication before airing issues at staff meetings.*
6. *The aim is problem solving, not judging.*

Community Norms

Recognizing that we each are responsible as individuals for our personal conduct with the goal of building community and maintaining civility, we ascribe to the following school norms governing interpersonal relations.

1. *Positive Communication:*
   - "I" statements
   - Not judging
   - Active listening
   - Validating the other person's experience

2. *Ply "Honest Stuff":*
   - Own your issues and concerns as your own.
   - Take the risk and deal with it.
   - Be timely in dealing with issues.

3. *Honor Responsibility and Commitment:*
   - You can't bail out when it isn't going your way or it gets uncomfortable.
   - Don't undermine group decisions or others' efforts.
   - Be part of the solution, not part of the problem.

4. *Practice Patience and Flexibility.*
5. *Reflect and Celebrate along the way.*
6. *Know the difference between "aggressive" and "assertive."*
7. *Maintain a sense of humor.*

MOST OF ALL, KEEP IN MIND WHY WE ARE HERE:
REMEMBER THE KIDS

Authentic Collegiality

In the process of confronting the realities of our schoolplace environment, the staff discussed an article by Carl Glickman (1990) that spoke powerfully to each of us and let us know that we were not alone. In this article, Glickman notes the finding that improving schools experienced conflict because such schools were willing to take the risk to confront the inevitable discomfort attendant to the improvement process. That has been our experience.

Many schools mistake *congeniality* for *collegiality*. Warm social relations, helpful attitudes, and a veneer of polite interchange are no doubt more comfortable than disequilibrium, conflict, and controversy, but when in human history did significant change ever occur in a risk-free, copacetic environment? Change signifies a disruption of the status quo. Given that the institution of education values stability and routine, how is it that we wonder why true reform is so elusive (Sarason, 1990)?

The Principal's Role in Community Building

In a truly collaborative environment focused on school improvement, more is asked of us. We have found that we must each place more of our authentic self on the line and that such a step can lead to friction. It is not the absence of conflict that marks a good school but the manner in which the school addresses and processes its conflicts. We feel authentic collegiality directed toward improving our school involves confronting hard truths and uncomfortable questions. Collaboration has enabled us to grow both personally and professionally, ultimately strengthening our work as individuals and helping us to build a school community.

As the principal, this is an interesting paradox. I must stand simultaneously within the community and, to a degree, outside of it. My role is multidimensional in that I must facilitate the building of community and help to maintain attendant group norms. Sometimes, I am a conscience, a cop, a mirror, or a problem poser as I strive to present individuals and the group with issues that we must address to support our community. At the same time, I have to be a group member, a follower of the community's direction, willing to acknowledge or at least be willing to learn when my own actions are wanting in the goal of building community.

Leaders often are, I believe, people who are dealing with strong "control" issues. I am no exception. Neither are our strong teacher-leaders. Many of us acknowledge a tendency to be a "control freak." I believe one of the lessons of our experience is learning how to marshall one's control needs for socially protective enterprise while, at the same time, being willing to suspend or defer those in the larger context of the community. Truly, you can't always get what you want! Again, a seeming paradox emerges; as I have learned to "control" less, I find myself actually increasing my effectiveness. The number of players willing to step forward and join me in taking responsibility for this environment has increased as others perceive the opportunity to enter the conversation at a substantive level. I believe other site leaders are learning the same lesson. It is a delicate personal and interpersonal negotiation that demands constant reflection and communication. It is a process of learning. In the long run, I think it has been one of the most energizing things I, and we, have learned. *We find our true personal effectiveness grows a community of others.*

CONCLUSION

I do not know what the future of schooling will be. We live in a transitional period. It is amazing to realize that an institution that emerged just prior to the Civil War is hobbling into the twenty-first century virtually intact. Even in its dated form, the public school still manages to function with some measure of success for the children of economic privilege. It does not work so well for the poor, the culturally diverse, or the child of special needs.

Schools will change. In some small way, the work of schools like Reyes in exploring new curricular approaches, redefined roles for teachers, and exploring new organizational structures, will contribute to that new vision of schooling. No doubt, the final transformation of the institution will not be realized within the time of most of our careers, but we are contributing to the dialog. Working to effect some small measure of improvement through reflective collaboration in a sustaining community will be the mark we leave behind. That's what our work at Reyes School seems to be about.

> *You can't be of another time and you can't be of the future. You can only be of what you are and, if you work very hard and you've known the past and you've learned your lessons there, and you've seen what's relevant in the past, then chances are it's going to have some connection to what will prove in the future to have been relevant now. Then you, in turn, are of service to the future, and that's the best you can do. It's all a continuum.*
>
> Twyla Tharp, Choreographer
> From *Dance*, a PBS Broadcast, 1993

Recap Notes: Some Things We've Learned along the Way

- Change is a learning process, constructivist in nature. We each bring our own lenses and can increase the learning curve if we make that learning a social process. In that collaborative enterprise, we cultivate collective norms that are an important impetus to school improvement and that provide a strong framework of spoken and unspoken accountability standards.

- Everyone, including the principal, must participate as co-equal learners, each with much to contribute to the learning process, and each with much to learn in the process.

- Authentic collaboration is often disorderly and uncomfortable. However, substantive change and significant school improvement cannot occur unless we are each willing to risk the personal loss and disequilibrium demanded of that endeavor.

- A sustaining community is an essential foundation for our individual efforts to improve teaching, learning, and schooling. As a forum for learning and as a source of interpersonal support, the trust we place in that community is the reassuring net that enables us to walk the tightrope challenges of ongoing personal growth, professional development, and school improvement.

- The role of the principal, like that of everyone in educational organizations, is in transition. It is a multidimensional role comprised of leader, learner, gatekeeper, linker, protector, negotiator, facilitator, broker, and choreographer. Less a function of linear and mechanistic policy implementation, the principalship engages one in activities of ongoing problem solving and creative design.

REFERENCES

Acheson, K. A, and Gall, M. D. 1987. *Techniques in the clinical supervision of teachers.* 2nd ed. New York: Longman.

Anderson, L. W., and Pellicer, L. O. 1990. Synthesis of research on compensatory and remedial education. *Educational Leadership* (September) 48(1): 10–16.

California Department of Education 1993. *Beyond retention.* Sacramento, Calif.: State Bureau of Publications.

Canter, L., and Canter, M. 1976. *Assertive discipline.* Los Angeles: Canter and Associates.

Clay, M. 1979. *The early detection of reading difficulties.* New Zealand: Heine-mann.

Cohen, M. D., March, J. G., and Olsen, J. P. 1972. Garbage can model of organizational choice. *Administrative Science Quarterly* 17:1–26.

Driekurs, R. 1964. *Children: The challenge.* New York: Penguin.

Edmonds, R. R. 1979. Effective schools for the urban poor. *Educational Leadership* 37:15–24.

Glickman, C. 1990. Pushing school reform to a new edge: The seven ironies of school improvement. *Phi Delta Kappan* (September) 72(1):68–75.

Goldhammer, R. 1969. *Clinical supervision.* New York: Holt, Rinehart and Winston.

Hunter, M., and Russell, D. 1981. Planning for effective instruction: Lesson design. In *Increasing your teaching effectiveness.* Palo Alto, CA: The Learning Institute.

Joyce, B., and Weil, M. 1986. *Models of teaching.* 3rd ed. Englewood Cliffs, N.J.: Prentice-Hall.

Keirsey, D., and Bates, M. 1984. Please understand me. Del Mar, Calif.: Prometheus Nemesis.

Lieberman, A., and Miller, L. 1984. *Teachers, their world, and their work.* Alexandria, Va.: ASCD.

Nelsen, J. 1981. *Positive discipline.* New York: Ballantine.

Pinnell, G. S. 1990. Success for low achievers through reading recovery. *Educational Leadership* (September) 48(1):17–21.

Purkey, S. C., and Smith, M. S. 1982. Too soon to cheer? Synthesis of research on effective school leadership. *Phi Delta Kappan* (December) 64(4):643–47.

Sarason, S. 1971. *The culture of the school and the problem of change.* Boston, Mass.: Allyn and Bacon.

Sarason, S. 1990. *The predictable failure of educational reform.* San Francisco: Jossey-Bass.

Weick, K. E. 1982. Educational organizations as loosely coupled systems. *Administrative Science Quarterly* 21:1–19.

Taking the Lead from Teachers:

Seeking a New Model of Staff Development

MITZI LEWISON

In recent years, authors of numerous articles and books in the field of teacher education have advocated teachers taking a reflective approach to professional practice. This literature is based on a body of research that describes how many of the theories that teachers hold about learning and teaching are implicit— unconscious and not readily open to examination (Smyth, 1989; Schon, 1987; Lester and Mayher, 1987; Lester and Onore, 1986; Peterson and Clark, 1986; Tom, 1985; Zeichner, 1983). The authors of these studies argue that helping teachers become aware of their implicit assumptions about life in the classroom will enable them to perceive and examine the beliefs they hold about learning and teaching, and that this act of reflection will enable them to become more skilled and effective educators. Reflection (or inquiry-oriented teaching, as it is often called) is generally described as distancing oneself from an engagement, taking a new perspective, seeing alternatives, and developing new understandings (Short and Burke 1989).

Over the past six years, I have been intrigued with exploring the relationship between reflective practice and classroom change. I wanted to see if it was possible to encourage in-service teachers to take a more reflective stance toward language arts instruction that would lead to these teachers taking a critical look at their beliefs about learning and teaching and, as a result, make changes in classroom practice.

At the same time, it seemed important to explore alternate models of

> ### Chapter 4 HIGHLIGHTS
>
> - Reflective Practice
> - Reflective Practice and Classroom Change
> - Professional Study Group Project
> - Study Group Participation and Collegial Interactions
> - Teachers Critique Practice through Professional Reading
> - Study Group Participation: Effect on Classroom Practice and Students
> - Changes in Beliefs and Teacher Expectations
> - The Principal's Role
> - The Outside Consultant's Role

staff development where the focus was on reflection (admitting problems, asking questions, exploring new perspectives, seeing alternatives, and developing new understandings) rather than the more traditional "transmission of information" model.

FORCES THAT DISCOURAGE A REFLECTIVE APPROACH

The majority of educational literature on reflective practice reflects an underlying assumption that some type of action must be taken to get teachers to be reflective. Since most teachers don't naturally take a reflective stance toward their practice; reflection must be encouraged, modeled, and worked on over time (Newman, 1988; Lester and Onore, 1986; Dewey, 1933).

There are a variety of explanations as to why reflective practice is not part of the professional tradition of most educators in this country. In their reviews of research literature on reflective practice, both Zeichner and Liston (1987) and Sparks-Langer and Colton (1991) point out that when teachers use a reflective approach, they are acting contrary to the commonplace goals of schooling. Teachers who question methods of instruction, the prescribed curriculum, the role of students, and the goals of education, may not only be challenging the norms of their particular school but those of society as well.

Our educational system is based on the concept of "transmission of knowledge" rather than one of interpretation and critical analysis (Lester and Mayher, 1987; Zeichner and Liston, 1987; Barnes, 1975). When society generally perceives teachers as technicians whose main role is to transmit knowledge to their students, the act of reflection (questioning) on the part of teachers could be viewed as subversive. In addition, when professional knowledge is perceived as coming from sources outside of the teacher (Sparks-Langer and Colton, 1991; Smith, 1981), there is no role for reflection. As Wehlage (1981) points out, neither the general public or many teachers themselves conceive of teaching as "a problematic effort, but rather as a technical and procedural task" (p. 109).

Dewey (1933) states that "routine [as opposed to reflective] action is guided primarily by tradition, external authority, and circumstance" (p. 24). The conventional wisdom in schools has been for administrators to tell teachers, either explicitly or through textbooks, what to teach and how to teach it (Eisner, 1985; Smith; 1981). Reflection generally has had little place in this top → down model of authority. Routine, not reflective thought, has been the norm.

Teachers, like most professionals, strive to fit into the social milieu of their workplace. New teachers who come out of teacher education programs that stress a reflective approach report that they reject university practice in order to engage in the socially acceptable behaviors expected by their school systems (Wehlage, 1981). They are generally rewarded for and socialized into a nonreflective stance. In addition, the typical isolation teachers experience—because of the "closed door" policy and not much team teaching—is counterproductive to encouraging collaboration and interaction, which are positively associated with promoting reflective practice (Bolin, 1988).

Thus it is not surprising that so few teachers take a reflective stance toward their work when so many forces seem to be acting against inquiry-oriented teaching.

CAN REFLECTIVE PRACTICE BE ENCOURAGED?

A number of strategies are described in both the research and theoretical literature that are reported to encourage reflective practice. These major strategies include **writing**—mostly journals (Kottkamp, 1990; Smyth, 1989; Newman, 1988; Lester and Onore, 1986; Eisner, 1982; Yinger and Clark, 1981), **reading and responding to professional literature** (Cutler, Cook, and Young, 1989; Gebhard and Oprandy, 1989; Ross, 1989; Newman, 1988; Lester and Mayher, 1987; Zeichner and Liston, 1987), **group discussions and study groups** (Anders and Richardson, 1991; Bishop, 1989), **observing and analyzing actual teaching events**

(Cutler, Cook, and Young, 1989; Gebhard and Oprandy, 1989; Zeichner and Liston, 1987), and **teacher-as-researcher projects** (Gebhard and Oprandy, 1989; Lester and Mayher, 1987; Zeichner, 1987).

However, the large majority of these studies were done with preservice teachers. Of those few that were done with in-service teachers, all but one took place in a university class. These informants were a "captive" group, with their course grades dependent on "going along" with the reflective agenda.

One other aspect of these studies was troubling. Although many did show "success," there was no indication as to whether the "reflective stance" that was documented "in class" had any effect on actual classroom practice. Only two studies of in-service teachers, Anders and Richardson (1991) and Lester and Onore (1986), showed a link between a reflective stance and change in classroom practice. In addition, many studies that attempted to encourage a reflective stance in preservice teachers showed no difference or mixed results after the intervention (Cook, Young, and Cutler, 1989; Zeichner and Liston, 1987; Wehlage, 1981).

TRADITIONAL MODELS OF PROFESSIONAL DEVELOPMENT

A huge body of school reform literature was generated in the 1980s that advocates new models for the structure and management of schools, the content and process of curriculum, and forms of professional development. But despite all of the calls for reform, the primary focus of staff development today is still on trying to raise the competency level of individual teachers (Goodlad 1991). Schools and districts plan their staff development programs using a deficit model, attempting to "train" the teacher to do the things (acquiring certain competencies and skills usually determined by administrators) that the teacher is *not* presently doing.

In addition, the specific forms of staff development have stayed pretty much the same. Teachers either attend staff development sessions at their school or district office where everyone receives the same training, or they go to conferences or university classes where they are usually the only person from their school attending. From my perspective, these forms ignore what we now know about the social nature of learning (Vygotsky, 1978) and the importance of groups of teachers working together (Short and Burke, 1989). The focus is still on individualistic learning.

In a recent article that documents what works and what does not in school reform, Fullan and Miles (1992) make a strong case for acknowledging the complexity of school reform:

> It is folly to act as if we know how to solve complex problems in short order. We must have an approach to reform that acknowledges that we don't necessarily know all the answers, that is conducive to developing solutions as we go along. (p. 746)

Most models of staff development don't take this complexity into account and simply offer quick, "band-aid" solutions to whatever the current problem is.

Fullan and Miles do offer what they call "propositions for success" in school reform. These propositions include:

- Change is learning—it is loaded with uncertainty.

- A climate that encourages risk taking is critical (if people don't venture into uncertainty, changes will not occur).

- Change is a journey, not a blueprint.

- Problems are our friends.

- All large-scale change is implemented locally.

It seems to me that these propositions for school reform can also serve as guiding principles for exploring new forms of staff development. What would a model of staff development look like that incorporates these principles? Is it possible to create a model that embraces a reflective approach (admitting problems, asking questions, exploring new perspectives, seeing alternatives, and developing new understandings) where teachers have a strong say in both the content and form of professional development?

ENCOURAGING REFLECTIVE PRACTICE AND CLASS-ROOM CHANGE: STARTING A STUDY GROUP PROJECT

During the 1991–92 school year, I developed a professional development project that was designed to implement strategies that have been shown to encourage teachers (mostly preservice) to become more reflective. I was interested in seeing if these strategies would be effective with in-service teachers and if using them would result in the teachers making changes in their language arts programs. I also wanted to experiment with forms of professional development that would be congruent with encouraging reflective behavior.

The project took place at a suburban K-5 elementary school in a middle-class neighborhood. The school, situated twelve miles from downtown Los Angeles, has a population of 700 students. In 1989–90, 25 percent of the school's students spoke a language in addition to, or instead of, English, with 16 percent demonstrating limited English proficiency.

Forrest School District and Pine Hill School (both fictitious names) were fairly traditional institutions. At the start of the project, the principal was beginning her third year at the site, having previously worked in a more progressive school district. She was in the process of encouraging the faculty to update the school's curriculum (in line with the California frameworks) and begin to engage in more participatory forms of management. This is her description of the school district:

> In Forrest School District for many many years everything has come from top down. The district office annual walk-through was a critical one to see if bulletin boards were done properly. There was a prescribed method for doing everything, even bulletin board titles which were to be hand written in the form of a question on sentence strip paper. One teacher during my first year, who had come from Arizona, covered the walls with student work and had missions displayed all over the room. The director of elementary education and the curriculum consultant were horrified. I told teachers they could have students as guides for the visitors. That was a mistake. They didn't want to talk to kids. They wanted to walk through the room and look at the products—not the producers! (Principal, journal entry 9/6/91)

There is now a new superintendent and curriculum director, but the legacy of years of restriction remains. "Up until last year, all teachers received lesson plans [from the district office] to follow for the first two weeks of school" (Principal, journal entry. 9/6/91). The principal describes the school staff as fitting into the tradition of teachers as the "transmitters of knowledge" that the district writes. She has three huge notebooks in her office that prescribe the curriculum the teachers are to follow, and each teacher has a large guide covering all subject areas. Even though district personnel have been reduced with budget cuts, these guides are still updated every summer. The district office stance is one of telling teachers what to teach.

The principal has been a long-time professional friend of mine. I first met Joan (fictitious name) in the early 1970s when she was hired as a reading specialist at the school where I was teaching second, third, and fourth grade. Over time, she became my mentor, working alongside me on joint classroom projects and sharing professional articles. I spoke to Joan casually one day, describing that I was interested in exploring reflective practice, classroom change, and new models of staff development. She made it clear that she wanted Pine Hill School to be the site of the project. Her personal goals for the project were to change the culture of the school by encouraging teachers to question their practice and support each other when trying new strategies. In addition, she wanted to become more transparent to her staff, allowing them to understand more fully her beliefs about learning and teaching and also to have a feel for what it's like to be a principal at Pine Hill (Principal, journal entries 9/7/91 and 9/22/91: Researcher, journal entry, 9/30/91).

MY ENTRY EXPERIENCE AT PINE HILL SCHOOL

The principal held a faculty meeting in December 1991 so I could meet the teachers on her staff and explain the proposed study. Joan started things off by introducing me to the teachers and describing why she wanted this project at her school. She also told the faculty about how she and I had been keeping a weekly dialogue journal since September in preparation for the project.

Then she turned the meeting over to me and I described how I was interested in experimenting with new forms of staff development that were different from the traditional top → down (expert/lecturer) model and gave a quick review of research literature on reflective practice and school change. I shared how I wanted to conduct a different type of research, using a more collaborative form of methodology than was usually found in school-based research. I read Elliot Eisner's (1988) quote: "Researchers need to go back into the schools, not to conduct commando raids, but to work with teachers" (p. 16).

I concluded by explaining exactly that participating in this project would involve attending regular study group meetings, writing journal entries once a week, and participating in pre- and post-project questionnaires and interviews. I also said that after we got started, it might be the case that someone would stop participating in one or more parts of the project. I made it clear that this would not be a problem as long as the person was willing to discuss why he or she had stopped.

I asked anyone who was interested in participating to let the principal know during the next week. It was also stressed that there was no pressure for teachers to participate and to do so only if they really wanted to.

I was hoping that at least six or seven people would decide to participate in the project, so getting sixteen of the twenty-five faculty members as volunteers was a pleasant surprise. Three of the sixteen did not fully participate in the project. One dropped out late in the project because of personal problems, another because of a class with a conflicting meeting time, and a third participated in all of the study group meetings but did not want to be a formal member of the project. Most of the participants had spent their entire teaching careers in Forrest School District.

Five of the participants were "novice teachers" being either first- or second-year teachers. Two were at midlevels of experience with seven and eleven years respectively. I designated them "experienced teachers." Six were "veterans" who had taught from eighteen to thirty-three years.

The fact that 60 percent of the teachers had seven or more years of classroom experience was a major concern for me because as McLaughlin and Marsh (1978) point out in their report on the findings of the RAND Change Agent Study, "years of experience" is negatively related to the successful implementation of innovative programs.

The teachers volunteered to be part of this project for a number of different reasons. It is interesting to note that twenty of the thirty-two reasons (62 percent) that teachers gave for participating had to do with issues of collegiality (want to discuss and share ideas with other teachers; will benefit from experience of colleagues; want/like to work with other staff members; want a support group; want to be with adults; get to meet people/share; have respect for principal and her interest in project; getting to know staff; getting closer to staff).

Lemlech and Kaplan (1990) have defined collegiality as "the establishment of a professional relationship for the purpose of service and accommodation through mutual exchange of perceptions and expertise" (p. 14). The desire for such collegial exchange was a very prominent concern for the staff members who decided to participate in this project.

In addition 25 percent of the responses indicated that teachers wanted to participate because of reasons centering around professional growth (desire to learn; to be a better teacher; get new ideas; not go stale). Idiosyncratic reasons for participating included: likes the idea of keeping a journal; service ("I have to participate in something"); and wanting to know if her fears about being a first-year teacher are normal. It is worth noting that this first-year teacher expressed the sentiments of uncertainty that so many of us felt when we first came into the profession:

> Being a first year teacher—sometimes you don't know if your feelings are right on, if your fears are like everybody else's . . . I think I'm going to learn quite a bit about what it is to be a teacher and what the feelings are of all the other teachers. (Ms. S., interview, 1/23/92)

COMPONENTS OF THE PINE HILL STUDY GROUP PROJECT

There were four major components of the Pine Hill study group project: negotiated-topic study group meetings, informal journal entries, dialogue journal writing, and reading professional literature.

Negotiated-Topic Study Group Sessions

Participating teachers, the principal, and myself met once a month after school for an hour from January to June (except for May, when an overload of special school activities made it impossible to find a day to meet). Topics for each session were negotiated by the teachers. At the first session, the teachers prioritized the most important issues in language arts that they wanted to discuss and "writing" came out on top. Different aspects of this topic were pursued over the five study group sessions. At the end of each session, topics and leaders for the next meeting were negotiated. I provided journal articles relevant to study group topics that the participants could read prior to the next study group. The "negotiated" topics were:

Session 1   Discussion of how their own journal writing was going; prioritizing of language arts issues; decision was made to pursue "writing" as the first priority for study group meetings.

Session 2   Getting a writing workshop started; inventive spelling.

Session 3   Continuation of inventive spelling; author's chair; mechanics/editing; writing conferences.

Session 4   Continuation of writing conferences.

Session 5   Publishing of student writing.

Informal Journal Entries

The teachers made weekly entries in a professional journal that served as the basis for deciding the topics and format of the study group sessions. The focus of these entries was left open-ended, starting with a suggestion that teachers write about issues they have concerning their language arts program, their students, their classroom environment, or responses to professional reading. The journals were confidential; even the principal did not see them.

Cook, Young, and Cutler (1989) conducted a study to find out if the amount of structure used in reflective writing makes any significant difference. They found that both more structured (specific reflective writing assignments) and less structured (informal journals) entries produced similar levels of pedagogical thinking, similar student teaching performance, and similar attitudes toward reflection. The authors recommended that the less structured journals be used, speculating that this type of writing would be a more conducive tool for lifelong reflection. Because of these data, less structured, informal journal entries were used in this study.

Dialogue Journal Writing

Dialogue journal writing is where two or more participants correspond by means of journals. The principal and I wrote to each other in dialogue in journal format once a week (by fax machine) for the entire school year, starting in September 1991. The principal began sharing her journal with the faculty starting in November 1991. This brought about a change in the format of the journal dialogue she was having with me:

> Writing my journal for teachers has changed how I think about several things. I can't be honest about some things and I have to be careful somewhat about my topics. (Principal, journal entry, 11/30/91)

As a result, for each entry the principal usually wrote a "private" portion of her journal for my eyes only. Joan found that she was not able to be as "transparent" with her staff as she had hoped.

After the second study group session, one of the participants spoke to the principal and was especially concerned about whether she was doing the journal entries "right." The principal wrote to me about this in a journal entry and as a result, I started dialoguing with the teachers. For every group of journal entries that I collected (once a month at the study group meeting) I responded in letter format to each teacher individually.

Professional Reading

Prior to each study group meeting, I selected three to seven articles that related to the negotiated topic for the upcoming meeting and sent them to the principal, who distributed them to staff members. These articles dealt with the study group topic from different perspectives or addressed a range of grade levels. It was not mandatory that teachers read these articles—they were provided as a resource.

STUDYING THE PINE HILL STUDY GROUP PROJECT

To establish a full picture of what was happening at Pine Hill School as a result of the study group project, I conducted a research investigation as a participant-observer at the same time the project was taking place. I used a number of data sources that were triangulated to help me gain an understanding of explicit changes in classroom practice (or lack thereof) that were made and also enable me to assess less visible changes such as those affecting personal relationships and school culture.

I used ten different data sources: (1) pre- and poststudy teacher questionnaires. (2) pre- and post-audiotaped teacher interviews, (3) pre- and poststudy *literacy beliefs profiles* (Kucer, 1991), (4) audiotaped negotiated-topic study group sessions, (5) journal entries, (6) classroom observations and photographs, (7) principal interview, (8) state program review findings, (9) district writing test data, and (10) group interview and discussion—one year later.

The data from these ten sources were initially coded and classified into five categories: (a) general reactions to the project, (b) study group meetings, (c) journal writing, (d) professional reading, and (e) change in practice. Then the data were recoded into significant "research stories" that emerged from the initial coding. After I had finished with these two levels of analysis, I shared the data with the principal of Pine Hill School, who offered a further level of review. From this layered analysis of data, the following "research stories" emerged.

Study Group Sessions: Learning and Growing Together

Negotiated-topic study group sessions proved to be the most valued part of the project by the staff at Pine Hill School. Twelve of the thirteen participants rated study group as the "most important" or one of the most important parts of the project. No one rated study group as the least valuable portion of the study.

Attendance Patterns   Attendance at study group meetings was very high. Five teachers attended all sessions, seven teachers missed one session, and one teacher missed two sessions. The reasons for missing a meeting included jury duty (2), a district meeting (2), class (2), and a doctor's appointment (1). The principal and I attended all the sessions.

Level of Participation   On a self-assessment measure, teachers rated their level of participation in study group higher than their participation in professional reading or journal writing. Table 4.1 shows their self-appraisals.

TABLE 4.1   Self-Assessed Level of Participation in Study Group

Self-Assessment	Number of Teachers
Low	0
Low/medium	2
Medium	2
Medium/high	5
High	4[a]

[a]Three of these four teachers were first-year teachers.

Desire to Participate in the Future   Another measure that assessed the value that teachers placed on study group sessions were their answers to the question: "Do you want to continue with any part of the project next year?" Eleven of the thirteen teachers expressed an interest in continuing with a study group.

Analysis of the Value Teachers Attributed to Study Group

There were six different explanations that accounted for the teachers placing such a high value on study group sessions. These include: learning from other teachers, learning more about colleagues, changing socially constructed norms, socializing novice teachers, providing professional growth, and implementing a teacher-friendly format.

Learning from Other Teachers   Through attending study group sessions, teachers came to see themselves as colleagues who learned from each other. Nine of the thirteen participants indicated that learning from other teachers was one of the positive outcomes of participating in study group. Three of these teachers felt this exchange of ideas among colleagues was more important than any other form of staff development:

> You learn more talking with other teachers, even if you pick up one idea you can use in your classroom. I think you can pick up more than you can sitting through a semester class. (Veteran teacher, poststudy interview, 6/92)

> Hearing about practical experiences is really helpful. It helps me more. You can get reading and journals in a class, but they aren't enough to get [me] started. (Novice teacher, poststudy interview, 6/92)

The third teacher makes a strong point of positioning study group sessions as being very different than traditional forms of staff development:

Staff development as it has been existing for the last few years has its good
points and its definite negative points. We're meetinged to death! Who
wants to go and listen to another person go "gr-r-r-r-r?" And if you just
go and sit down with these people that you work with all the time, they've
got lots of good ideas. It's just a meeting of the minds. It's certainly as valuable as anything else. (Veteran teacher, poststudy interview, 6/92)

Learning More about Colleagues   The study group sessions seem to
have given teachers a window from which to view the practice of their
colleagues, even though they did not actually observe each other. Seven
of the thirteen teachers mentioned that the study group gave them an
opportunity to learn more about other teachers. A second-year teacher
gave a very precise description of how the study group counteracted
some of the traditional isolation associated with being a classroom
teacher:

> The most valuable part of the project was the actual meeting of the group. I
> enjoyed meeting with other teachers. I learned a great deal about some of
> my co-workers. Teaching can be an almost secretive profession. No one
> really knows what goes on in another teacher's room. (Novice teacher, post-
> study interview, 6/92)

A few teachers were surprised, in a positive way, about what their colleagues were actually doing in their classrooms:

> You know, it was amazing to hear Ms. Flower [fictitious name] talk about
> the writing workshop. I had no idea [what she was doing]! That whole
> thing was so different from what my impression was of her as a teacher. I
> never would have thought she did that [writing workshop]! (Novice
> teacher, poststudy interview, 6/92)

In addition, this particular group of teachers really enjoyed the social act
of "getting together." Yet as the reader will see in the next section, the way
they "got together" in study group was very different from what had previously been the case at the school.

Changing Socially Constructed Norms   It became very clear after interviewing the teachers at the end of the project, that the study group format had provided a forum for discussing successes and actual classroom
practice that was generally not previously present in the school. There
were a few instances of grade-level planning, but this was not the norm.
    The best way to understand the previous norm and how this changed
is to hear the voices of the teachers:

Usually the only time we talk is either at a staff meeting (there are all these things we need to discuss), or in the lunch room. And people just don't talk about what's going on in their classrooms in the lunch room. They talk about children, maybe behavioral problems and things like that, but they really don't talk about their teaching. (Novice teacher, poststudy interview, 6/92)

[I like] to just be with the people I'm working with where it's *not* in the lunch room where we're complaining about certain students or something . . . It's a time to sit—to have that time, not for a faculty meeting or anything [else]—to talk and share. (Novice teacher, poststudy interview, 6/92)

A lot of times, I don't know if it's modesty or whatever, but you don't come in and say, "Look at what I did today." But you want to hear what other people do . . . It's OK to gripe in the lunchroom, but you can't brag. (Experienced teacher, poststudy interview, 6/92)

This last teacher went on to explain how she would share ideas and successes with another teacher in private, but never in public. Another teacher discussed how she felt it was hard for a few people to explain things about their classroom programs even in study group because of this previous tacit norm of not "bragging" about successes or discussing pedagogy.

Socializing Novice Teachers   Although my objectives for this project were to explore the possibility of being able to promote a reflective stance toward learning and teaching and to see if classroom changes were made as a result, the five novice teachers seemed to get something very different out of the project. For them it proved to be a way to connect, in positive ways, with more experienced and veteran staff members.

At the beginning of the study, they expressed concerns which included not being able to find someone at Pine Hill School to share ideas with, feeling very isolated from other staff members, being concerned about the disinterest of other (more experienced) teachers, and the possibility of these experienced teachers not wanting to participate in the project.

At the same time, these newcomers said they would love to find someone to collaborate with, to have a support group, and to share and get feedback on what they are doing in their classrooms.

All of these novices found the study group was a good way to get to know their co-workers and to feel more a part of the staff. The principal and I feel that the study group provided an avenue to help the new teachers become socialized into the school community in a much quicker fashion than would have been the case without study group meetings.

Here are Joan's comments on what happened to one first-year teacher during her second year at Pine Hill:

> As a first-year teacher, Ms. Rose had a very difficult time adjusting to the other teachers at her grade level. They were all very traditional and she wanted to experiment with the whole-language techniques she had learned in college. She felt isolated and rejected. The year following the study group project, I was able to change her grade level to one where she knew all the teachers from study group. When they met at the beginning of the year to make long-range plans, Ms. Rose freely suggested an innovative way to deal with spelling that the other teachers at her grade level really liked. Everyone used this strategy during the school year. She felt comfortable with the teachers at her grade level, and they shared all year. (Principal comments, August 1993)

Providing Professional Growth   The teachers at Pine Hill had all taken part in traditional forms of staff development, including university and district classes. Through the study group, they found that learning together could become a regular part of the workplace culture. They seemed to be surprised by the growth that they made as a result of participating in study group. Seven of the thirteen teachers attributed study group sessions to furthering their professional growth:

> It kind of opened up a whole new way of teaching, which I think will influence other subjects, too. (Veteran teacher, Poststudy interview, 6/92)

> I have grown so much from this, professionally. I have never before got into [teaching] writing in so many new and inventive ways. (Veteran teacher, poststudy interview, 6/92)

> It helps keep us up-to-date. (Novice teacher, poststudy interview, 6/92)

Implementing a Teacher-Friendly Format   Teachers who admitted that they complained about meetings after school found that the after-school study group sessions renewed their energy and enthusiasm for teaching. Nine of the thirteen participants cited the structure and format of study group meetings as one of the reasons for its success. The specific explanations for the teacher-friendly format were as follows:

> Low-key and relaxed atmosphere.

> Safe setting to share positive ideas.

> Nonthreatening atmosphere.

> You don't need to have a polished performance to talk.

Some structure, but nonrigid.

Voluntary.

Always had a chance to talk.

All grade levels met together.

The voices of a few of the participants helps to elaborate and clarify this list:

> I normally don't share personal experiences, but I felt comfortable enough to do it here. (Veteran teacher, poststudy interview, 6/92)

> I liked having a structure, but not so [much] that we couldn't vary [it] and get into other discussions. (Veteran teacher, poststudy interview, 6/92)

> I have come to the study group tired, and yet before it's over I am enthused and anxious to try a new idea. (Experienced teacher, poststudy interview, 6/92)

> It was really low-keyed and relaxed. You could talk about what was going on in your class, anything funny or interesting that happened—something great or something awful. (Novice teacher, poststudy interview, 6/92)

> You don't always get a chance to talk about things unless you have a set time. Somehow on our kind of crazy schedule you're always running somewhere and at lunch you're eating and rushing to get things done. When you set aside this time to reflect, then you get it done. A specific time is important, otherwise it's just moaning and groaning. (Novice teacher, poststudy interview, 6/92)

Three additional factors should be noted in this section. First of all, the principal attended all study group sessions and contributed in a very relaxed and reflective manner that I feel served as a model for the teachers.

Second, although I tried to get teachers to facilitate the sessions, I couldn't get volunteers and ended up leading all study group meetings. I tried to lead in a very informal fashion and to encourage everyone to participate with questions like, "Does anyone else have experience with peer conferencing that you could share?" I also made connections between a practice that a teacher was sharing with what had been explored in the professional readings for that session.

Last, and maybe most important, there was food for the teachers at the meetings provided by the principal and myself. After a long day of teaching, a cool drink and a snack may have been part of the appeal, although no teacher mentioned this in the poststudy interviews.

Problems with Study Group

On the whole, study group sessions were the part of this project most valued by teachers. However, these meetings did not prove to be valuable for everyone. One of the teachers felt they were of little value and that the sessions were not of much interest to her. It is interesting to note that this teacher volunteered for the project because of "service." ("I have to do something this year"), so it is not surprising that she didn't get much out of the group. This teacher and one other said they would not like to continue with study group if it were offered next year.

Among those teachers who were happy with study group and expressed an interested to continue, they still had some problems with the group that they discussed in the postinterviews:

■ "We need more practice talking in front of peers about our successes. A few of us are still afraid of bragging."

■ "After I made changes in my classroom, the meetings weren't as valuable."

■ "It was hard to get to meetings after school, but once I got there it was great."

■ "I missed one meeting and I felt like I had really missed something. I didn't feel as comfortable at the next meeting."

■ "I would have liked it if more people shared."

■ "Time was limited."

■ "Sometimes it took long to get 'into' a topic."

Despite the problems, study group sessions were definitely the most successful and valuable part of the project in the eyes of the teachers.

Critiquing Practice through Professional Reading

Professional reading proved to be the second most valued part of this project by the staff at Pine Hill School. Eight of the thirteen teachers rated professional reading as one of the "most important" parts of this study. One of the eight teachers rated professional reading as the only valuable portion of the project. Two first-year teachers rated professional reading as the least valuable component of the study, an understandable response given the intense demands of practice beginning teachers must

TABLE 4.2   Self-Assessed Level of Participation in Professional Reading

Self-Assessment	Number of Teachers
Low	3
Low/medium	2
Medium	4
Medium/high	1
High	3

meet. Taking time to read may be more than many first-year teachers can deal with.

Prior to this project only four of the thirteen teachers had done any type of recent professional reading aside from idea magazines (*School Days, Arts and Activities, Instructor, Scholastic,* and *Creative Classroom*). I classified only one of these teachers as being an avid reader of professional books or articles.

It is important to note that by the end of the study five teachers who had not done any recent professional reading were not only doing it but highly valued it as a part of this study.

Level of Participation   On a self-assessment measure, teachers rated their level of participation in professional reading lower than their involvement in study group sessions. Table 4.2 shows their self-appraisals. All three teachers who rated their level of participation as "high," were veteran teachers with 18, 23, and 35 years of experience.

Desire to Participate in the Future   Another measure that assessed the value that teachers placed on professional reading were their answers to the question, "Do you want to continue with any part of the project next year?" Five of the thirteen teachers expressed an interest in continuing with professional reading.

Analysis of the Value Teachers Attributed to Professional Reading

Five explanations accounted for the eight teachers who rated professional reading as one of the most valued parts of the study. The first three were:

■ "It kept us up-to-date with current teaching trends and topics."

■   "The articles clarified points that I was unclear about."

■   "I used ideas from the readings in my classroom."

Professional Articles to Keep   Having articles to read on curriculum issues in language arts that could be referred to at a later date held great appeal for teachers:

> What I like about the reading is that I have it and I do a lot of reading over the summer and it *will* get read. And I like being given things. You know I have my limited number of professional books, but there aren't a lot of stores where you can go and get them. I like being given things to read because I can put them away and go back to them. (Novice teacher, post-study interview, 6/92)

> I've got them [the articles] all read and I've highlighted a lot of information. I hope to give myself a date before we come back to school . . . to sit down and go back over the articles and refresh everything so that I can come back [in the fall] thinking the way I am now. (Veteran teacher, post-study interview, 6/92)

Providing a Focus   The professional readings gave the study group a new lens from which to view practice and provided a focus for the meetings. Two veteran teachers felt very strongly that the study group sessions would not have worked without the readings. I think their explanation might hold one of the keys to understanding the overwhelming success of the study group sessions:

> I don't think the discussions would have been as valuable without the literature to read . . . I loved hearing what everyone else was doing [at study group sessions], but I think the professional reading gave us things to think about and talk about and follow through with. (Veteran teacher, poststudy interview, 6/92)

> I have grown so much from this [project] professionally. I have never before got into [teaching] writing in so many new and inventive ways. I think that it's [because of] the professional readings that you gave me . . . hearing them discussed in the groups helped to motivate me to get into the reading and take the time to do it. (Veteran teacher, poststudy interview, 6/92)

Even those teachers who did not read the articles themselves seemed to benefit from hearing them mentioned in study group:

> I liked hearing the articles discussed. I think there were good ideas in them,

I just didn't take the time [to read them]. Time was the real issue. (Novice teacher, poststudy interview, 6/92)

Professional reading also turned out to be highly valuable to me in the role of facilitator. Here is a journal entry I wrote to the principal on 2/24/92:

Finding articles to send you [to distribute to the teachers] is like a staff development session for me. It has got me into rereading articles and books that I hadn't looked at in a long time. Also, along the way, I have found some articles on other subjects that look really interesting that slipped through the cracks.

Additional Factors   Two additional factors should be noted in exploring what happened at Pine Hill School with regard to professional reading. First of all, the principal has always been an advocate of keeping up with current journals. She still has a high regard and value for reading educational literature and she modeled this regard for her staff. Here is an example of one of her journal entries that was shared with the staff:

I read three of the articles M. sent. Two were chapters from Lucy Calkins' book. I love her writing and ideas. She makes writing conferences so natural. I'm afraid I would have made a list of questions for peer conferences and required everyone to answer them all—more like the editing she described. I like the idea of a content conference being a simple conversation based on listening. (Journal entry, 3/15/92)

There is one other item of interest to note here: The knowledge base of teachers at Pine Hill School changed because of this project. The names of researchers like Donald Graves and Lucy Calkins (whose articles were used extensively in the project) were mentioned numerous times by the teachers during the course of this study. Everyone came to know who these writers were, their theoretical perspectives, and the concepts they advocated for teaching writing in the schools. They became household names and part of the new knowledge base of this community of teachers.

One teacher actually was able to go to a conference and hear Lucy Calkins. Here is part of her reflection about the value of this study:

The information [readings] and discussion [study group]—I got so much out of that. If nothing else, I've really changed my whole way of thinking . . . and this led me to know [who] Lucy Calkins [is] and going to a conference with her that I would have never signed up for [before]. I got so much out of that, she's incredible! (Veteran teacher, poststudy interview, 6/92)

Problems with Professional Reading

Six teachers reported problems with professional reading. These problems included not having enough time to read (3 teachers); too many articles handed out at one time (2 teachers); difficulty in getting ideas from the articles (1 teacher); the articles did not help with implementation (1 teacher); and having little regard for educational writers (1 teacher).

The last three responses are worth exploring in some detail. Although only one teacher said that it was hard to get "ideas" from the articles, two others mentioned that the set of articles they liked the best was the last one. This packet contained a series of practical ideas on publishing children's writing but no theoretical or research articles. These teachers still place a very high value on "practical ideas."

The teacher who said that the articles did not help with implementation was a first-year teacher who told me that she was already familiar with many of the articles or ones like them from her preservice program. Commenting on them, she said:

> I skimmed the highlights. It [the content of the reading] seemed very obvious because in my training, that's what we studied. I could have quoted you on those articles, but it doesn't matter if I read it five times or ten times, there are things that are going to work practically for me and things that aren't—even if I know it's the right thing to do. (Novice teacher, poststudy interview, 6/92)

As a first-year novice, it is not surprising that this teacher cannot implement everything that's "right," but her response reveals more than her ability to implement new ideas. The tone in her remarks conveys a mild disdain for what educational researchers have to say.

There is still a very strong orientation toward the "practical" at Pine Hill School, yet by the end of the study, 60 percent of the teachers valued professional reading as one of the most important parts of the project.

THE CHANGING FACE OF PINE HILL SCHOOL

Five different kinds of change took place at Pine Hill over the course of this study and in the year following the project.

Change in Classroom Practice

Eleven of the thirteen teachers in the project made some type of change in classroom practice as a result of participating in the study. (The level of change will be discussed later.) The two teachers who made no changes were novices. Both of these teachers reported that although their language arts programs incorporated many of the strategies discussed in study group, they would have implemented them anyway. The changes in practice that were made by the other eleven teachers included:

Student journal writing.

Encouraging kids to use inventive spelling in their journals on drafts.

Student choice of writing topics.

Daily writing time.

Students sharing their writing.

Peer conferencing.

Implementing "writing workshops."

Publishing student writing.

Peer editing.

Using the writing process.

Teachers sharing their own writing with students.

Here is a fairly typical example of how one teacher articulated the changes she had made in her classroom to her colleagues:

> I started kids writing in journals about two weeks ago . . . It's just really exciting, they love to do it. They can do whatever they want. If they don't want anyone to see it, no one will see it. Some of them are drawing pictures, some of them are writing words. They're not spelled correctly, but I had one little girl write—she wrote all the words to "My Country 'Tis of Thee." It was fairly easy to read the words, she had all of the sounds down. They really enjoy it! We do it every day for about five minutes. They can volunteer to share them with the class. (Novice kindergarten teacher, study group, 3/18/92)

In addition to the changes that were made during the year of the study, three teachers made further substantial changes during the following year. During the principal's interview, nearly a year after the end of the study, Joan reported that one of the kindergarten teachers had influenced and become a mentor to the two kindergarten teachers who were not part of the project. Now students in all four kindergarten classrooms are writing journals and using inventive spelling.

In addition, Joan reported that two other teachers who were part of the study made "radical" changes in their classroom writing programs. Both of these teachers are building on the small-to-moderate changes they made during the year of the project. In one class, students are now choosing their own topics for writing, and they have a classroom publishing center where they have published more than a hundred books.

All three of these teachers proudly shared their successes at the group interview held a year after the end of the project.

Level of Change   A rating of the level of change that each teacher made in her classroom writing program was arrived at by combining my observations of the teacher's change, the principal's observations, and the teacher's self-perception of change. I kept these ratings on the conservative side, so when their were discrepancies between the three ratings, I took an average or assigned the lower designation. Table 4.3 shows the ratings in relation to the years of teaching experience.

The veteran teacher who rated "high" on level of change not only transformed her writing program in significant and substantial ways but was an inspiration for other teachers, three of whom mentioned her numerous times in the poststudy interviews.

It is interesting to note that four of the six teachers who made no change or little change in classroom practice were novice teachers. This is not surprising, since they were spending so much time just getting acclimated to teaching and were concerned with so many issues at the same time. In addition, these novice teachers were already acquainted with

TABLE 4.3   Level of Classroom Change in Writing Programs

Level of Change	Years of Teaching Experience		
	Novice (1–2)	Experienced (7–11)	Veteran (18–33)
No change	2	0	0
Low	1	0	2
Low/medium	1	0	0
Medium	1	1	0
Medium/high	0	1	3
High	0	0	1

similar literature and teaching techniques discussed in study group from their preservice experiences.

There was an interesting commonality between the two veteran teachers who made few changes in their classroom writing programs. I classified their style of relating to this project as "isolationist." They both had areas of interest outside of language arts instruction and seemed very insulated from their colleagues in this setting. Although different in many ways, they were both loners and did not use this setting to establish collegial relationships with other teachers on the staff.

At the other end of the scale, four of the five teachers who were rated "medium/high" or "high" on the level of change in their classroom writing programs were veteran teachers. The fifth teacher had taught for seven years. This is a very encouraging outcome of the study.

How Students Were Affected by the Project

To understand the type of classroom change that took place during this project, it is instructive to hear how the teachers describe the effect the project has had on their students:

> Well, I was really tentative to do inventive spelling, I really was. So then I just went with it and that's what we've done most of the year and my kids, compared to my other classes—I have kids writing three and four pages now. I mean front and back. (Experienced grade 1 teacher, poststudy interview, 6/92)

A second-grade veteran teacher feels her kids have gained more confidence in their writing this year:

> They write more, they worry less about mistakes, and they help each other with ideas and corrections. (Poststudy questionnaire, 6/92)

And more evidence of students being positively affected:

> We've been having writing workshop each day. I know it has paid dividends because on Friday one of my students . . . said, "We've been writing a lot, haven't we?" I answered, "Yes, we write in reading, social studies, and writing time." I thought he was complaining about it until he said, "Last year I didn't know how to write that well, but now I can write real easily. It's easy now!" The more I think about his comment, the more I realize what giving the students time to write is doing. I love it! The completed stories they are beginning to turn in are more original and more interesting, too. (Veteran teacher, journal entry, 3/22/92)

I had them [the students] conference on a few stories they'd written with specific questions. I'd never thought of having the reader responsible for answering specific questions. They took it seriously and did it well. As I looked around the room they were smiling and enjoying the experience. Some said to me, "Wait until you read_____'s story—you'll love it." (Experienced teacher, poststudy questionnaire, 6/92)

My ESL student who is just learning the language has gotten excited about writing! He has a two-part story that he has been working on. He started out working with a friend. They worked together several times on it. Then he wrote part 2 by himself. It is quite amazing. It is in sequence and has all the parts of a story. He needed help with the past and present tense verbs, but learned a lot about this. He's publishing the story now and it's twenty-two pages long! (Veteran teacher, journal entry, 6/1/92)

Many of the changes made by the teachers in this study were not simply implementing a set of "cookbook" ideas. Changes in practice such as inventive spelling, student choice and ownership of writing topics, writing workshop, and peer conferencing require the teacher to examine her beliefs about how kids learn, her role as a writing teacher, and how classrooms should be organized.

While observing writing-workshop time in the classroom of the teacher who made the most change in her writing program, I wandered around the room and randomly interviewed students. These kids were involved in all stages of the writing process, including prewriting and planning, revising their writing, informal conferences with the teacher, peer conferences, using writing folders, and publishing. I asked individual students how writing was different in this class compared to other rooms. Here are their responses:

- "We write every day."
- "We publish hardbound books."
- "I didn't get to publish before."
- "Ms. Flower encourages us to write."
- "Ms. Flower helps us get started."
- "We want to write stories and we didn't get to write stories in other classrooms."
- "We do more writing."
- "I never had writing workshop before."

- "You used to have to write on a certain paper."

- "We didn't conference or use the edit and revise sheets in other rooms."

- "Conferencing helps us get better."

- "We publish real books."

I was amazed at how articulate these students were in not only expressing how writing was different for them this year, but in understanding what made them better writers.

Change in Beliefs about Literacy Learning and Instruction

Seven of the thirteen project teachers moved five or more points closer toward a whole-language orientation on the *literacy beliefs profile* continuum (92 total points). Two additional teachers reported changes in their belief systems, but these changes did not show up on the profile.

In trying to interpret why these seven teachers showed significant gains on the literacy beliefs profile, I could find only one trait in common: Six of these seven teachers identified professional reading as one of the most valuable parts of the project. I have labeled these teachers as "scholars." From the data I examined, this is the only interpretation I could make of the change. The one teacher whose score on the profile changed who was not a "scholar" was a novice teacher who had a preprofile score that was lower than any other participant. I suspect that her score rose because of sharing and discussion at study group sessions.

Change in Teacher Expectations for Students

Two teachers, one veteran and one experienced, expressed a marked difference in the expectations they held for their students before and after the study. Although I never asked a question about expectations on the questionnaire or in the interview, here is what these teachers have to say:

> I couldn't believe how much the kids could write when they didn't have to worry about spelling. I'm amazed at what I'm getting out of these kids. Having grown up in the Forrest School District schools and being a product of them—you learned how to spell [in a traditional manner] or that's it. (Experienced teacher, poststudy interview, 6/92)

> I was the only one who limited their writing and I thought I was doing an excellent job, I really did! . . . I never thought that second graders could peer conference: they do it very well. (Veteran teacher, poststudy interview, 6/92)

Principal's Perception of Teacher Change

The principal observed a number of changes at the school site during the year after the study that she attributes to this project.

Book Publishing Center   During the year of the study, the principal worked with parent volunteers to establish the Pine Hill School Publishing Center in the school library. She reported that in the year following the study, twice as many bound books were published than during the prior year. She says that more teachers have students engaged in book writing and so they are more student products to take to the publishing center.

Grade-Level Planning Meetings   Although some grade-level planning meetings were taking place at Pine Hill School during the year of this study, in the following year they became a regular feature at Pine Hill School. The principal feels the meetings are very productive, and they have actually taken the place of most staff meetings. Joan attributes most of the "collegiality thing" to study group. Now it is okay for teachers to sit down and talk and plan. The main problem that she sees currently is that grade-level planning meetings do not allow for cross-grade collaboration and discussion based on professional reading. Joan is planning to start up study group again next year to remedy this.

Inventive Spelling   The principal reported that inventive spelling, which allows students to write their ideas down on first drafts without worrying about correct spelling, is "rampant" around the school and has really made a radical change in how teachers teach writing. This is evident in both project and nonproject teachers. The principal used one of the study group articles on inventive spelling with parents at a workshop, and she reported they understood and were extremely supportive of the process.

State Program Review   In March of 1993, a team of reviewers representing the California State Department of Education (Instructional Support Services Division) conducted a three-day Program Quality Review at Pine Hill School. Here is what they said about the school's writing program and level of collaboration among teachers.

> Students write in all areas of the curriculum as evidenced by writings displayed in classrooms . . . The team examined portfolios at various stages of development in every class. Collections of journals, class books, individual books, reports and poetry all written by students were accessible. Volun-

teers of the Pine Hill School Book Publishing Company assembled books authored by students.

Grade level planning strengthens and unifies the language arts curriculum. It is evident that teachers' sharing of ideas and approaches increases possibilities for student interest and understanding. (California State Department of Education, 1993)

Test Data   In the spring of 1993 Forrest School District administered the Forrest School District Integrated Reading/Writing Assessment to all fourth grade students. The holistically scored test was designed to get students ready for the new State of California Language Arts Assessment and assigned students a score from 1 to 6. A 1 designated an unacceptable response while a 6 a truly outstanding one. The students at Pine Hill School received 31 percent of the level-6 reading scores in the district. The principal had predicted they would score about the same in writing, but this was not the case. The Pine Hill School students received 44 percent of the level-6 scores in writing. She attributes this difference to the change in classroom writing programs at her school.

CONCLUDING RESEARCH STORIES

Although there are a multitude of "concluding stories" to be told as a result of this project, the five most significant themes that emerged were:

1. Study group as a forum for collegiality.

2. Professional reading—viewing practice through a new lens.

3. The changing culture at Pine Hill School.

4. The role of the principal.

5. Transforming traditional staff development.

Study Group as a Forum for Collegiality

The most concise way to explain the immense value that teachers attributed to study group sessions was the role they played in fostering collegiality. During the course of the project and poststudy interviews, it became clear that for the overwhelming majority of project teachers at Pine Hill School there was a real hunger to meet and discuss teaching and learning in informal settings. The teachers felt that study group sessions cut down isolation and created closer bonds with their colleagues.

At one level, study group seemed to reinforce a built-in bias toward the "practical" among these teachers (something that is the norm in most elementary schools). The staff wanted "new ideas" and they wanted to get them from their colleagues. But the inclusion of professional reading and journal writing as a part of the project served to broaden the role of study group to include more critical and theoretically based discussions. Study group sessions alone probably would not have led to teachers moving toward examining practice from a critical perspective.

At the end of the study I developed a profile for each teacher that described his or her style of relating to the project. The descriptive terms I used were:

Practitioner	Concerned with the practical, finding new ideas, values the experience of colleagues.
Scholar	Uses theory to inform practice, values professional reading.
Writer	Enjoys and uses journal writing as a way to reflect on practice, readings, and beliefs.
Reluctant writer	Kept a journal for this project, wrote reflectively, but did not enjoy keeping a journal.
Isolationist	Did not value meeting with colleagues or their contributions.

The profile for most teachers consisted of more than one descriptor (i.e., practitioner/writer). At the end of the study only three of the thirteen teachers were classified as having *only* a "practitioner" profile. Thus, even though there was a built-in bias toward the practical, many of these teachers came to value using theory to inform practice.

Another important role that study group played, was to alter some of the socially constructed norms at Pine Hill regarding what was okay to discuss and what was not. The ethos at the school before the project was one of complaining in the lunch room and of its *not* being socially acceptable to discuss "successes" (a phenomenon that I have observed at a number of schools). These "rules" of behavior are not set in stone, but rather agreed upon by the communities who abide by them. They are social constructions (Kuhn, 1962) and open to renegotiation. Although study group did not eliminate complaining in the lunch room, it did provide a forum for teachers to talk about successes, share problems, question beliefs, and discuss pedagogy. Most teachers mentioned how much they appreciated this aspect of the study group during poststudy interviews.

An unexpected finding of this study was the rapid way that new teachers became part of the school community. As Lemlech and Kaplan (1990) point out, in most cases, new teachers are socialized to be isolates. At the beginning of study group sessions in January (four months into the school year) these newcomers expressed feelings of isolation and distrust of the experienced staff. Study group provided a venue for new teachers not only to get to know other staff members quickly, but to engage in meaningful dialogue about teaching and learning.

PROFESSIONAL READING— VIEWING PRACTICE THROUGH A NEW LENS

Professional reading proved to be a critical element related to the positive outcomes of this project. The journal articles provided teachers new perspectives from which to view their writing programs and critique classroom practice. The articles became the subject of reflection and provided the "meat" of what was discussed during study group and written about in journals. As a couple of teachers put it, the study group was great, but it would not have worked without the reading.

Reading professional articles seemed to serve an especially important role for experienced and veteran teachers. Six of the eight teachers who valued reading journal articles as one of the "most important" parts of this project had taught for seven, eleven, eighteen, twenty-three, twenty-five, and thirty-three years, respectively. Experienced and veteran teachers have traditionally been seen as a group who is reluctant to make shifts in practice or beliefs (McLaughlin and Marsh, 1978). Yet in this setting these more experienced teachers proved to be "stars" in terms of their ability to critique their practice and make changes in their writing programs. Providing a forum for professional reading may prove to be key in working effectively with more experienced teachers.

At Pine Hill, the traditional stance of not placing much value in what researchers and scholars have to say about classroom practice has been significantly altered.

The Changing Culture at Pine Hill School

In the year following this study, there were changes at Pine Hill School that spread beyond the individual teachers who were involved in the project. Grade-level planning meetings, an active book publishing center, and the schoolwide use of inventive spelling in journals and on drafts were evident across the school community. The Program Quality Review document from the California Department of Education review team and Pine Hill's test scores on the district integrated reading/writing test confirm that there is significant cohesion in the language arts program at Pine Hill. The principal is still sharing her journal with the entire staff, and the study group members want to start a group up again next year.

The Role of the Principal

In looking at the changing culture at Pine Hill School, the role of the principal cannot be overlooked. This principal truly values the teachers on her staff as professionals, and they know it. She has high expectations for them as both learners and teachers and has created an atmosphere that supports professional growth. She was an active participant in every phase of the project, modeling and engaging in the type of thinking and behaviors that she wanted to encourage in her staff. I believe her positive and supportive leadership style strongly influenced the way teachers involved themselves in this study. She led through example rather than coercion.

Transforming Traditional Staff Development

The study at Pine Hill can offer a new lens from which to view established forms of staff development. Unlike traditional programs of professional growth, the teachers at Pine Hill had control over the topics of study group sessions and which parts of the project (study group, professional reading, journal writing) to participate in. The atmosphere was relaxed and there was no coercion to move or change in any particular direction. This model values teachers as professionals who can make wise decisions about their own professional growth, and the study group provided a safe and supportive environment for this growth to take place. The model also provided multiple ways for teachers to participate and still be a part of the group. For example, one teacher was not keen on study group, but really enjoyed the professional reading. The teachers had the options whether to participate and, if so, at what level.

However, this type of model offers no "quick fixes" for a staff, because it acknowledges the complexity of teachers moving toward more theoretically based practice. In his introduction to Judith Newman's book *Finding Our Own Way, Teachers Exploring their Assumptions* (1990), John Mayer's explanation of Newman's book title serves to describe some of the dynamics that were present at Pine Hill:

> The metaphor of a journey of exploration . . . embodies the most fruitful
> kind of response by educators to . . . new challenges. It recognizes that since
> there are no maps or signs on the road to change, we must find our own
> way. It further emphasizes that while more experienced practitioners and
> theorists may provide us with a new vision of the road ahead, we are finally
> responsible for our own choices within our own teaching and learning con-
> texts. We can learn with and from each other, but not in the sense of adopt-
> ing wholesale a gimmick, recipe, or lesson plan . . . What we can learn are
> the values of collaboration, of taking seriously the fundamental questions
> of learning and teaching, and most important of all, of the kinds of rewards
> that can come from risk taking in our teaching. (p. xiv)

The teachers at Pine Hill were definitely risk takers, but the importance of having the collegial setting of the study group to support risk
taking cannot be overemphasized.

The Role of an Outside Consultant   The principal felt that my role as an
outside consultant was critical in understanding what happened at Pine
Hill. My role was not important because I was such a "wonderful" group
leader, but rather because I was able to support the direction the teachers
took by providing journal articles on the topic of each upcoming study
group meeting. Because of the demands of teaching and running a school,
the principal was adamant in her belief that neither she nor any teacher
had the time to gather this type of professional literature on a regular basis.

From my perspective, I was seen as a safe "outsider" by the staff, even
though I had a prior relationship with the principal. Aside from being
the "provider of articles," I was also very careful about how I led the
study group meetings and responded to teacher's journal entries. I made
a commitment to respect the path that a teacher was on, even if this was
in opposition to my own beliefs about learning and teaching. In trying to
encourage these teachers to "find their own way," I also invited the teachers to critique the articles we read and discuss parts that went against
their own beliefs. The organizational style that developed in this group
was one of exploring teaching and learning issues together, with no
authority keeping the group on the "right" track. This framework was
extremely important in creating an atmosphere that was safe and that
encouraged risk taking.

Another interesting aspect of this project is that it has caused me to
rethink the role I have usually played as an outside consultant: transmit-
ting "the word" to the masses. Just as I would like to see teachers increasing
their level of reflectiveness and professionalism, those of us who consult
and work with teachers need to find new vantage points from which to
view and critique our practice.

Staff Development in a Whole-Language Model   It seems that the Pine Hill study group project has implications for informing staff development in the whole-language movement. Unlike the more traditional skill-based models of literacy instruction, the whole-language model takes a constructivist stance toward learning. Some principles that underpin the model include:

A student-centered curriculum.

Personal construction of meaning.

Multiple interpretations of text.

Emphasis on the social nature of learning.

Use of "authentic" literacy activities.

Self-selected topics of study.

Ongoing, informal assessment.

A whole-language model of literacy instruction requires more reflective, inquiry-oriented teachers who are keen observers and able to provide a flexible learning environment that is ever-changing and based on the needs of the students.

New models of staff development are necessary to help teachers become more reflective and inquiry-oriented. We need to look at models that:

- Are teacher-centered and based on self-selected topics of inquiry.

- Encourage personal construction of meaning and multiple interpretations of phenomena.

- Encourage taking a reflective stance toward beliefs about learning and teaching.

- Emphasize the social nature of learning.

If teacher educators, school districts, and even some state departments of education are expecting teachers to move toward a whole-language model (as we see happening at this time), then staff development practices must also change. The traditional top → down, transmission model will need to give way to more collaborative and empowering forms of staff development (Monson and Pahl, 1991). Short and Burke (1989, p. 193) very insightfully point out that until teacher educators explore more fully how to live their own models, they will have a limited effect on changing the current course of education.

Recap Notes: Issues to Consider When Designing Professional Development Programs

Does the professional development program
- Attempt to foster collegiality?
- Provide a way for teachers and the principal to negotiate topics, structure, and format?
- Provide alternative modes of participation by faculty?
- Attempt to encourage a reflective stance toward practice?
- Encourage participants to consider actively how issues explored in professional development sessions can impact practice?
- Acknowledge that teachers at different stages in their careers have diverse needs?

REFERENCES

Achilles, C. M. 1989. *Challenging Narcissus, or Reflecting on reflecting.* Paper presented at the Annual Meeting of the University Council on Educational Administration, Scottsdale, Arizona.

Anders, P. L., and Richardson, V. 1991. Research directions: Staff development that empowers teachers' reflection and enhances instruction. *Language Arts* 68, 316–21.

Barnes, D. 1975. *From Communication to curriculum.* Portsmouth, N.H.: Heinemann.

Bean, T. W., and Zulich, J. 1989. Using dialogue journals to foster reflective practice with preservice, content-area teachers. *Teacher Education Quarterly*, 16(1): 33–40.

Bishop, W. 1989. *Teachers as learners: Negotiated roles in college writing teacher's learning logs.* Paper presented at the Annual Meeting of the Conference on College Composition and Communication, Seattle, Washington. (ERIC Document Reproduction Service ED 304 690)

Bodgan, R. C., and Biklen, S. K. 1982. *Qualitative research for education: An introduction to theory and methods.* Boston, Mass.: Allyn and Bacon.

Bolin, F. S. 1988. Helping student teachers think about teaching. *Journal of Teacher Education* 39(2): 48–54.

Borg, W. R., and Gall, M. D. 1983. *Educational research, an introduction.* New York: Longman.

Boud, D., Keogh, R., and Walker, M. 1985. *Reflection: Turning experience into learning*. Vols. 7–17. London: Kogan Page.

Bruner, J. 1990. *The Karplus Lecture*. Paper presented at the Annual Meeting of the National Conference of Science Teachers, Atlanta, Georgia.

Burgess, R. C. 1984. *In the field, an introduction of field research*. London: Allen and Unwin.

California State Department of Education. 1993. *Elementary school program quality review report of findings*. Sacramento, Calif.: Instructional Support Services Division.

California State Department of Education. 1987. *English/language arts framework for California public schools, kindergarten through grade twelve*. Sacramento, Calif.: State Department of Education.

Canning, C. 1991. What teachers say about reflection. *Educational Leadership* 48(6): 18–21.

Clark, C. 1979. Five faces of research on teaching. *Educational leadership* 37(1): 29–32.

Clark, C. M., and Peterson, P. L. 1986. Teachers' thought processes. In *Handbook of research on teaching*, ed. M. C. Wittrock, pp. 255–96. New York: Macmillan.

Connelly, F. M., and Clandinin, D. J. 1990. Stories of experience and narrative inquiry. *Educational Researcher* 19(5):2–14.

Cook, P. F., Young, J. R., and Cutler, B. R. 1989. *The effect of structured training vs. less formal journal writing on the quality of thinking, classroom teaching performance, and attitudes toward reflective teaching during preservice training*. Paper presented at the Annual Conference of the Northern Rocky Mountain Educational Research Association, Jackson, Wyoming. (ERIC Document Reproduction Service No. ED 325 464)

Cooper, J. E., and Dunlap, D. M. 1989. *Journal keeping as an example of successful reflective practice among administrators in government, business, and education*. Paper presented at the Annual Meeting of the American Educational Research Association. (ERIC Document Reproduction Service No. ED 307 681)

Crandell, D. P., Eiseman, J. W., and Louis, K. S. 1986. Strategic planning issues that bear on the success of school improvement efforts. *Educational Administration Quarterly* 22(3): 21–53.

Crowhurst, M. 1989. *The role of writing in subject-area learning*. Vancouver: University of British Columbia. (ERIC Document Reproduction Service No. ED 303 805)

Cutler, B. R., Cook, P. F., and Young, J. R. 1989. *The empowerment of preservice teachers through reflective teaching*. Paper presented at the Annual Convention of the Association of Teacher Educators, St. Louis, Mo. (ERIC Document Reproduction Service No. ED 325 473)

Deford, D. 1978. *Theoretical orientation to reading profile*. Unpublished document, University of Indiana.

Deford, D. 1985. Validating the construct of theoretical orientation in reading instruction. *Reading Research Quarterly* 20(3): 351–67.

Dewey, J. 1933. *How we think*. Lexington, Mass.: D. C. Heath.

Duffy, G. 1977. *A study of teacher conceptions of reading.* Paper presented at the National Reading Conference, New Orleans.

Eisner, E. W. 1988. The primacy of experience and the politics of method. *Educational Researcher* 15–20.

Eisner, E. W. 1985. *The educational imagination: on the design and evaluation of school programs.* New York: Macmillan.

Eisner, E. W. 1982. *Cognition and curriculum: A basis for deciding what to teach.* New York: Longman.

Fielding, N. G., and Fielding, J. L. 1986. *Linking data.* Beverly Hills, Calif.: Sage.

Fowler, F. J. 1984. *Survey research methods.* Beverly Hills, Calif.: Sage.

Fullan, M. G., and Miles, M. B. 1992. Getting reform right: What works and what doesn't. *Phi Delta Kappan* 73(10): 745–52.

Gebhard, J. G., and Oprandy, R. 1989. *Multiple activities in teacher preparation: Opportunities for change.* Indiana University of Pennsylvania, Evaluative Report. (ERIC Document Reproduction Service No. ED 307 813)

Glaser, B. G., and Strauss, A. L. 1967. *The discovery of grounded theory.* New York: Aldine.

Goodlad, J. I. 1991. Why we need a complete redesign of teacher education. *Educational Leadership* 49(3): 4–10.

Hall, G. E., and Hord, S. M. 1987. *Change in schools: Facilitating the process.* New York: State University of New York Press.

Hall, J. L., and Bowman, A. C. 1989. *The journal as a research tool: Preservice teacher socialization.* Paper presented at the Annual Meeting of the Association of Teacher Educators, St. Louis, Mo. (ERIC Document Reproduction Service No. ED 306 218)

Hammersley, M., and Atkinson, P. 1983. *Ethnography: Principles in practice.* London: Tavistock.

Harste, J. C. 1989. *New policy guidelines for reading: Connecting research and practice.* Urbana, Ill.: National Council of Teachers of English.

Harste, J. C. 1984. *Excellence: Multiple realities.* Paper presented at the Annual Meeting of the Political Issues Affecting Literacy Interest Group of the International Reading Association.

Holmes, E. W. 1989. *Student to teacher: A naturalistic profile.* Paper presented at the Annual Meeting of the American Educational Research Association, San Francisco. (ERIC Document Reproduction Service No. ED 312 224)

Huberman, and Miles, 1984. Why school improvement succeeds or fails. Beverly Hills, Calif.: Sage Publications.

Kemmis, S. 1985. Action research and the politics of reflection. In *Reflection: Turning experience into learning,* ed. D. Boud, R. Keogh, and M. Walker, pp. 139–63. London: Kogan Page.

Killion, J. P., and Todnem, G. R. 1991. A process for personal theory building. *Educational Leadership* 48(6): 14–16.

Kottkamp, R. B. 1990. Means for facilitating reflection. *Education and Urban Society,* 22(2): 182–203.

Krashen, S. 1990. How reading and writing make you smarter, or, How smart people read and write. In *Georgetown University Round Table on Languages and Linguistics,* ed. Washington, D.C.: Georgetown University Press.

Kucer, S. B. 1991. *Literacy beliefs profile.* Unpublished document. University of Southern California.

Kucer, S. B. 1983. *Theoretical orientation to writing profile.* Unpublished document, University of Wyoming.

Kuhn, T. S. 1962. *The structure of scientific revolutions.* Chicago: University of Chicago Press.

Lemlech, J. K., and Kaplan, S. N. 1990. Learning to talk about reaching: Collegiality in clinical teacher education. *Action in Teacher Education* 12(1): 13–19.

Lester, N. B., and Mayher, J. S. 1987. Critical professional inquiry. *English Education* 198–210.

Lester, N. B., and Onore, N. B. 1986. From teacher-teacher to teacher-learner: Making the grade. *Language Arts* 63(7): 698–704.

McLaren, P. 1989. *Life in schools.* New York: Longman.

McLaughlin, M. W., and Marsh, D. D. 1978. Staff development and school change. *Teachers College Record* 80(1): 69–74.

Monson, R. J., and Pahl, M. M. 1991. Charting a new course with whole language. *Educational Leadership* 48(6): 51–53.

Neisser, U. 1976. *Cognition and reality.* New York: W. H. Freeman.

Newman, J. M., ed 1990. *Finding our own way: Teachers exploring their assumptions.* Portsmouth, N.H.: Heinemann.

Newman, J. M. 1988. Sharing journals: Conversational mirrors for seeing ourselves as learners, writers, and teachers. *English Education* 134–188.

Osterman, K. F. 1990. Reflective practice, A new agenda for education. *Education and Urban Society* 22(2): 133–52.

Peterson, P. L., and Clark, C. M. 1986. Teachers' reports of their cognitive processes during teaching. *American Educational Research Journal* 15(4): 555–65.

Pytlik, B. P. 1990. *Collaborative learning in a teacher training class: A case study of a teacher-researcher's experience.* The Annual Meeting of the Conference on College Composition and Communication, Chicago. (ERIC Document Reproduction Service No. ED 317 999)

Rainer, T. 1978. *The new diary.* Los Angeles: J. P. Tarcher.

Richardson, V. 1990. The evolution of reflective teaching and teacher education. In *Encouraging Reflective Practice in Education,* ed. R. T. Clift, W. R. Houston, and M. C. Pugach, 3–19. New York: Teachers College Press.

Ross, D. D. 1989. First steps in developing a reflective approach. *Journal of Teacher Education* 22–30.

Schon, D. A. 1987. *Educating the reflective practitioner.* San Francisco: Jossey-Bass.

Schon, D. A. 1983. *The reflective practitioner.* New York: Basic Books.

Short, K. G., and Burke, C. L. 1989. New potentials for teacher education: Teaching and learning as inquiry. *The Elementary School Journal* 90(2): 193–206.

Simmons, J. M., Sparks, G. M., Stark, A., Pasch, M., Colton, A., and Grinberg, J. 1989. *Exploring the structure of reflective pedagogical thinking in novice and expert teachers: The birth of a developmental taxonomy.* Paper presented at the annual conference of the American Educational Research Association, San Francisco.

Smith, F. 1981. Demonstrations, engagement and sensitivity: The choice between people and programs. *Language Arts* 58(6): 634–42.

Smyth, J. 1989. Developing and sustaining critical reflection in teacher education. *Journal of Teacher Education* 2–9.

Sparks-Langer, G. M., and Colton, A. B. 1991. Synthesis of research on teachers: Reflective thinking. *Educational Leadership* 48(6): 37–44.

Spradley, J. P. 1980. *Participant observation.* New York: Holt, Rinehart, and Winston.

Surbeck, E., Han, E. P., and Moyer, J. E. 1991. Assessing reflective responses in journals. *Educational Leadership* 48(6): 25–27.

Stenhouse, L. S. 1985. *Research as a basis for teaching.* Portsmouth, N.H.: Heinemann.

Tama, C. M., and Peterson, K. 1991. Achieving reflectively through literature. *Educational Leadership* 48(6): 22–24.

Tom, A. R. 1985. Inquiring into inquiry-oriented teacher education. *Journal of Teacher Education* 35–44.

Van Manen, M. 1977. Linking ways of knowing with ways of being practical. *Curriculum Inquiry* 6: 205–28.

Vygotsky, L. S. 1978. *Mind in society.* Cambridge, Mass.: Harvard University Press.

Walker, D. 1985. Writing and reflecting. In *Reflection: Turning experience into learning,* ed. D. Boud, R. Keogh, and M. Walker, pp. 52–68.

Wehlage, G. G. 1981. Can teachers be more reflective about their work? A commentary on some research about teachers. In *Studying teaching and learning: Trends in Soviet and American research,* ed. B. R. Tabachnick, T. S. Popkewitz, and B. B. Szekily, pp. 101–13. New York: Praeger.

Wellington, B. 1991. The promise of reflective practice. *Educational Leadership* 48(6): 4–5.

Wibel, W. H. 1991. Reflection through writing. *Educational Leadership* 48(6): 45.

Yinger, R. J., and Clark, C. M. 1981. *Reflective journal writing: Theory and practice.* Michigan State University, Institute for Research on Teaching, East Lansing. (ERIC Document Reproduction Service No. ED 208 411)

Zeichner, K. M. 1987. Preparing reflective teachers: An overview of instructional strategies which have been employed in preservice teacher education. *International Journal of Educational Research* 11(5): 565–75.

Zeichner, K. M. 1983. Alternative paradigms of teacher education. *Journal of Teacher Education* 34(3): 3–9.

Zeichner, K. M., and Liston, D. P. 1987. Teaching student teachers to reflect. *Harvard Educational Review* 57(1): 23–48.

Zumwalt, K. K. 1982. Research on teaching: Policy implications for teacher education. In *Policy making in education,* ed. A. Lieberman and W. McLaughlin, pp. 215–48. Chicago: University of Chicago Press.

Means to Actualize Professional Roles

5 Teacher Research

Laurie MacGillivray

A couple of years ago, I left my position as an elementary school teacher in order to conclude my doctorate in literacy studies. My graduate courses prepared me to conduct research in schools, to identify a problem or focus, review the literature, design a study to explore the issue further, analyze the data, and then write up my conclusions, all this as an outside researcher, as one looking in on another's teaching. Curiously, the first study I found myself carrying out after graduating was on my own teaching, although teacher research had never been discussed in my classes. As the instructor of two reading classes at the university for preservice teachers, I wanted to offer my students more choice in their learning. These college students were frustrated that this class was different and that they were expected to participate in literature discussion circles and even to propose their own grades. I believed in how I was teaching and that most students by the end of the semester would also come to value their larger participatory roles, so I began to take notes during class of what students were saying to each other during small and whole-group discussions. After each class, I spent some time reflecting in a journal. Also, I collected each piece of writing the students turned in, including both formal papers and "free writes" (students immediate written thoughts to questions posed during class, such as "Why did our discussion go better today than yesterday?"). When

Chapter 5 HIGHLIGHTS

- Teacher Research, What It Is
- Interviews, Questionnaires
- Written Products, Daily Work
- Anecdotal Records
- Informal Assessment
- Journal Writing
- Generating Research Questions
- Interpretive Studies
- "Looking Back" Research
- Hurdles, Dissemination, Coping Strategies

I realized that my reflections upon my own and the students' learning could actually be considered research (for a while I was blind to my own inquiry), I went through the typical college process to receive permission to "conduct a study." Questions from the university research committee such as "*You* are the teacher and the researcher?" and "You've already started the study?" revealed unfamiliarity and a lack of understanding for teacher-researcher inquiry. It took much explanation and repeated phone calls to get through the process, but finally approval was granted.

As I looked over the students' writing and my journal entries, I looked for telling moments, such as when a student shared that she had been told this was an "easy class" and was annoyed that it was not, or when a student talked about how a book we had just read reminded her of when her father died. These moments served as cornerstones to the class's shift from a place where students came expecting a lecture to a place where learners gathered to wrestle with the role of print in their own lives and ways to share the power of print with children. The processes of reflecting in the journal and rereading students' writing served as lenses in which I could look again not only at my own but also my students' teaching and learning. Their responses to my instruction helped me become aware of some ways that I had made the transition to a more student-centered approach more difficult for my students.

As I began to make sense of the "data," the need to discuss it with others was growing, yet other instructors at the university did not seem particularly interested. Luckily, I had met a teacher in Florida who was interested in examining his own teaching of preservice and in-service

---

TABLE 5.1   Six Tips for Getting Started

1. Read teacher research studies.
2. Tap into or create a support system. Maybe just a buddy down the hall will work.
3. Build a study around something that you have a passion for or a burning curiosity.
4. Be flexible. Assume adjustments are part of the process.
5. Enlist aid from knowledgeable folks around you, other teachers, administrators, district-level personnel.
6. Make your students co-researchers.

---

teachers, and we began to talk and exchange ideas. Also, the work of Donald Graves, who has written extensively about teachers and children as writers, was helpful. He encourages teachers not only to reflect on their own teaching but to share their wondering, collecting, and analyzing with the students. So I talked with both classes about what I was focusing on and how I was learning about myself as a teacher through examining what occurred in class. They offered feedback that allowed me to refine my insights and perceptions continually (See Table 5.1).

This is the most recent tale of my teacher-researcher work. It has many similarities with those of classroom teachers who find themselves asking a question, then collecting various sources of data such as student work, finally working to construct an answer or answers, and usually formulating more questions. Unfortunately, the similarities persist, such as feeling isolated from other teachers at times, needing to go beyond the immediate circle of peers to find someone to share ideas with collegially, and overcoming the barriers in the educational system for teachers to research their own teaching and learning. Possible ways to conduct classroom studies will be the heart of this paper, but, first, I will describe what I mean by the term *teacher research*.

DEFINING TEACHER RESEARCH

Teacher research is the examination of teaching and learning by teachers in their own classrooms. In *Inside Outside: Teacher Research and Knowledge* (1993) by Marilyn Cochran-Smith and Susan L. Lytle, teacher research is defined as "systematic and intentional inquiry carried out by teachers." Although teacher research has been published since the 1950s, during the last two decades there has been a great increase in activity in the field. In the seventies there tended to be a focus on joint efforts between teachers and college researchers, and the trend for "partnerships" has continued. In the field of composition, Don Graves, Susan Sowers, and Lucy Calkins's study as researchers-in-residence at Atkinson Academy in the early eighties validated the importance of watching children as they wrote. Both teachers and researchers published findings from this joint project.

Although collaborative projects between researchers and classroom teachers have continued to flourish, teachers have begun to claim their right to do research independently of university personnel. As teachers become curious about specific aspects of learning and teaching, they often decide to carry out investigations themselves (see Cochran-Smith and Lytle, 1993, and Goswami and Stillman, 1987, for numerous examples). Also, some academics have been asserting that it is only natural for teachers to conduct classroom research. Nancy Martin (1987) has stated that "Teachers and their students are the essential sources of information . . . It is they who are in the position to initiate inquiries into learning and to gain the confidence to develop this potential" (p. 21). From both inside and outside the classroom, there is growing recognition of the role that teacher research can play in increasing our understanding about learning and teaching.

The next section will offer someone new to the practice of research an understanding of various ways to gather data and will describe how to go about undertaking a study.[1] For the more experienced researcher, this section will illustrate possible ways to discuss data collection with those less familiar with traditional research terms. After examining several approaches to teacher research, the chapter will conclude with a section on the hurdles to teacher research and the techniques for overcoming them.

WAYS TO COLLECT DATA

Following is a description of five of the most common techniques of the many used to collect information, with examples of how they might play a role in teacher research. Included are illustrations of how I have used and at times misused these techniques myself. It is important to stress that not every question I set about answering became a full-fledged study—a consequence of the frustrations and time constraints many classroom teachers feel.

---

[1]For an in-depth discussion of how to conduct teacher research studies, see Hubbard and Power's *The Art of Classroom Inquiry: A Handbook for Teacher-Research* (1993).

Interviews and Questionnaires

One of the best known teacher-researchers, at least in the field of literacy, is Nancie Atwell. Her book, *In the Middle,* which came out in 1987, detailed how she ran a writing classroom with adolescents. An essential part of the book describes how she interviewed her students to learn about them as composers. More and more teachers are beginning to use interviews as a way to collect information about a certain process, such as composing, or a set of beliefs. When I was teaching first grade, I wondered how students felt about themselves as readers and writers, so while conferring with them about a piece of writing or a text, I would say something like, "Tell me about yourself as a reader." After fine-tuning the wording during different informal talks, I would type up several questions to use as a framework for interviewing each child. Writing down the children's comments as they spoke was critical, since it would have taken an enormous amount of time to transcribe audiotapes later. While I attended to the individual responses, I could have read through them, looked for patterns or types of responses, and formed some summary statements. Knowing what I do now about the power of feedback, I wish I had analyzed the answers this way and then shared my findings with the children.

As many teachers are encouraging children to work more independently and collaboratively, the possibility to conduct interviews on a regular basis increases. Besides interviewing children orally, teachers can give children *written questionnaires.* For example, at the end of the year with my second graders I asked them three questions to which they responded in writing: "What was a favorite moment from the year?" "What's something that I [the teacher] need to work on?" and "Do you have a memory of when I was a good teacher for you?" Ugo wrote that he liked when my stepfather came to visit and wrote with the students, that I needed to work on my handwriting, and that he liked the day that I told him he looked nice. Those simple three questions and Ugo's responses reminded me not only of the need to improve my handwriting but of how important it is to spend one-on-one time affirming a child. Unfortunately, I did not ask these questions until the end of the year or analyze the students' responses, but I would remember the potential of interviews and questionnaires as a source of rich data when I conducted research later. (See Figure 5.1 for an example of a reading survey for young children.)

Oral or written interviews can serve a wide variety of information-gathering purposes, both general and specific. A reading survey, for example, can include questions about how often and what kinds of books one reads as well as elicit in-depth knowledge about a specific

READING SURVEY

NAME _____   DATE _____

Draw a line reflecting how strongly you would say "Yes" or "No".

1) I am a good reader.   NO   •————————→   YES

2) I like to read.   NO   •————————→   YES

3) I like to read alone.   NO   •————→   YES

4) I like to read with my friends.   NO   •——————————→ YES

5) When I'm reading a new book,
   I'm reminded of other books.   NO   ←—•   YES

6) I like to read hard books.   NO   •————→   YES

7) I read at home.   NO   •————→   YES

8) I skip words I don't know.   NO   •——————————→   YES

9) I sound out words I don't
   know.   NO   •————→   YES

10) I read a sentence again
    if I get confused.   NO   •————————→   YES

11) I think about ways that I am
    like the characters in the book. NO   ←—•   YES

12) I work at a word until I get it.   NO   ←—•   YES

13) I read with my family.   NO   •————→   YES

14) I think about books during
    the day when I am not
    reading.   NO   ←—•   YES

15) I get so involved when I am
    reading that I don't hear
    people around me.   NO   ←——•   YES

16) When I am an adult, I am
    going to be a good reader.   NO   •——————————→ YES

FIGURE 5.1   Reading survey for young children.

issue or process. In addition, as teachers are coming to value the importance of out-of-school experiences, they are beginning to ask parents questions as well as children. Interviews can be a key technique in collecting data for teacher research. Ken Macrorie's essay "Research as Odessy" (Goswami and Stillman, (1987), which details one of his own studies using interviews, is worthwhile reading for those interested in conducting interviews.

Written Products/Daily Work

Another research procedure is to *collect samples of children's work.* This technique can document many facets of learning and teaching. **Writing folders,** often used to house all of a child's writing pieces throughout a year, reveal a student's exploration of genres, development of graphophonemic understandings, evolution of audience awareness, and much more. **Portfolios,** the year-long gathering of select samples of children's work, are sweeping the country. These means of collecting examples of children's work are similar to and, in some cases, identical to the research procedure I am proposing here. One difference is that researchers tend to collect products on a regular basis, whereas teachers tend to emphasize that the portfolio contain the "best" of a child's products, similar to an artist's portfolio. Clearly, samples of work do not need just to capture the ability to produce a product but also children's processual learning. Many math teachers are getting children to write not only the answer to a problem but also how they went about solving it. Similarly, science teachers are creating frameworks in which children document the thinking they did while conducting an experiment. For example, if children are simply given a cloud-shaped piece of paper, they can write down things they wonder about but do not have time to discuss. These can be discussed briefly at the end of class and, if collected by the teacher, offer insight into children's thinking processes. (See Figures 5.2A and 5.2B for examples of ways to encourage children to reflect on their own thinking processes.) A teacher-researcher might collect a single type of product, a variety from many children, or just one or two. For example, a math teacher might collect a variety of written products weekly, such as a sample of homework, a center activity sheet, and brain teasers from five children who represent diverse abilities.

Three important issues are what to collect, how to collect it, and how much to collect. Teacher-researchers need to ask first, "Which, if any, of the children's products address the focus of my research?" Don Graves (1991) talks about this as "knowing where to put your bucket." Sometimes the answer will emerge by just musing over it throughout the day.

Our minds are constantly working during a science experiment. Today jot down your thoughts, including questions and new learning.

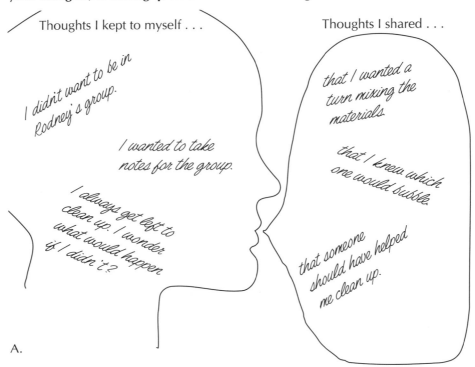

Thoughts I kept to myself . . .

I didn't want to be in Rodney's group.

I wanted to take notes for the group.

I always get left to clean up. I wonder what would happen if I didn't?

Thoughts I shared . . .

that I wanted a turn mixing the materials.

that I knew which one would bubble.

that someone should have helped me clean up.

A.

Use this as a record sheet while you are at math center today. By writing down what we are thinking, we learn more about math and about ourselves as mathematicians.

?QUESTIONS?

How many ways could this puzzle be solved? (I found 3!)

Why do marbles roll faster than cotton balls?

Why do they weigh more?

Why is there more than one word for the same thing? Like minus and subtraction

!SURPRISES!

Tim said he found 6 ways to solve the puzzle!

Cotton balls stick in my hair!

B.

FIGURE 5.2   Worksheets designed to encourage reflective thinking.

Students and our peers may also offer helpful suggestions. Another option is looking at others' research that addresses similar questions. The answer is necessarily context-specific, so ultimately the teacher-researcher is left to make the final decision on this as the real expert about her or his classroom.

Don Graves has also impacted my notions of *how* to collect samples. Years ago, I would have looked through a child's work, taken some samples, and tucked them away. Now, I cannot imagine collecting a sample without involving the creators, the children, and asking them about the process of creating it. Writers' input is integral to the emerging notions of a portfolio. For example, when second grader Ugo had spelled *AND* with just an *N,* I assumed he did not yet know how to spell it conventionally. Luckily, I asked him about it and he said, looking disgusted with my ignorance, "It's an abbreviation!" Repeatedly, when I am wise enough to put my assumptions aside and ask the children about their products and thoughts, I come away with new understandings. Also, as the power of metacognition, thinking about our own thinking, is being recognized, more emphasis is being placed on having learners reflect about what they produce and how. There might be times when a teacher-researcher chooses the samples, but it is crucial to be aware of the role that the student can play in their choosing.

"How many samples are needed to offer variety yet not overwhelm me?" As a teacher interested in how children's writing evolves, I thought I would save everything, even abandoned papers with only initial scribbles. What a mistake! Although initially excited about the quantity of my data, I was soon overwhelmed. Also, I had not yet heard Don Graves's talk of sharing research with students. Sitting alone surrounded by students' work and besieged by parent conference forms that needed to be filled out by morning, I abandoned yet another attempt at systematic inquiry. My eagerness for quantity and also my notion of research as separate from teaching had crippled my endeavor (the integration of teaching and research will be discussed further in the closing section.) Since then I have learned to stress the idea of *sample,* although I still wrestle with the problem of how much is enough.

This issue of appropriate sampling is also debated by academic researchers. One advantage of teacher-researchers is that we hold class every day. Even though we may collect samples of "free writes" in social studies on a weekly basis, if a child creates something interesting, we are there to collect it regardless of the collection schedule. I think the best way to know how much is the right amount is to get in and try something, then be ready to adjust. Viewing research as a flexible process is critical to success.

For all researchers, what, how, and how much to collect are ongoing issues. Sustained, systematic inquiry demands continual analysis of the quality of the investigation. Though some researchers would encourage sticking rigidly to a procedure and simply learning lessons from it for the next study, I would tend to stress the flexibility of the process. As long as I keep an accurate account of collection procedures, gathering more or less or changing how I compile data seems integral to making the most of each inquiry. Although rarely used in isolation from other forms of gathering information, the technique of collecting samples can assemble a great deal of data.

Anecdotal Records from Observations

A procedure that often accompanies the collection of samples is the compiling of anecdotal records. The teacher-researcher's equivalent of an anthropologist's field notes, these records are written on the scene, unlike journals, which are usually written after the fact. In these brief jottings, teachers can capture a student's behavior in a math center, an interaction between two students while reading, or a child's comment during a science lab. Such events tend to reveal many facets of learners not documented in grade books or written work. This kind of note taking has been promoted as part of the current movement to attend to children's processes as well as products.

Once a teacher decides to try anecdotal records, logistical problems arise. "Where should these notes be written?", How can I keep up with all of them?" and "How and what should I write?" are questions commonly asked. It is clear that teacher-researchers must find a method that works for them, as I had to myself. Having individual folders that could be accessed each time a child made a noteworthy comment was written was my first method, but it was much too slow a system. A friend recommended using sheets of mailing labels, which were a great improvement. I just clipped several sheets of these to my lesson plan book, which I usually carried with me throughout the day. Noticing something to write down, I would jot the child's name, the date, and then a couple of sentences. Each child's name was at the top of both sides of a sheet of construction paper in a file. So at the end of the week, I would peel off the labels with notations and stick them to each child's file. One side was designated for reading and writing, the other for math. These were my target areas for anecdotal records.

This procedure not only chronicles specific moments in each learner's life, it also highlights which students a teacher tends to notice more or less. Upon realizing there was less documented about certain children than others, I would write their names at the top of some of the address labels as a reminder the next day to attend to those children. Another way to keep track of anecdotal records is to have an index card box divided into sections by the children's names. Notes can be jotted down on the index cards, which are filed when time allows.

The focus of your research determines what you write down. When I was teaching first grade and seeking to document each student's academic growth, I learned the most from my colleague Colleen Buddy. We shared some students, so one day I read over her anecdotal records. There was so much information! Many of my records were the same length but offered much less. She had a knack for being very specific and descriptive, while holding off what I call teacher commentary. Anecdotal notes should capture the moment. Here are a few examples of what my early anecdotal records were like:

> "Curtis is still not reading during silent reading time."

> "Cynthia is happy while she reads an easy book."

> "James changes his spelling of Robocop, still not conventional but a little closer."

> "Ikeshia worked with adding coins successfully today."

Vague labels like "easy book" and "inventive spelling" can easily be made more informative. Here are these four comments revised:

> "Curtis is hitting his book against his leg and has been doing that for the first five minutes of silent reading time."

> "Cynthia is smiling as she reads *Dan, Dan, the Flying Man,* a predictable book."

> "James changes "REOY" to "kBreoy" for Robocop."

> "Ikeshia adds two pennies and a nickel to make 7 cents."

Notice that the note now states what Curtis is doing rather than what he is not; Cynthia's book has a title and a descriptive label, not a judgmental one; James's exact spelling is given; and a specific example of Ikeshia's work with coins is detailed. I realized I could take out the commentary because specific anecdotal records actually said more. Since I was attending to academic growth, details relating to inventive spelling were critical.

Also, these could then be shared with both children and their parents without what would have been for some children a punitive message. A side note: When children realize their teacher cares enough about their learning to record the specific details, there is often a renewed sense of pride and attention to detail.

Besides being used in conjunction with written-product sampling, anecdotal records are often used alongside journals, interviews, and questionnaires. Just as field notes tend to be the heart of ethnographic or naturalistic work, anecdotal records can be the mainstay for teacher research. Flexibility is crucial to the success of this procedure just as it is with collecting samples. It may take a while to figure out what information is most valuable to record, so adjusting as needed only makes sense.

Informal Assessment Measures

Informal assessment measures continue to grow in number and popularity. In literacy assessment, teachers are using retellings (children's retellings of books) as well as miscue analysis (analysis of children's deviations from text while reading orally) as types of data. For example, a teacher-researcher might ask a child to write a list of words that have various spelling patterns. The test may reveal that the child is developing an awareness of double vowels but is not using them accurately yet. Nine weeks later, a similar request might document that the child is now consistently making accurate decisions about the use of double vowels. Because informal assessment tends to be diagnostic, it gives more information about the learner than formal assessment procedures. Many informal assessments reveal the underlying processes a child is using when attempting various tasks and thus offer insight into directions for further instruction.

A teacher-researcher has a range of options when applying assessments. A single assessment might be used at the beginning of a study and then at the end. For example, a teacher might want to explore the role of manipulatives in increasing fourth graders' understandings of division and choose to assess each child before and after a six-week unit, using various manipulatives. A second option would be to assess repeatedly throughout a study, such as every two weeks. For example, the development of children's problem-solving skills could be documented by having them attempt to solve the same kind of problem periodically. A teacher could create an observation sheet upon which vital information could be recorded, such as time elapsed (for speed and/or tenacity), the process of solving, and the solution.

Yet a third option would be to use more than one type of assessment, allowing for both a wider range of data and potentially corroborating data. In other words, two different tasks might document a child's understanding of the same concept. For example, a paper-and-pencil test could document increased understanding of a concept by revealing a higher number of correct answers than was evident before the intervention, and a one-on-one assessment with the child demonstrating the processes involved in computation with manipulatives could corroborate this fact. Without seeming redundant, I would like to assert again the importance of monitoring and adjusting the research as needed. If upon looking at the results of an assessment, the information does not seem accurate or does not capture the aspect you are focusing on, use a different assessment technique.

Journals

Journals are composed of regular written comments on a teacher's day. Though they serve as a contributive method of data collection, journals are also a viable form of research. Because of this, they are presented in the following section.

HOW TO CONDUCT TEACHER RESEARCH STUDIES

Five different ways to go about teacher research are delineated below. The first section describes journals, which as previously stated can be either one of many procedures or the sole method used to collect data.

Journals

Many teachers have been keeping journals for years as a way to wind down at the end of a day, to think on paper, to keep track of their evolving teaching processes, and to capture interesting interactions with specific students. Often including teachers' thoughts, plans, and wonderings, journals are now being considered a form of research in and of themselves. Cochran-Smith and Lytle (1993) assert, "Teachers' journals provide a unique blend of observation and analysis in which classroom vignettes are juxtaposed with more general assertions and interpretations" (p. 30). A journal can be a collection of "snapshots," five-minute notes on a moment of the day; a retelling of the day's events; or a response to regular questions such as, "What did I do well today?" "What did I learn about a particular student?" and/or "What would I have done differently and how?" Thus a journal can be many things, the content being determined by the teacher-researcher.

Personally, I have attempted at various times in my teaching to keep a journal before I even considered it a form of research. While teaching fifth grade, I began to shift toward focusing on reading and writing as processes as opposed to focusing merely on products by offering the students more choice in their literacy activities. I began a journal but then my attentiveness waned. However, I encouraged a few teachers interested in similar issues to gather together on a regular basis. We read professional books and talked about our reactions to the text and issues we were struggling with in our own teaching. I see now that I needed an audience for my journal and this group might have served that purpose; instead I put down my pencil in favor of talk. Addressing this need for another's response, two colleagues of mine have recently explored the use of dialogue journals as a form of teacher research. While Rebecca Anderson was attempting to change her teaching style in an undergraduate education class to be more student-centered, she exchanged dialogue journals twice a week with Suzanne Reid, who also sat in on the class. They both found the process rewarding and useful as a way to study systematically their own instructional assumptions and practices.

For many teachers interested in beginning research, journals may be the least daunting method to try. There is room within this methodology to create a kind of inquiry that is both personally and professionally rewarding. For some, like myself, forming a support system would not only add the benefit of an audience but also enable long-term commitment. This might take the form of encounters with a peer across the hall whom you have breakfast with on Monday mornings and share aloud interesting journal entries; a long-distance exchange of journals with an old college buddy who also went into education; or discussion of parts of your journal with a neighbor who is interested in education from the perspective of a concerned parent.

It is clear that in many schools networks within which teacher researchers can talk are not in place. But just as teachers have historically been ingenious about finding supplies for our rooms, we need to do the same in building support systems that nurture our teaching and learning. This sharing can serve the dual purpose of strengthening the analysis and supporting the efforts of the reflective teacher. Deborah Jumpp and Lynne Yermanock Strieb (1993) write of their experience:

> Journals have linked our separate inquiries as teacher researchers and have connected us in new ways with our students' inquiries as well. We have used

journals to guide our decision making, and they have helped us expand the lines of communication between teachers in very different settings and between teachers and diverse students in important but unexpected directions. (p. 149)

Clearly, journals can serve as a tool for systematic, sustained inquiry.

Generating Questions, Then Seeking Answers

Generating questions first and then designing a study to explore the answers is what often comes to mind when teachers hear about research. Along with the questions, there might also be hypotheses, that is, predictions about what the study will find. For example, a teacher may ask, "If children are allowed to choose their own books, will they increase their reading?" A likely hypothesis would be that, "Yes, when children are allowed to choose what they read, they tend to read more." Two reasons for the teacher-researcher posing such questions are, first, see if a hypothesis proves correct and, second, in order to be able to share his or her findings with others.

After forming a question, it is essential to ask, "Is the answer attainable?" This refers to focus and scope of the question. Often, initial questions are too broad, requiring data that would be impossible to gather and/or exhausting to pursue thoroughly. Especially for beginning teacher-researchers, I would recommend keeping the question narrow and specific to avoid being overwhelmed. This is a good point in the process in which to share thinking with others, if this has not already occurred. The teacher-researcher may check the clarity of the question and consider her or his hypotheses with other educators. Examining other studies that have had a similar focus may also be helpful.

Four Facets of Designing a Study   The next step is designing the study. Four facets of this process will be discussed here. Many academics spend a lifetime studying research design; the following discussion is definitely and necessarily only a sliver of what designing a study can involve. As an emerging genre, teacher research has not formulated guidelines for designing a study. Unfortunately, the only guidelines available are those that have been established by university-based researchers and that I believe are inappropriate for teacher research.

Clearly, the research question or questions guide decisions about the study. One key issue is that of duration: How long will the study be? Will the impact of an intervention, such as math manipulatives, be examined for two weeks? Or will the effect of teacher conferences be examined over the course of a year? One way to address the issue of duration is to consider the focus of the research. If a process of change is being described or measured, then a relatively long period of research is typically appropriate, if a type of interaction is being described or its impact measured, then a short time period may be adequate.

Second, how many students will be a part of the study? Some teacher-researchers prefer "case studies"; that is, a few children are the focus, whereas others utilize their entire class. One way to determine this aspect of your design is to examine how this problem has been addressed in similar studies.

A third issue is that of collecting data, specifically, determining what data will be important and how it will be gathered. For example, a study may be based solely on information gathered in interviews or may combine this technique with product samples and classroom observation. This requires figuring out what information is relevant to the research question. As a preliminary step to deciding, a teacher-researcher may use several collection techniques for one week and then decide which processes gathered the most useful information.

The fourth facet of designing a study is determining how the data will be analyzed. Of the many ways to make sense of data, one of the most common is to count things and compare quantity, for example, the number of books read when choice was not offered and number of books read when it was. Besides comparing numbers before and after an intervention, a teacher-researcher can track a change by collecting information throughout a process known as a time series analysis. For example, a survey on reading attitudes could use Likert scales (1 to 5, 5 being "the best"). If given monthly, responses to various questions could be charted over an extended period of time. "Talk" can also be categorized and quantified. Students' comments during shared reading time may be categorized and counted. A read-aloud session could be described by breaking down the talk by topic, such as the number of comments about the illustrations, those related to personal experience, those directed to the text, and those considered "other," including requests to go to the lavatory. Further examples within each category could be given to enrich the commentary. More ways to analyze data will be discussed in subsequent sections.

Studies That Begin without a Hypothesis

Not all studies that begin with a question have an hypothesis. Many begin with an open-ended question without a prediction of the outcome being made. For example, Colleen Buddy (1993) conducted a study with her multi-age primary classroom in Colorado. She set out to investigate the role of imagination and its relationship to authentic writing. This question emerged because the literature on authentic writing stressed the connection to personal experience, yet this did not gel with what she was seeing with one student in particular who seemed to engage authentically with his imaginary worlds. Choosing this student, Nelson, as a focal point, Colleen gathered his writing samples, documented his comments while talking with his peers and his behavior during literacy events, interviewed him repeatedly, and interviewed his mother.

Continually, as Colleen collected the data, she analyzed the information by asking, "What does this say about the role of imagination and its relationship to authentic writing?" As she began to develop an answer, she would pursue issues through more specific interviews and repeated observation. Thus, her hypotheses emerged during data collection and were constantly shaped and refigured by the incoming data. Concluding her article, Colleen states:

> Nelson reminds me of the importance of focused classroom inquiry. His statement, "I live in the world of my imagination" caused me to pose questions and rethink notions. Focusing on one child as a springboard for my own learning helped me think more deeply about my teaching.

Teacher-researchers like Colleen find value in attending to questions that emerge as they teach and following through with a systematic inquiry.

Descriptive/Interpretive Studies, or Letting Issues Emerge

Though descriptive interpretive studies also start with a question they tend to be very open-ended and the field of application very general, such as writing time or parent interviews. The teacher-researcher begins by asking, for instance, "What is really happening during X?" then collects data that address this question. It is after data gathering has occurred for a period of time that issues emerge that narrow the research. For example, my research with undergraduates that I mentioned in the opening of this chapter began with the question, "What is going on here?" To answer this question, I took anecdotal records, wrote in my journal after each class, and collected students' writing. About half-way into the study, I realized that a key issue was the role of expectations in teaching and learning. Both the students and myself had previously unexamined assumptions about the roles of teachers and students in college learning and teaching. When these formal role assumptions emerged from the data as a reoccurring theme, I began to direct my research toward this issue. Thus, through describing and interpreting what was going on in general, I became aware of one specific issue that I believed warranted attention. If a more specific question had guided the initial data collection and analysis, I believe that this issue of unexamined assumptions might not have been recognized.

That sort of study was clearly interpretive because I, as a teacher-researcher, was making sense of the data through my own lens. Most researchers will agree that it is impossible to describe, or gather any data for that matter, without revealing a bias. For example, in my anecdotal records, I did not write down the color of the students' socks because I did not view that as information that would address the issue of what was going on. In fact, no mention of clothes is made in either my journal or anecdotal records. Another researcher might have pursued how assumptions about teachers and students are revealed in the way both teachers and students choose to dress. Even through surveys, researchers reveal what is important to them through what is asked, not asked, and the way in which questions are framed.

Unlike research that begins with narrow questions, in descriptive interpretive studies data must be continually analyzed in order for the focus points to emerge. Yet in many ways, the two means of going about research are similar. The studies are designed using various data collection techniques and relevant literature is traditionally considered. Findings can be quantified and/or categorized, but there is a tendency to use more of the students' talk to support the findings, which are often presented as patterns that were prominent in the data. For example, in my study with the undergraduates, in the analysis I am looking for ways that the students shared their assumptions with me. There seem to be three ways that I have discovered so far (I am still analyzing the data). Specifically, some students asked questions, others reported a dislike in their written responses, and yet others waited until they had made the adjustment and did not share their discomfort until after the fact. One way I may choose to share these findings is to present this "typology" or categorization and several examples of each instance. This discussion could be extended by examining the impact of each way to share and explore how these ways further reveal assumptions about teacher-student relationships. For further information on this type of research, see the excellent book by Spradley (1980), entitled, *Participant Observation*. Although it is not specifically written for teacher-researchers, it offers a great deal of information that is easily accessible.

Position Pieces, or Looking Back

The final type of teacher research to be discussed here is that of "looking back." Smith-Cochran and Lytle (1993) refer to this as conceptual research or essays. The process involves the teacher-researcher articulating a specific stand or concept and then providing supporting data. I refer to this as "looking back" because the general assertions are articulated first, then teacher-researchers review previous experience and select relevant examples. The research cycle in a sense is flipped, because the conclusion is asserted, then the data the teacher already has is examined for supporting information.

I wrote a study using this process the summer after I taught second grade. In reflecting on the year, I came to the conclusion that my students had learned about how to care for each other within the framework of a writing-process classroom. The literature I was reading seemed to be discussing socialization as another area of curriculum that needed to be addressed separately from academics. However, I believed socialization could be a critical facet of learning addressed through general academic frameworks, such as process classrooms. So I thought back through the year to critical moments when our classroom seemed to move toward a sense of community and also individuals' progressions toward an increased social awareness, an increased sensitivity to others. Looking back through the children's writing folders and notes they had written to me helped to jog my memory; also I found some writing samples that reflected this socialization process. From these remembered instances and children's notes and products, I crafted an argument for my stance that socialization, like high-quality writing could be an outcome of a writing-process classroom. Like journals, this "looking back" process of teacher research may also serve as an entry point for interested teachers.

HURDLES TO TEACHER RESEARCH AND DISSEMINATION; COPING STRATEGIES

The previous sections focused on tools and ways to go about teacher research. What we all know as teachers is that even those that are interested in research get discouraged. This section will address the difficulties and offer some ways to overcome the barriers. There are two primary areas of difficulty for any kind of research: the conducting of the study and dissemination of the information. First, I will discuss the difficulties of classroom teachers as they seek to carry out their own inquiries. In relation not just to research but simply to reflective teaching, some of these problems have been delineated repeatedly, both in the literature as well as in teacher lounges.

Time Restraints

First is the problem of time restraints within which teachers must function and second is the feeling of isolation that most practitioners experience. These related hurdles inhibit the wonderings that often prompt initial forays into teacher research. As I mentioned earlier, Don Graves's invitation to share inquiries with the students has enabled many teachers to overcome the frenzy and loneliness they experience. If questions, data collection, and analysis are incorporated into classroom life, teachers can explore issues alongside twenty-plus fellow investigators. A team of interested students might gather data on the different genres that are being explored by their classmates, for example. They might create a list of the different genres represented, the frequency with which they appear, and even explore the relationship between what books students are reading with what genres they are using in their writing. In fact, this stance of reflecting on learning processes can become the life blood of the classroom rather than an add-on. Nancie Atwell discusses this integration of teaching and research in terms of thoughtfulness:

> When teachers ask questions about students' learning, observe in their classrooms, and make sense of their observations, schools become more thoughtful places . . . When teachers invite students to become partners in inquiry, to collaborate with them in wondering about what and how students are learning, schools become more thoughtful places. And when teachers act as scholars, closely reading, heatedly debating, and generously attributing the published work in their field, schools become more thoughtful places. In short, the most thoughtful practitioner is the teacher who acts as a researcher. (1991, p. 3)

Embedded in Atwell's words is the notion that inquiry can make a difference not only in the students' lives but also in the teachers'. Sharing inquiry with the students can serve as a sustaining force for educators.

Research Criteria

A less frequently mentioned obstacle to teacher research is the criteria for research in general. Cochran-Smith and Lytle (1993) stress that "teacher research is an emerging genre wherein researchers are striving to render their ongoing analyses of classroom and school data in ways that are inventive rather than imitative and that are accessible and meaningful for multiple rather than specific audiences (p. 116)." Not only should teachers naturally conduct studies but they should also be involved in establishing the criteria for this genre, such as what literature should be considered for review or what research designs are most appropriate. Teachers need to make decisions not only about their classrooms but about what type of inquiry is fundamental to teaching and learning.

Support Systems

Finding colleagues and creating support systems through which teachers can explore and develop their own ideas of research is yet another critical issue and is being addressed on multiple fronts. There are nationwide organizations, such as whole-language groups, that enable teacher-researchers to communicate both through newsletters and conferences. At the local level, many schools are encouraging teachers to gather on a regular basis to read professional books and reflect on their teaching. These sorts of gatherings often serve as springboards for teacher-researchers. Not only do they encourage professional reading and reflective teaching, but they offer colleagues that are interested in similar issues a chance to talk. As I have experienced both at the university and the elementary level, it is easy to feel lonely and isolated as one explores the world of the teacher-researcher. In yet another attempt to break down barriers, some districts and principals are offering release time so that teachers may observe other classrooms and have observers in their own. Offering teachers more flexibility in their schedules obviously nurtures collegial sharing.

Dissemination

The other key area of difficulty in teacher research has been that of dissemination. Teacher-researchers have often been their own audience. Inquiry has been conducted in order to inform one's own teaching. Yet as the genre develops and teachers become more self-assured researchers, more diverse audiences are being sought. Teachers are sharing their learnings with colleagues (through the outlets discussed earlier); with parents through letters and meetings; with their students often as co-investigators; with school and district administrators, sometimes to support teacher-based curricular decisions; and finally nationwide through professional journals.

Unfortunately, the established forums for disseminating educational research have been created by academics. This has occurred naturally, not maliciously, since teachers have not traditionally been considered researchers. Also, a layer of language has been created by academic researchers, but terms such as *analysis of variance* and *randomization* are often foreign to teacher-researchers. This creates a situation in which the voices of teachers who breathe the life into our schools are denigrated unless an academic vocabulary is learned and utilized. Researchers from universities, some of whom rarely enter classrooms, let alone experience the larger ethos of schools created during lunch and dismissal, officially own the language of educational research through their key roles as editors and reviewers of professional journals. In validating this notion of teacher alienation, Fredrick Burton, one of the two teacher-researchers represented in the *Handbook of research on teaching the English language arts* (1991), asserts:

> It is no secret that positivistic research, which traditionally emphasizes quantitative measures and experimental designs, has not only been ignored by public school teachers, but has alienated them as well . . . These studies have failed to make visible the rich complexity of classroom life as children and adults experience it. For many teachers, these studies have findings but no meaning. (p. 226)

Nancie Atwell similarly disclaims the prevalent model of research; "Teacher research is not theory-stripped, context-stripped method testing. We need to reject impoverished models that turn classroom research into a pseudoscientific horse race (1991, p. 328)." She goes on to urge teachers to know what has already been written and to study previous research. This can be done in the field of composing if one attends to the work of the last two decades, which tends to be more naturalistic and more practitioner-oriented. I wonder, though, how teacher-researchers in other fields can come to know previous research when it demands an entirely different vocabulary. This circles back to Cochran-Smith and Lytle's (1993) point that teacher-researchers need to further define this emerging genre rather than be compared to existing standards as set by academics. Clearly, I am not calling for a less rigorous inquiry, simply one that is deemed appropriate by classroom researchers.

Fortunately since the 1980s publishers such as Heinemann have begun to respond to this field by offering edited volumes of teacher research work. In fact, within these texts the diversity and complexity of teacher research are often celebrated. Professional journals are also responding to the new genre of teacher research, and teachers are increasingly staking their claim to the right to publish studies about their own classrooms. These trends not only allow teacher-researchers to share their studies but also raise the status and understanding of the genre. Each article simultaneously redefines the genre and further establishes the work of teachers as generators of theory-based knowledge and pedagogy.

CONCLUSION

Teacher research is an emerging genre. It represents a movement of teachers acknowledging their ability and right to design and conduct inquiries into learning and teaching. While not supplanting the work of academic researchers, teacher research claims equal rights for classroom educators to be the generators of knowledge. Several barriers hinder both the conducting of studies and the dissemination of findings, but determined practitioners are causing change. Teacher research is becoming integral to many classroom teachers' understanding of the processes of schooling. Forever changed are what it means to be a teacher and student, and the body of knowledge on teaching and learning, as teachers continue to find their voices and join with others to pronounce their passion for reflective teaching and declare their insights, discovered through systematic inquiry.

Recap Notes: Six Tips for Getting Started

- Read teacher research studies.

- Tap into or create a support system–maybe just a buddy down the hall will work.

- Build a study around something that you have a passion for or a burning curiosity about.

- Be flexible. Assume adjustments are part of the process.

- Enlist aid from knowledgeable people around you, other teachers, administrators, district-level personnel.

- Make your students co-researchers.

REFERENCES

Atwell, N. 1991. "Wonderings to pursue": The writing teacher as researcher. In *The Heinemann reader: Literacy in process,* ed. B. Power and R. Hubbard. Portsmouth: Heinemann.

Atwell, N. 1987. *In the middle: Writing, reading, and learning with adolescents.* Upper Montclair, NJ: Boynton/Cook.

Buddy, C. 1993. Imagination and passion: Rich sources of authentic text. *Primary Voices* 1:26–32.

Burton, F. 1991. Teacher-researcher projects: An elementary school teacher's perspective. In *Handbook of research on teaching the English language arts,* ed. J. Flood, J. Jensen, D. Lapp, and J. Squire. New York: Macmillan.

Cochran-Smith, M., and Lytle, S. 1993. *Inside outside: Teacher research and knowledge.* New York: Teachers College Press.

Goswami, D., and Stillman, P. 1987. *Reclaiming the classroom: Teacher research as an agency for change.* Portsmouth: Heinemann.

Graves, D. 1991. Donald Graves of teacher as researcher. *Gazette,* 3:1, 2, 5 (Spring).

Graves, D. 1991. *Build a literate classroom.* Portsmouth: Heinemann.

Hubbard, R. S., and Power, B. M. 1993. *The art of classroom inquiry: A handbook for teacher-researchers.* Portsmouth: Heinemann.

Jumpp, D., and Strieb, L. 1993. Journals for collaboration, curriculum, and assessment. In *Inside outside: Teacher research and knowledge,* ed. M. Cochran-Smith and S. Lytle. New York: Teachers College Press.

Macrorie, K. 1987. Research as odyssey. In *Reclaiming the classroom: Teacher research as an agency for change,* ed. D. Goswami and P. Stillman. Portsmouth: Heinemann.

Martin, N. 1987. On the move: Teacher-researchers. In *Reclaiming the classroom: Teacher research as an agency for change,* ed. D. Goswami and P. Stillman. Portsmouth: Heinemann.

Spradley, J. 1980. *Participant observation.* New York: Holt, Rinehart, and Winston.

6 The Professional Teacher in a School-University Partnership

HILLARY S. HERTZOG

E̲ver since *A Nation at Risk* (National Commission on Excellence in Education, 1983) was published, there has been a call for the improvement of teaching through a restructuring of how new teachers are taught and inducted into the profession (see Carnegie Forum 1986; Holmes Group, 1986). Severe criticism of traditional teacher education and the quality of new practitioners entering the ranks has been directed at universities. Teacher education has been accused of focusing on theory over practice and thereby educating novice teachers who cannot handle the demands of the classroom. At the same time, research has shown that the most powerful influence on the novice teacher is the modeling provided by the "master" teacher during the traditional student teaching experience and that the quality of the student teaching experience in these "master" teachers' classrooms is uneven (Griffin et al., 1983). Scrutiny of the quality of experiences for preservice teachers has resulted in a reexamination of how preservice teacher education needs to change.

Teacher education institutions have begun to examine their programs for the purpose of changing the curriculum and teaching experiences they offer preservice teachers. Valli describes seven teacher education institutions who have moved from a traditional program to a "reflective orientation which emphasizes the knowledge, disposition, and analytic skills needed to make good decisions about complex classroom

Chapter 6 HIGHLIGHTS

- Apprenticeship Model
- Clinical School Model
- Characteristics of Professional Development Schools (PDS)
- Teachers' Roles in a PDS
- Collegial Relationships
- Mentoring Preservice Teachers
- Exemplary Practice
- Study Group Participation
- Teaching Cases
- Peer Coaching

phenomena" (1992, p. xii). At other universities, especially those associated with the Holmes Group, a different type of school-university partnership is being conceived in which school-based faculty work closely with university faculty to shape teacher education experiences for preservice teachers. Termed *professional development schools (PDSs)*, these sites are rapidly being formed as results from initial projects are being reported (see *Journal of Teacher Education*, 1992).

As schools and universities examine the partnership concept and the impact of closer collaboration on teacher education, it is critical that consideration be given to which in-service teachers should be involved in the education of tomorrow's teachers. What are the professional characteristics these teachers need to possess that will aid in the success of these new partnerships? How do you identify these professional teachers as they engage in their daily routine of classroom teaching? Once this cadre of professionals is identified, how can their development as a teaching professional in a school-university partnership be supported by the district and university? The purpose of this chapter is to describe the qualities teachers need to have to be successful in partnerships and how those teachers can be supported as they prepare the teachers of the future.

SCHOOL-UNIVERSITY PARTNERSHIPS

There are almost as many types of school-university partnerships being designed, defined, and defended as there are university teacher education programs. It is not the emphasis of this chapter to discriminate among the many variations; however, some common themes of current partnerships help us to understand the role that the classroom teacher might be asked to play in a redefined teacher education program.

To understand how the present school-university partnerships vary from what has been done in the past, it is important to understand how a "traditional" teacher education program prepares new teachers and what the traditional role of the cooperating experienced teacher is. Most programs engage the preservice teacher in course work that studies theories of teaching and learning and culminates in a "student teaching" experience. Termed the *apprenticeship model,* the student teacher is sent out to the classroom of an experienced teacher to learn and practice techniques. The experienced teacher is expected to model teaching strategies; for the student teacher, success is equated with how well the experienced teacher's techniques are duplicated. As a novice teacher entering the profession, the former student then replicates the curriculum and instruction learned from the experienced teacher in his or her own classroom. Teachers that are educated in this manner tend to do little reflective thinking about their own practice and find it difficult to move beyond maintaining the status quo (Lanier and Little, 1986). In recent years, this tradition has been challenged as the call for more reflective practice was heard (Schon, 1987).

Though the concept of school-university partnerships has been around for many years, the idea was revived in 1986 with the publishing of the Carnegie Forum proposal for creating clinical schools as a way of infusing teacher education with a reflective approach to teaching (Winitzky, Stoddart, and O'Keefe, 1992):

> Clinical schools would link faculties in elementary and secondary schools, colleges of education, and colleges of arts and science to provide the best possible learning environment for teacher preparation . . . The clinical school was seen as analogous to a teaching hospital . . . Participants in this partnership would have opportunities to reflect upon teaching and learning within the clinical school environment. (Stallings and Kowalsi, 1990, p. 255)

More recently, the Holmes Group (1990) has defined the new and more rigorous partnership of the PDS as follows:

> By "Professional Development School" we do not mean just a laboratory school for university research, nor a demonstration school. Nor do we mean just a clinical setting for preparing student and intern teachers. Rather we mean all of these together, a school for the development of

novice professionals, for continuing development of experienced professionals, and for the research and development of the teaching profession. (p. 1)

Development of PDS represents a substantial departure from the traditional apprenticeship model that universities and schools have used in the past. It has been proposed that the development of PDSs may result in the teaching profession actualizing professional status (Darling-Hammond, in press). To understand the roles and responsibilities of faculty members who will serve in a PDS, it is important to examine the idealized characteristics of a PDS suggested by its current proponents.

Characteristics of Professional Development Schools

The PDS described by the Holmes Group is guided by six principles: (1) teaching and learning should reflect greater understanding and students should participate in meaningful experiences that promote lifelong learning; (2) PDSs should be organized as a democratic community of learners; (3) all students, including minority students, should be engaged in learning for understanding; (4) all adult participants should be engaged in continual professional growth; (5) reflection and research on practice should be the norm; and (6) new organizational structures should replace the traditional university-school relationship. Actualizing the principles represents a major change in current practices for educating future teachers. Building a PDS has been referred to as a substantial restructuring effort and implementation of an innovation (Darling-Hammond, in press).

What would we see happening in a PDS? Houston (1988) proposes nine standards by which PDSs could be described and assessed: (a) Students would be provided opportunities to demonstrate their knowledge in diverse ways through authentic learning experiences. (b) Teachers would collaborate to use the best possible teaching methods to meet the learning needs of the students. (c) Teachers would participate in designing the mission of the school, taking responsibility for guiding its implementation. (d) Governance of the school would be shared by participants. (e) Assessment of all aspects of the school's operation would be collaborative and continuous. (f) Professional development activity would happen as a result of identified needs specific to the site, and would collaboratively involve all participants in design and implementation. (g) New funding structures would be developed jointly between school and university partners, reflecting fiscal support for the joint venture. (h) The induction of novice teachers would be structured to provide maximum opportunity for responsible experimentation and reflection about teaching and learning. (i) Ongoing research and experimentation would be a fundamental component of PDS daily life and would be used to improve teaching and learning at the site.

Creation of a PDS that embodies the aforementioned principles offers the possibility of dramatically changing the way teachers are inducted into professional practice by involving preservice teachers and in-service teachers more deeply in the teacher education process and bringing university faculty out of the "ivory tower" to work in schools alongside teachers. In a PDS, expert teachers and university faculty would share responsibility for educating new teachers as they "encounter state-of-the-art practice and a range of diverse experiences under intensive supervision so that they learn to teach diverse learners effectively" (Darling-Hammond, in press). In addition, first-year teachers would complete internships at the PDS site in an attempt to acquire the necessary support to develop into successful teachers who would stay in the profession. To be able to provide this type of teacher education experience, expert teachers and university faculty would collaborate to deepen the knowledge base for teaching by conducting practice-based research and translating the knowledge base into improved experiences for preservice teachers. The PDS would provide opportunities for learning by teaching, learning by doing, and learning by collaborating. Through articulation of common goals and shared decision making about which educational experiences preservice teachers need to become successful, the expert teachers and university faculty would assume joint responsibility for shaping the next generation of teachers. Proponents of PDSs see the expert teachers named as clinical faculty in universities; they also envision formal university recognition of school-based work as sanctioned activity by university faculty. Collaboration would result in the redesigning of both teacher preparation and the practice of teaching. (Darling-Hammond, in press).

There are numerous sites attempting to implement the Holmes principles as they build PDSs. Their efforts, in terms of embryonic successes and, sometimes, massive failures, are descriptive of the multitude of challenges those trying to implement this innovation have experienced. Although the projects often vary greatly in their case descriptions, analysis of their work informs us about how teachers involved in the PDSs have found their roles changing. This information is helpful in thinking about who might be successful as a teacher-leader in a school-university partnership. Sirotnik (1991) describes lessons learned in several PDS projects: authentic collaboration is crucial; development of shared activity is time-consuming; and leadership develops as a result of shared responsibility. The teacher-leader can anticipate being asked to function as a true collaborator, spending much time engaged with partners in the development of shared activity, and is expected to demonstrate leadership in an area of expertise. Darling-Hammond (1994) describes the characteristics of successful collaboration in PDSs: there must be common goals, mutual trust and respect, shared decision making, a clear focus, and information sharing and communication. Realization of these characteristics requires that a substantial portion of the teacher-leader's daily life (and one's energy) be spent away from the classroom, valuing time spent in collaboration with school and university partners and understanding that collaboration will translate into better teaching practice at the PDS. The teacher who cannot see the value in spending time constructing belief statements, setting goals, examining problems, brainstorming solutions, and acting upon decisions will be unable to function as a teacher-leader in a PDS.

Much of what is shared in this chapter about the role of the professional teacher in a school-university partnership comes from a project I have participated in for the past three years. As a coordinator of student teaching for a university, I was asked to help create a type of PDS with other teacher education colleagues and the faculty of an elementary school. What we learned, beyond the fact that collaborative relationships require much time and energy, was that the professional teacher who participates in this kind of partnership represents a new kind of teacher-leader, one whose skills must extend beyond the domain of the classroom.

THE TEACHER-LEADER IN THE SCHOOL-UNIVERSITY PARTNERSHIP

The role of the teacher in a school-university partnership is very different from that of the traditional teacher. The professional teacher in this type of collaborative venture will be expected to (1) spend time engaged in studying teaching and learning processes with peers, university partners, and preservice teachers; (2) be reflective about teaching and learning; (3) apply inquiry-based thinking to teaching and learning theory and methods; (4) be truly collegial with others; (5) make and act upon decisions; and (6) mentor novices. These skills become as important as the ability to promote student learning in the classroom. This represents a significant departure from traditional indicators used to identify "master teachers."

Reflection about Teaching

Reflection in teaching has been a frequent topic of discussion ever since Schon (1987) described the concept of "reflection-in-action" as an antecedent to quality teaching. Further study has expanded on the types of reflection that characterize teachers' professional lives. Sparks-Langer (1992) describes three types of reflective thinking: (1) a focus on the knowledge and processes involved in teacher decision making; (2) a focus on knowledge that is socially constructed by the examination of a dilemma and possible consequences; and (3) a focus on the personal circumstances under which decisions are made.

The need for teachers to participate in all three types of reflection was observed in the PDS project in which I was involved in for the past three years. Focusing on the knowledge and processes for making decisions dominated discussions of curriculum needs among school and university partners. Time spent in joint planning sessions frequently centered on curriculum and instructional planning for the PDS classrooms. Teachers were also frequently asked by student teaching partners to describe curriculum and instructional planning decisions. To do this, they needed to verbalize their thinking schemata—how they came to make decisions about what happened in their classrooms. For all of the teachers, this represented a higher level of reflection than the typical self-analysis of lessons. It required them to reflect "in public" with others, a task that seemed exhilarating to some and intimidating to others.

Reflection on dilemmas that result from the "reflection-in-action" of others constitutes another type of thinking and teaching. Termed the *critical approach to reflection,* this type of thinking is applied as teachers examine ethical, moral, and justice issues in education, clarify beliefs, and examine curriculum and methods for hidden lessons about equity and power (Sparks-Langer, 1992). In our PDS project, we asked teachers to participate in "problem-solving clinics" with student teachers by using a case method approach. Participants read a case that depicted a dilemma and described the response of a hypothetical teacher. The teachers and students then analyzed the case, discussing beliefs and implications of teacher decision making. Case method has been described as a way for master teachers to engage beginning teachers in the process of solving complex teaching problems and to model step by step how experts solve problems

(Carter 1988). This type of reflective activity represented a significant departure from the traditional discourse that takes place in most schools.

The decisions teachers make that influence the learning of their students are the result of personal circumstances that affected reflection about a situation. To grasp the rationale of teachers' decisions, one must understand how situational factors contributed to reflection. Working with student teachers engenders this sort of understanding. The students see a situation unfold, watch the decisions made by the teacher, and then ask the teacher to explain why a decision was made. This happens to some extent in the traditional "apprenticeship" relationship between a master teacher and a student teacher. However, in our PDS project, in which master teachers worked with teams of student teachers, we found that it happened even more frequently (Hertzog-Foliart and Lemlech 1993). This context for reflection requires that the thinking of the professional teacher be performed in a public forum, a substantial departure from the apprenticeship model.

Being asked to reflect aloud in the presence of others is not always easy. In our partnership, those teachers who were able to participate in the types of reflection described above frequently indicated that reflective thought, even about hypothetical dilemmas, resulted in further self-reflection. The more they participated in reflective dialogue with others, the more inwardly reflective about their own practice they became.

Inquiry-Based Thinking

It is not purposeful for the partnership teacher to reflect about practice, whether it be in a social or personal context, unless it results in inquiry about curriculum, instruction, and learning. In the words of Lieberman and Miller (1990):

> In a school where teachers assume leadership in curriculum and instruction and where reflective action replaces routinized practice, providing opportunities and time for disciplined inquiry into teaching and learning becomes crucial. Unlike traditional school settings, [PDSs] are places where teachers, sometimes working with university scholars and sometimes working alone, do research on, by and for themselves. (p. 96)

The "teacher as researcher" concept discussed in Chapter 5 by MacGillivray describes the rationale and process for this new dimension of teaching. It is a critical role for the professional teacher in the school-university partnership. Teacher education programs must make a choice whether the preparation of new teachers will be for the purpose of maintaining the status quo or for the purpose of moving forward with new knowledge about teaching and learning. Programs will need to be structured to reflect that philosophy. Universities that choose to create school-university partnerships begin by embracing new models for teacher education. Teachers who work in these partnerships are expected to be (or become) knowledgeable about current trends and research about teaching and learning, and willing to experiment with this knowledge in their classrooms. The university needs the classroom-based partner to participate in reflective inquiry about how theory or generalized research findings translate into contextual practice. This results in valuable content to be shared with preservice teachers.

An example of this took place in a school site where I was working with student teachers and serves as an illustration of the impact that disciplined inquiry has on classroom teaching. Two student teachers were placed in an urban elementary school with a large population of speakers of English as a second language. They were to work with a teacher named Amy whose class included students at various levels of English proficiency, from non-English-speaking to fluent second language ability. At the university I had been studying language acquisition intensively as background for a course I was teaching on literacy. My interest in the subject had an impact on my weekly seminars with the group of student teachers I supervised. The two student teachers who were working with Amy began to respond with interesting insights about their class, which motivated me to observe more carefully what was happening in their classroom. Subsequent conversations with Amy revealed that she too was interested in language acquisition theory and was quite knowledgeable about recent advances in the field. She was beginning to apply research in her classroom by examining the effect of asking different types of questions to students with varying English production abilities in order to discover the effect on attention level, comprehension ability, and subsequent verbal interactions. Her transformation of theoretical constructs in the context of her own classroom resulted in valuable learning for all of us. I shared her insights with others at the university, and the student teachers shared what they had learned with their peers. By the end of the experience, the student teachers were skilled at including speakers of limited English in lessons and assessing the learning that had taken place. A professional teacher such as the one just described becomes a valuable asset in the school-university partnership. Through inquiry in the classroom context, the teacher provides the link that teacher education needs between theory and practice.

Decision Maker/Decision Enactor

Participation in a school-university partnership increases the likelihood that teachers will be involved in group decision making. Beyond curriculum and instructional decisions made in the classroom, PDS teachers become active in the decision-making process for setting schoolwide goals and in determining ways to include preservice teachers in the school program. *Group* decision making takes time, and the professional teacher must be willing to spend time in a group setting discussing school and professional issues in order to participate meaningfully in the decision-making process.

To remain a part of the decision-making cohort, the teacher is also obligated to follow through on decisions. Patterson (1993) describes the relationship between the two when he says, "if I choose to opt out of our group's decision-making process, I by default opt into endorsement of the decision and its implications for my work life" (p. 55). Implicit in the decision-making process is the expectation that the decision maker will act on the decision, following through with implementation. An individual's failure to enact decisions impedes the group's ability to move toward implementation and reduces trust and respect between the teacher and other group members. In a PDS, such failure has serious implications. Both the university and school partners need to believe that decisions, often reached after much investment of time and effort, will be realized.

Many teachers and professors are unfamiliar with participation in group decision making. Much of our professional lives has been spent in traditional organizations where decisions are made in traditional top-down hierarchies. Darling-Hammond (1994) asserts that the traditional bureaucratic view of teaching that has prevailed since the late nineteenth century will be one of the greatest hurdles for PDS success. In the bureaucratic approach to teaching, teachers are expected to implement the decisions of others, handed down through policy and reflected in curriculum and teaching materials. Without doubt, in the school-university partnership, decision making and decision enacting require that the teacher accept both a new role and greater responsibilities.

Collegiality

A school-university partnership in which student teachers and university personnel enter the classroom of the professional teacher to work collaboratively constitutes a major change from traditions of privacy, practicality, and isolation (Lieberman and Miller, 1984). Different types of collaboration are needed for the partnership to be successful. In a PDS, the professional teacher will be expected to participate in shared work, shared problem solving, mutual assistance, and teacher leadership in curriculum and instruction (Lieberman and Miller, 1990).

Collegiality is defined as more than the friendly exchange of materials, lesson ideas, and emotional support when one has had a difficult day. In the words of Lemlech and Kaplan (1990), collegiality is "the establishment of a professional relationship for the purpose of service and accommodation through the mutual exchange of perceptions and expertise" (p. 14). Collegiality requires the establishment of openness and trust among colleagues as they examine their collective teaching and learning practices.

Collegiality is not an immediate state of being. One cannot express the desire to be collegial and therefore exhibit collegial behavior. Becoming collegial has been described as a process composed of states (Lemlech and Kaplan, 1990). Little (1990) conceptualizes the ability to be collegial as falling on a continuum and asserts that to be collegial, teachers' propensities lie within a range of collegial behavior. There are skills associated with the ability to be collegial. These can be described as being able to recognize other's proficiencies; demonstration of one's own expertise through teaching and/or propositional knowledge; the ability to coach, support, and provide consultant services to others; and the recognition that one can profit from the expertise, coaching, and support of others (Hertzog-Foliart and Lemlech, 1993). The professional teacher in the university partnership needs to be willing to participate in activities that will help develop colleagueship, openness, and trust with other partnership members.

Mentoring Preservice Teachers

Mentoring preservice teachers in a traditional setting is hard work. In the PDS, expectations that are espoused for teachers become goals for teacher education. It is hoped that PDS preservice teachers will learn how to be reflective about practice, approach teaching and learning from an inquiry-based model of thinking, develop skills of collegiality, and become skilled in the best methods of teaching available. Helping preservice teachers reach those goals is an arduous undertaking for master teachers. In addition to practicing expert teaching, the master teacher must be proficient in helping preservice teachers develop the new professional skills demanded of teachers in restructured school settings.

For example, in a PDS, helping preservice teachers learn the skills of collegiality becomes an important part of the master teacher's work. Lemlech and Kaplan (1990) confirmed that preservice teachers can achieve collegial relationships with each other. In our PDS project, preservice teaching partners demonstrated various levels of collegial behavior. What role did the master teacher play in helping preservice teachers develop collegiality? In a study of supervision of collegial preservice teacher teams, we were able to describe the behavior of master teachers who fostered collegial behavior among student teaching partners (Hertzog-Foliart and Lemlech, 1993). Each master teacher was responsible for working with a team of student teaching partners.

Table 6.1 compares traditional supervision with collegial supervision of preservice teachers, as evidenced in our study. The role of the master teacher varied substantially during the planning, lesson enactment, and

TABLE 6.1   Roles and Responsibilities of Master Teachers

	Traditional Supervision	**Collegial Supervision**
Planning	Directs "what" to teach	Engages in "process" of planning what to teach
	Identifies goals and desired environments	Engages in team planning, choosing goals and learning environment
		Explores subject matter possibilities
Lesson Enactment	Sits, watches	Assists, aids in teaching, guides partner observation
	Emphasizes current school district practices	Helps to examine alternatives and eclecticism
	Shows	Facilitates examination own and colleagues lessons
Feedback	Tells	Guides reflective thinking of colleagues
	Critiques	Models the language of critiquing, listens to feedback
	Demonstrates, models	Demonstrates, models, responds to two viewpoints
	Evaluates "mastery" of specific practices	Evaluates developmental competencies, collegial relationship

Source: Hertzog-Foliart and Lemlech, 1993.

feedback phases of teaching, especially during conferencing time. We observed master teachers engaging in several different types of conferences that facilitated the development of collegiality between partners. A *planning* conference engaged the team in long- and short-term planning that focused on content, context, and process. It was a shared experience with the master teacher acting as a facilitator of reflective thinking about the planning process for the preservice teachers. A *feedback* conference occurred with the master teacher leading professional critique of a lesson that had just been concluded with both student teachers. The teaching partner discussed the intent of the lesson. The observing partner provided additional information from observation notes. The master teacher facilitated discussion between partners, modeled appropriate language for suggestive feedback, and offered additional observations. A *facilitating* conference occurred when the observing partner provided feedback to the teaching partner while the master teacher listened in and asked questions to guide reflection. A *teaching* conference occurred when the master teacher discussed pedagogical techniques, modeling, demonstrating, and sharing of ideas and resources with the student teachers. The ability of the master teacher to facilitate successfully these types of conferences positively impacted the developing collegial behaviors of the preservice teachers.

Exemplary Classroom Practice

What is exemplary classroom practice? If you asked that question to fifty different educators, you would probably get fifty different ideas of exactly what it would look like demonstratively through students' work. In the past, teaching was described as a process-product paradigm that related specific teaching behaviors to specific student achievement measures. Current understandings about teaching and learning describe it as a process co-constructed by teachers and students that reflects a teacher's response to many elements in the school and classroom setting (McLaughlin, 1991). However, certain common principles that undergird curriculum and instruction can be used as indicators of exemplary practice.

As the restructuring movement has grown over the past few years, much has been written about how schools need to change to improve education. Some researchers, like Newmann and Wehlage (1993), caution those involved in the movement to focus on increasing student achievement as the primary goal for improving schools. They argue that school change often takes place organizationally without affecting student learning. Schedules, teacher responsibilities, conduct, and content during faculty meetings change, but student achievement remains unaffected. These researchers advise those involved in school change "to distinguish between achievement that is significant and meaningful and that which is trivial and useless" (p. 8). There is a message embedded in their logic for identifying exemplary classroom practice in any setting. For example, when visiting a partnership school, I often spend time updating the principal on how the preservice teachers are doing while they are on site. One elementary school principal I met with on a regular basis consistently made comments about teachers' curriculum based on her visual perusal of classroom environment as she walked the halls. During one visit she asked if I had visited a particular classroom and seen the new bulletin board that had been put up after a writing lesson. The principal then explained that an increased use of writing across the curriculum is one of the school's goals for the year. When I visited the classroom my eye was caught by a beautifully displayed bulletin board with neatly written letters on it. As I began reading the letters, it became evident that, while the lesson (and the resulting product) represented a change in the language arts curriculum to include more writing, the change was trivial and useless. Each writing sample was a business letter, each written to the same organization. All the letters contained the same content using the same language patterns. It was obvious that the letters were written as a classroom exercise in which the teacher controlled the topic, to whom the letters would be addressed, and how the language contained in the letter would be formatted. How much more significant it would have been to have taught the students how to write a business letter and then permitted them to correspond with a person or organization with whom they were genuinely interested!

To understand what exemplary practice should be, we must examine the learning goals for students. The current restructuring movement has articulated these goals in what Newmann and Wehlage (1993) describe as authentic achievement. It happens when "(1) students construct and produce knowledge, (2) students use disciplined inquiry to construct meaning, and (3) students aim their work toward production of discourse, products and performances that have value or meaning beyond success in school" (p. 8). Achieving these goals happens as the result of the curriculum and instruction taking place in each classroom. When teachers are successful, we consider them to be purveyors of exemplary practice.

Can teachers who practice exemplary teaching be easily identified? Are there common elements in their programs which can be used to describe exemplary curriculum and instruction? Frequent observation in classrooms has demonstrated to me that the answer is a definite "yes." Exemplary teaching is the result of three types of exemplary thinking by the teacher:

Curriculum thinking.

Instructional thinking.

Social system thinking.

Curriculum Thinking　How does the teacher organize curriculum for the students? Is it made relevant for them? Does it connect with knowledge learned at other times (inside or outside the classroom)? What do students do with the content they learn? Evidence of this type of thinking on the part of the teacher can be observed in the classroom.

For example, upon entering the fourth grade classroom of a teacher we will call Vera, you can see that she provides this kind of curriculum experience for her students. Vera is responsible for teaching her students the history of the state in which they live. This subject isn't particularly difficult to teach; an excellent textbook that students can read and discuss suffices to teach the necessary content. But Vera has obviously gone beyond the recall of content. On the back wall, there is an unfinished mural divided into panels depicting the history of the state. Two panels are finished. The first depicts the state as it presently exists. You can identify the state capital and the city in which the students live through artistic likenesses of famous landmarks. The flora and fauna of the region are visible. Even modern transportation systems that show how the students could get from their city to the capital have been sketched in. Below the panel is a class description of daily life in their city—how the people meet their basic needs of food, clothing, and shelter; how they spend leisure time; how they provide for their health; and how they "feel" connected to other parts of the state. Nearby is a graph that shows which state landmarks different class members have visited. On top of the bookcase, student-authored books are displayed that reflect different areas of individual interest. One student has researched where the best fishing streams and lakes are located. Another has written a book about the major league baseball team his father works for. The second panel of the mural illustrates the life of the Native Americans who lived hundreds of years ago in the same area. The mural depicts Native Americans in a village wearing traditional clothes, Native Americans cooking food over an open fire, a map of trails that ran through the area, and a dance/ritual of some kind. The class description under the panel describes Native

American life and discusses the same concepts as were in the first chart. On some tables along the side of the room are group projects about Pre-Columbian Native American life. There is a collection of live plants, all native to the region, with cards describing how to cultivate them and how the Native Americans used them. There is a collection of handmade "toys" that Native American children would have played with and a booklet describing different games. In the class library, there is a collection of biographies on famous Native Americans in the United States and a story map of a biography the class read together. On the day of the observation, the students were conducting research in small groups to answer questions they had formulated that would result in the construction of the third panel, a depiction of how the arrival of early American explorers to the region changed life as it was known during the Early Pre-Columbian period. Clearly, Vera has the ability to make curriculum come alive for her students in a relevant and meaningful way. She makes the content relevant by comparing it to the students' own lives; she integrates subject areas when it makes sense to do so; and she allows students to follow their own research interests.

Instructional Thinking   How students are taught is equally as important as what they are taught. The research suggests that exemplary instruction is probably more difficult to achieve than exemplary curriculum because it is so difficult to change the way teachers initially learn to teach. Teachers are highly influenced by how they were taught as students and how instruction is modeled for them during the student teaching experience (Guyton and McIntyre, 1990). This body of research supports the rationale for the modeling of exemplary teaching by master teachers in the university partnership.

What should exemplary instruction consist of? Newmann and Wehlage (1993) describe standards of instruction that promote authentic student achievement. Understanding these standards gives us observable characteristics to look for in the classroom. (1) *Higher-order thinking* requires students to manipulate information and ideas that transform meaning and promotes implications. Students are able to synthesize, generalize, explain, hypothesize, or interpret data to solve problems and discover new meanings. For example, Vera helped organize the curriculum study for her students to promote higher-level thinking. She encouraged them to solve problems and interpret data about various aspects of modern and Native American life. (2) *Depth of knowledge* refers to the character of the ideas in a lesson and the level of understanding with which students consider them. Knowledge is deep when it centers on important topics or themes and encourages students to develop distinctions, make arguments, solve problems, and construct explanations. In Vera's classroom, students were well on their way to being able to compare their needs to those of the Pre-Columbian Native Americans and the early colonial settlers. If the study continued as one might anticipate, they would probably be able to hypothesize the effect of the arrival of settlers on the Native American settlements. (3) *Connectedness to the world beyond the classroom* concerns the extent to which the class has value and meaning beyond the curriculum context. Activities assessed by students as having little or no value beyond the classroom result in poor student achievement. Exemplary instruction helps students to connect what they learn in the classroom to their lives beyond the classroom. For Vera's students, her inclusion of personal research topics and her availability to help her students see their research through to the production of a product, as depicted by their personal books, demonstrates that she organized a component of her instruction to allow students to make highly personal connections to their world. (4) *Substantive conversation* refers to the opportunity students have to participate in discussing and questioning topics, themes, and issues. Exemplary practice in this requires a movement away from the lecture-recitation format of traditional instruction. In Vera's classroom, this was not directly observed but is depicted in the students' products. The class charts describing life during the various time periods reflects much discussion that must have taken place prior to composition. Clearly, Vera has moved away from an instructional format that promotes the simple imparting of knowledge and assessment of factual content.

Social System Thinking   Social system support for student achievement is probably the most important element of exemplary teaching. The social system in the classroom describes how individuals and the collective classroom "family" interact with one another. Perceptions and beliefs about control, power, and authority in the classroom mold the teacher's thinking and decisions that affect the social system. Interaction in the classroom can take place between individual students, groups of students, the teacher and individuals, and the teacher and student groups. In order to teach in the co-constructed environment that promotes high achievement, it is essential that the teacher be able to share control, power, and authority with students. Vera is an example of a teacher who has been able to achieve this for herself as a teacher and, perhaps more important, who *promotes* shared control, power, and authority among the students in her classroom. This can be seen in how she has moved away from directed lesson activities to activities such as the panel mural with chart stories, which give students control over the development of their product, the power to make decisions concerning the product, and the authority to direct their own learning. By giving her students the opportunity to be genuinely in charge of their own learning, Vera has demonstrated to her students the sense of respect she feels for them. Respecting students by sharing control in the classroom may be the single most important skill a teacher can have. In the words of one teacher, "Respect allows and promotes choice, trust, and independence. Respect accepts children where they are and encourages and congratulates them for their attempts. Respect values children as unique individuals . . . if they feel respected, they will feel secure and be able to take risks (Routman, 1992).

Newmann and Wehlage (1993) use the social system constructed by a teacher as an indicator of high authentic achievement. Using their scale to rate authentic instruction, social support is considered low when "teacher or student behavior, comments, and actions tend to discourage effort, participation or willingness to express one's views" (p. 10). Support is high when the teacher conveys high expectations, including risk taking, high levels of effort to complete challenging assignments, and a climate of mutual respect that all class members can contribute meaningfully to projects.

When preservice teachers enter the classroom of a teacher where support is high, what will the effect be on them? Beyond the obvious fact that the experienced teacher is modeling effective strategies for the novice and providing an ideal environment for practicing teaching, the preservice teacher experiences the effects of the environment as a learner. Student teachers were placed with Vera, who accepted them into her social system as part of the classroom family. Rather than control their learning, Vera supported their attempts to teach meaningfully, which weren't always successful. One of the student teachers wrote in her journal, "I can't believe how much I am learning in this experience. Vera supports me in the same way she supports her students. I did a really horrible lesson today, but rather than tell me how I should have done it, Vera guided my thinking and encouraged me to think of alternatives and make choices about what I would do next. She let me know that she trusted me to take the risk and try again." Clearly, the teacher who can mold an environment with a high social support system has the potential to influence profoundly the preparation of new teachers.

The role of the teacher-leader in the school-university partnership is critical to the survival of the partnership and very demanding of the teacher. A willingness to reflect about teaching with others, participate in disciplined inquiry about teaching and learning, function as a decision maker, and enact skills of collegiality with peers and university partners (including preservice teachers) is needed. In addition, the teacher-leader needs to demonstrate exemplary classroom practice that reflects not only excellent curriculum activities but also instruction that enriches the curriculum by helping students to assume authority and control over their learning.

MEETING THE NEEDS OF THE PROFESSIONAL TEACHER IN THE SCHOOL-UNIVERSITY PARTNERSHIP

To become the kind of teacher-leader described in the first part of this chapter requires a tremendous amount of energy and reconceptualization of effort on the part of teachers and those supporting teachers. Fullan (1993) cautions that "the teacher of the future . . . must be equally at home in the classroom and in working with others to bring about continuous improvements" (p. 17). As we consider the demands that a restructured professional setting such as the university partnership puts on the teacher, we must attend to the increased demands on the teacher's time. University partners, school administrators, other support personnel, and teachers themselves must carefully allocate time and energy to worthwhile endeavors that will help teachers define their professional personality. For the teacher, there must be careful consideration of value structures that have been in place for many years. Years after the norms of privacy and isolation in the classroom were first described, they still persist (Lieberman and Miller, 1991). Replacing them with norms of collaboration, colleagueship, and trust among peers and other professionals is time-consuming and energy-sapping. In a very real sense, the teacher-leader is expected to act as a change agent in adopting an innovation, and the innovation is the teacher's own expanded role (Fullan, 1993). This represents a monumental undertaking for teachers. Teachers are expected to continue practicing their craft while struggling with changing the parameters of the professional role. An old adage sums it up best: It's very difficult to fly an airplane while simultaneously trying to build a new one. What kinds of activities and what type of support will help professional teacher-leaders be successful in their expanded role?

Opportunity for Inquiry and Reflection

It is very easy to state the argument espousing the benefits of teacher inquiry about teaching and learning and reflection on one's own practice.

It is very difficult to create situations that actually allow teachers the opportunity to study teaching in meaningful ways. It takes a great amount of time, something teachers do not have much of. In addition, we are cautioned that if teachers are to integrate successfully the efforts of their inquiry and reflection on their teaching practice, they must be involved in inquiry about something that has meaning for them (Schwartz, 1991; Smith et al., 1991). The activities described below afford teachers that opportunity.

Study Groups/Networks   Participation in a teacher study group is an example of a teacher's quest for inquiry about teaching and learning to improve his or her craft. If participation is voluntary and focuses on a teacher's personal areas of interest, it can result in high levels of personal growth.

Organizationally, study groups can be structured in several ways. Holly (1991) describes a study group structure based on similar interests of teachers in action research projects. He argues that participation in action research promotes inquiry about teaching, reflection about practice, and collaboration among colleagues. The groups cluster around similar interests and conduct action research in their classrooms while meeting on a regular basis to share insights.

In a PDS, it is very possible that university- and school-based participants will come together to form a study group. Miller (1990) tells a compelling story of her participation as a university faculty member with a group of teachers who shared similar interests in curriculum theory. Her group was originally formed to address research concerns, but the struggles of becoming collegial and of carving out new roles soon took precedence over research. Perhaps the most important lesson to be learned from her story is that when group members come from backgrounds that have been traditionally hierarchical in role definition, the group must confront and redefine established roles. In Miller's case, although she wanted to participate as a peer in the study group, as a "professor" she found that she was considered the leader (by herself and the teachers), and much of the group's initial energy was spent breaking out of that traditional role definition to become truly collegial. This could certainly be a consideration when classroom-based and administrative school-district participants form study groups.

Study groups do not have to focus on research. One type of group that is growing in popularity is the Socratic seminar, in which a leader who has been trained in Socratic discussion techniques helps a group focus on an article or piece of literature that has been read by the group.

The discussion tends to be lively and can lead to a great amount of reflection about teaching and learning. Not only does the process cause self-examination of personal beliefs but also involves participants in understanding the perspectives of others. When a project such as a school-university partnership brings together traditionally diverse groups, this can serve as a very worthwhile activity.

Study groups may be formed from among members of a group, such as a PDS, or they may form across groups (perhaps school sites) that have similar interests. The richness of interaction when groups are mixed, as described by Miller (1990), attests to the fact that "cross-pollenization of ideas and perceptions across sites by members whose job responsibilities vary can be very fruitful. The greatest barrier to maintaining a study group with diverse membership is the element of time— just finding a regular time to meet that accommodates everyone's schedule is a challenge.

Networks differ from study groups in that they usually represent a group of people who have come together as a result of having studied some aspect of teaching and desire mutual support as they attempt implementation. Participation in a network can be a highly worthwhile professional activity. Smith and Wigginton (1991), in their description of the development of the Foxfire network discuss the opportunities such networks provide for teachers to develop leadership and the empowerment they gain to function in school-based governance settings. Most important, Smith and Wigginton (1991) state that:

> Participating in a network gives a teacher the sense of being able to make a difference by *being part of something larger, of being connected with other movements that are complementary to Foxfire, as well as with the other networks.* Many network members claim to have a bigger picture of school, reforms, and opportunities in education—and a realization that there is a place in which to share those discoveries as a consequence of networking (p. 206; italics theirs).

It is interesting to note that participation in the Foxfire network for teachers results in an expanded professional role for teachers since they are expected to serve as members of committees with specific roles, such as planning showcases, reviewing grant proposals, assisting other members with instructional problems, conducting in-service programs for school districts, participating in presentations to educational organizations, writing case studies that are published in journals, giving speeches (with students), and representing the network at professional meetings.

The teacher-leaders described in the Foxfire network are obviously well skilled in implementing the approach. There seems to be a logical connection between participation in a study group to inquire about and reflect upon an approach to teaching and learning which, in turn, leads to involvement in a network once the approach has been integrated into a teacher's craft. Membership in either certainly affects the individual's level of inquiry and reflection about teaching.

Using Teacher Cases for Reflection   Using teaching cases to stimulate inquiry and reflection is not new in the fields of business, law, and medicine. Each has taken the concept of using cases as a fundamental component of curriculum and adapted it to the needs of each particular discipline with great success. However, using teaching cases in education as a way of bringing together theory and practice in the context of real classroom situations is relatively new. Teaching cases are narratives consisting of first-person accounts, case reports, or case studies that have been written or edited for teaching purposes (Shulman, 1992). Cases vary in length and usually describe real events in a vignette style. The narratives have a plot; are particular and specific; place events in a frame of time and place; and reveal the decisions, motives, conceptions, and needs of the participants (Shulman, 1992). Tending in education, to focus on issues related to teaching and learning, contextual application of theory, policy implementation, and moral and ethical issues, cases are used by applying a case method of teaching. Case methods refer to the methods of pedagogy employed to "teach" the written cases. The method most commonly used is a Socratic-type discussion with high levels of student participation, led by skilled questioning from a leader.

Participation with others in studying a teaching case is a highly reflective experience. In discussing the actions (or inaction) taken by participants in the case, an individual begins to reflect about what should have been done, what they would probably do in the same context and, most important, why decisions were made (or neglected) and their effect on the situation described. Depending on the content, participation in the discussion of a case can be a highly charged experience, energizing the mind and draining the emotions at the same time.

Most of the writing being published about the use of the case method refers to its use in preservice or novice teacher education (see Kowalski, Weaver, and Henson, 1990; Schulman and Colbert, 1988; and Silverman, Welty, and Lyon, 1992 for collections of teacher education cases). Similar to its use in medicine, the case method has been lauded as a way to bridge theory and practice by providing situational relevance from which practitioners can reflect on their own decisions. Shulman (1992) states:

> I envision case methods as a strategy for overcoming many of the most serious deficiencies in the education of teachers. Because they are contextual, local, and situated—as are all narratives—cases integrate what otherwise remains separated. Content and process, thought and feeling, teaching and learning are not addressed theoretically as distinct constructs. They occur simultaneously as they do in real life, posing problems, issues, and challenges for new teachers that their knowledge and experiences can be used to discern. (p. 28)

Participation in case methods need not be saved for new teachers. Richert (1991) describes using case methods, in a graduate-level university class with experienced teachers. She reports the reactions of several of the teachers, who all state that the discussion of cases had a great impact on their sense of "self" as a teacher. Similarly, some participants in our PDS project were invited to experience the case method approach at a professional meeting. All were experienced teachers and all responded, following a lengthy group discussion of the case, that they had experienced one of the most intentional, focused, and reflective experiences they had ever shared with their peers.

Establishing a case-based discussion group may be susceptible to traditional organizational constraints that impede teachers' professional development. For example, the issue of time must be addressed. Most leaders report that cases generally require a minimum of ninety minutes' discussion time; lengthy cases require more. Another problem is who will choose the cases to be discussed. Cases can be found in a variety of places, including journals and books. Casebooks, or collections of cases for the purpose of applying the case method, are appearing with more frequency, but it takes time to find cases and they reflect a multitude of issues. Finally, who will serve as a leader? Instruction with cases is a skill that must be mastered, like any other teaching strategy.

In our PDS project, we attempted to use the case method with a group of preservice and experienced teachers. The method was lauded by the preservice teachers, but it was difficult to free up the experienced teachers to participate. The method did positively impact reflection and inquiry about practice. An unexpected outcome of the experience was that the cases forged a common knowledge base the preservice and experienced teachers could draw upon. When the master teachers needed to call attention to issues in the student teachers' lessons, they used the characters, situations, and issues in cases to address problems. This invariably contributed to the comfort level of sensitive discussions.

The potential for using the case method is only beginning to be explored in education. It seems to have value as a learning tool for both preservice and experienced teachers; it is a way to bridge theory and practice in situation contexts and promote thinking about one's own teaching.

Opportunity for Peer Coaching

Wasley (1991) describes a teacher named Gwen whom she observed as part of her study of teacher-leaders. Gwen's school district created a new type of leadership position to facilitate implementation of an instructional improvement program in which all the district teachers were required to participate. Gwen was removed from the classroom to serve as a mentor teacher. During the morning she ran the library. In the afternoon, Gwen's primary responsibility was to visit classrooms to provide peer coaching. During one observation, Wasley reported that Gwen visited two classrooms, observed for approximately eight minutes, during which time she took notes on what happened, and left notes on the teachers' desks to schedule a follow-up conference at their convenience. She was also in charge or organizing peer coaching among other teachers. She assigned partners and scheduled release time. Each partner was to observe the other, then participate in a postobservation conference. The participants were having difficulty sustaining the effort. Is this a good example of peer coaching? If one listens to Joyce and Showers (1988), who have popularized the concept of peer coaching, Gwen is not actually peer coaching. Understanding why helps us to understand how peer coaching can be a powerful tool for reflection, how it builds professional expertise, and why it should be sustained in school-university partnerships.

According to Joyce and Showers (1988), peer coaching has several purposes. Though the major purpose of peer coaching is the implementation of innovations, coaching also builds communities of teachers who continuously study their craft, develops the shared language and common understandings necessary for collegial study of new knowledge, and provides a structure for the follow-up to learning that is essential for acquiring new skills. Coaching programs are characterized by several conditions. They are attached to a learning situation in which a community of learners is attempting to master and implement new knowledge, skills, and strategies. The study is continuous; coaching is a set of continuing relationships and structures for self-help. Coaching is experimental. Teachers not only master new skills but explore when and how to use them. Coaching must be separate from supervision and evaluation cycles. According to Joyce and Showers (1988) "the norms of coaching and evaluation practice are antithetical and should be separated in our thinking as well as in practice" (p. 85).

When implemented appropriately, peer coaching has several beneficial effects. Coached teachers generally practice new strategies more frequently and develop greater skill than do uncoached teachers. Coached teachers use their newly learned strategies more appropriately than uncoached teachers. This happens because they have been given the opportunity to reflect on the application of a strategy with a colleague. Coached teachers exhibit greater long-term retention of knowledge and skill using a strategy. Finally, coaching facilitates professional and collegial relationships through the development of a shared language and norms of experimentation.

In Gwen's case, there is a conflict between her coordination of the peer coaching program and her new evaluative role as defined by her school district. When Wasley (1991) interviewed Gwen's peers, they had mixed feelings about the new position and Gwen's role. This case clearly demonstrates the incompatibility of peer coaching and evaluation.

When peer coaching is conducted as a supportive, collaborative activity it can help teachers participate in a continuous cycle of renewal and growth and help foster collegial relationships. In the school-university partnership peer coaching has the potential to help teachers not only maintain personal growth for classroom teaching but also help them define and learn the skills necessary for working with preservice teachers.

Opportunity to Build and Share Expertise

Feeling like a professional means knowing that you have professional expertise that is valued by others. Being able to share expertise is a factor in being able to build collegial relationships with peers. Expertise, however, is more than self-perception. And expertise is not static. For example, it is not enough to say that you have expertise in cooperative learning techniques. Colleagues must be able to identify you as expert (probably through your teaching), and your expertise must continue to grow as your research and the research of others continue to inform you. For that reason, it is critical to provide teachers both the opportunity to identify areas in which they feel expert and support for continuous study in that area.

Support for building and maintaining expertise can come from restructuring professional responsibilities and evaluation procedures. Schwartz (1991) describes the success of a *teacher center* in reconceptualizing staff development by focusing on the individual and collective expertise of teachers. Expert teachers work with administrators to provide staff development opportunities for teachers. The expert teachers develop a course or seminar, manage the budget, hire consultants or teach the course themselves, and evaluate work of the participants. As one aspect of the teacher center, a professional growth model was developed to support development of expertise. Former administrative evaluation procedures were replaced with individually tailored "personal growth" evaluation. Teachers identified an area in which they wanted to become expert and were helped to pursue study and classroom implementation. Yearly evaluation cycles were then tied to the ongoing establishment and maintenance of expertise.

Nurturing teacher expertise is important; valuing it is essential. How can teacher expertise be valued in the school-university partnership? Teacher expertise can be used as the foundation for staff development. In the words of Lieberman and Miller (1991), "coupling staff development with the growing move to professionalize teaching puts teachers at the center of helping to create and participate as central figures in their own development." (p. vii) In this conception, staff development is not defined as workshops where content focuses on effective teaching strategies taught by outside consultants. Instead, it becomes an important part of the school culture, continuous in nature, owned by the faculty that direct it, and responsible for creating the environment for real change in teaching and learning. Griffin (1991) describes this as "interactive staff development."

In the school-university partnership, the concept of interactive staff development could encompass the joint faculty at the site, including both university- and school-based partners. By providing teachers and university faculty the opportunity to share expertise as colleagues in meaningful ways with others in an interactive setting, the school-university partnership has the potential to achieve true colleagueship among the teacher-leaders *and* between university and school partners.

Finding the "Time" to Take Advantage of Opportunities

Recommending that teachers be given opportunities to participate in inquiry and reflection about teaching, peer coaching, and the possibility of building and sharing expertise, this chapter advocates a serious commitment to professional activities that take place outside the classroom. Probably the most important thing that was learned in the PDS project I participated in was the following caveat, which affected all planning, decisions, and implementation of any ideas: *It really doesn't matter what kinds of wonderful opportunities we make available to ourselves—if we don't find the time to take advantage of them, they are worthless.* Unfortunately, the classroom teacher is often at the mercy of organizational and administrative time constraints that render them powerless to make changes. They must rely on the support of others—district administrators, school administrators, and school-based resource personnel (curriculum specialists, off-norm mentor teachers)—to help them operationalize ways to gain time.

Time must be gained in ways that fit the goals and purposes of the school mission. Gaining time may mean reconceptualizing traditional roles and responsibilities in a school. It is worth the time it takes to explore possibilities. It takes much creativity to break out of previous time-restricting norms. Some suggestions follow:

1. Take better advantage of time as it is currently used. Examine the tasks of teachers. What takes the most time? Alter management strategies to free the teacher from previous "out of class" time constraints. For example, if the teacher documents that he or she is spending an hour a day (or a few hours a week) grading and recording homework, find ways to reduce that time, such as training parent volunteers or changing classroom management strategies to allow students to self-monitor progress. Use technology to assist in paperwork. Computer-assisted grading programs can substantially cut the time a teacher spends calculating grades. An electronic-mail system can help reduce the amount of time it takes for teachers to communicate with each other, the principal, and so forth.

2. Reschedule the school day. In secondary schools, add a period. Change the way teachers are scheduled to reinforce participation in professional activities by clustering teachers who are teaming, planning together, or participating in a study group or network, perhaps by slotting a free period next to a lunch period. Use that time weekly or biweekly for collaboration. Bank time by extending the students' school day four days a week and using the pupil-free time on the fifth day for staff development, faculty meetings, and so forth.

3. Redesignate existing time. Examine faculty meetings for streamlining. What information can be disseminated in writing? Can the frequency of faculty meetings be reduced and replaced with staff development or planning meetings? How can existing staff development days be reconfigured to make the best use of time? Does the state allow for a specific number of shortened days for students? How are those days currently used? Help teachers use some of those days to pursue professional endeavors.

4. Support teacher time outside the classroom. Use substitutes or part-time substitutes to release teachers. Build in classroom coverage time as part of an administrator's duties. If each administrator at a moderately sized school contributes three hours a week to coverage for peer coaching, the coaching program will probably be successful! Examine the

current use of teaching assistants. In one elementary school, teachers were freed up for two hours per week by grade level when teaching assistants were trained to conduct physical-education lessons under the direction of administrators. In another, teaching assistants were used to relieve teachers of lunch duties so meetings could take place during lunch. In a school-university partnership, use student teachers to take classes. In our PDS, we used student teachers once a week for one hour to teach "clubs" during the last hour of the school day. Teachers were freed to meet for professional activities. Team with other teachers for activities extending beyond a single classroom. For example, in one elementary school, the fifth-grade classrooms invited the first-grade classrooms to visit weekly, as part of an activity that was generated from the curriculum being studied and that the fifth-grade students could share with their first-grade "partners." This activity took forty-five minutes, backed with a twenty-minute recess, all of which gave the first-grade teachers an hour to use for professional activities.

5. Promote volunteer time. Provide child care (a few volunteers can do this) while volunteers work with teachers. Group volunteers with certified teachers and large groups of students to provide release time for other teachers. Provide funding to attend relevant training for volunteers. Seek out volunteers trying to earn credit. One school sought out community college students enrolled in child development classes that had observation requirements and worked with the college to develop a schedule that released teachers. Another school used high school students earning community service credits to help staff assemblies, the library, and so forth. Volunteers can substantially cut down the amount of "busy work" teachers find themselves doing. Sending a volunteer to the library or the Xerox machine is a time saver.

Once time for professional activities has been carved out of the teacher's day, reevaluate periodically how time is being spent. Reassess the goals for time use; address whether the time gained was used productively. Time can be the enemy, or a great asset if used creatively. It is perhaps the one variable on which the success of innovations such as school-university partnerships most depends.

CONCLUSION

School-university partnerships represent new kinds of professional opportunities for teachers. Their success will depend on the quality of professional teacher-leaders that can be recruited to work with university partners to transform teacher education. Partnerships will need highly skilled teachers who can interact collegially with peers and university personnel, have the knowledge base to transform theory and practice, and mentor novices in learning the craft of teaching. The partnership role requires teachers who seek expanded professional responsibility and activity beyond the classroom. School-university partnerships will flourish only if they are supported institutionally by support personnel who can help teachers gain access to professional development activities. Partnerships offer the promise of improving teacher education—of helping novice teachers learn professional skills as a component of the art of teaching. That is reason alone for supporting the professional teacher in the school-university partnership.

Recap Notes: On Developing Professionalism

- Increasing the professionalism of teaching improves teaching and learning in all classroom situations.

- There is a growing demand for professional teachers who can model inquiry-based teaching, reflective practice, and collegiality for novice teachers.

- New professional roles for teachers must be supported by providing them opportunities to participate in reflective activity, develop expertise, and learn skills of collegiality.

- Time for professional development must be gleaned by reconstructing the professional teaching day. Professional development can no longer be considered an "add-on."

REFERENCES

Carnegie Forum on Education and the Economy, Task Force on Teaching as a Profession. 1986. *A nation prepared: Teachers for the 21st century.* New York: Author.

Carter, K. 1988. Using cases to frame mentor-novice conversations about teaching. *Theory into Practice* 27: 214–22.

Darling-Hammond, L. 1994. Developing professional development schools: Early lessons, challenge, and promise. In *Developing professional development schools,* ed. L. Darling-Hammond, New York: Teachers College Press.

Fullan, M. G. 1993. Why teachers must become change agents. *Educational Leadership* 50(6): 12–17.

Griffin, G. A., Barnes, S., Hughes, R., O'Neal, S., Defino, M., Edwards, S., and Hukill, H. 1983. *Clinical preservice teacher education: Final report of a descriptive study.* Austin: University of Texas, R & D Center for Teacher Education.

Griffin, G. 1991. Interactive staff development: Using what we know. In *Staff development for education in the 90's* ed. A. Lieberman and L. Miller, pp. 243–60. New York: Teachers College Press.

Guyton, E., and McIntyre, D. J. 1990. Student teacher and school experiences. In *Handbook of research on teacher education* ed. W. R. Houston, pp. 514–34. New York: Macmillan.

Hertzog-Foliart, H., and Lemlech, J. 1993. *Collegial teacher preparation: Impact on the supervising teacher's role.* A paper presented at the annual meeting of the Association of Teacher Educators, Los Angeles, 1993.

Holly, P. 1991. Action research: The missing link in the creation of schools as centers of inquiry. A. Lieberman and L. Miller, *Staff development for education in the 90's,* 2nd ed., pp. 133–157. New York: Teachers College Press.

Holmes Group. 1986. *Tomorrow's teachers.* East Lansing, Mich.: author.

Holmes Group. 1990. *Tomorrow's school: Principles for the design of professional development schools.* East Lansing, Mich.: author.

Houston, H. 1988. Professional practice schools: How would we know one if we saw one? In *Professional practice schools: Building a model,* ed. American Federation of Teachers, pp. 103–18. Washington, D.C.: American Federation of Teachers.

Journal of Teacher Education. January-February 1992, 43:1. [Theme of issue is professional development schools.]

Joyce, B., and Showers, B. 1988. *Student achievement through staff development.* White Plains, N.Y.: Longman.

Kowalski, T. J., Weaver, R. A., and Henson, K. T. 1990. *Case studies on teaching.* New York: Longman.

Lanier, J., and J. Little. 1986. Research on teacher education. In *Handbook of research on teaching,* ed. W. C. Wittrock, pp. 527–69. New York: Macmillan.

Lemlech, J. K., and Kaplan, S. N. 1990. Learning to talk about teaching: Collegiality in clinical teacher education. *Action in Teacher Education,* 12(1): 13–19.

Lieberman, A., and Miller, L. 1984. *Teachers, their world, and their work: Implications for school improvement.* Alexandria, Va.: Association for Supervision and Curriculum Development.

———— 1990. Teacher development in professional practice schools. *Teacher College Record* 92: 105–22.

———— 1991. Revisiting the social realities of teaching. In *Staff development for education in the 90's,* ed. A. Lieberman and L. Miller, pp. 92–112. New York: Teachers College Press.

Little, J. W. 1990. The persistence of privacy: Autonomy and initiative in teachers' professional relations. *Teachers College Record* 91 (4): 509–32.

McLaughlin, M. W. 1991. Enabling professional development: What have we learned? In *Staff development for education in the 90's,* ed. A. Lieberman and L. Miller, pp. 61–82. New York: Teachers College Press.

Miller, J. 1990. *Creating spaces and finding voices: Teachers collaborating for empowerment.* Albany: State University of New York Press.

National Commission on Excellence in Education. 1983. *A nation at risk: The imperative for educational reform.* Washington, D.C.: U.S. Government Printing Office.

Newmann, F. M., and Wehlage, G. G. 1993. "Five Standards of Authentic Instruction." *Educational Leadership* 50(7): 8–12.

Patterson, J. L. 1993. *Leadership for tomorrow's schools.* Alexandria, Va.: Association for Supervision and Curriculum Development.

Richert, A. E. 1991. Using teacher cases for reflection and enhanced understanding. In *Staff development for education in the 90's,* ed. A. Lieberman and L. Miller, pp. 113–32. New York: Teachers College Press.

Routman, R. 1992. *Invitations.* Portsmouth, N.H.: Heinemann.

Schon, D. 1987. *Educating the reflective practitioner.* San Francisco: Jossey-Bass.

Shulman, J., ed. 1992. *Case methods and teacher education.* New York: Teachers College Press.

Shulman, J. H., and Colbert, J. A., eds. 1988. *The intern teacher casebook.* San Francisco: Far West Laboratory for Educational Research and Development.

Schwartz, J. 1991. Developing an ethos for professional growth, politics and programs. In *Staff development for education in the 90's,* ed. A. Lieberman and L. Miller, pp. 184–92. New York: Teachers College Press.

Silverman, R., Welty, W. M., and Lyon, S. 1992. *Case studies for teacher problem solving.* New York: McGraw-Hill.

Sirotnik, K. A. 1991. Making school-university partnerships work. *Metropolitan Universities* 2: 19–23.

Smith, H., Wigginton, E., Hocking, K., and Jones, R. 1991. Foxfire teacher networks. In *Staff development for education in the 90's,* ed. A. Lieberman and L. Miller, pp. 193–220. New York: Teachers College Press.

Sparks-Langer, G. M. 1992. In the eye of the beholder: Cognitive, critical and narrative approaches to teacher reflection. In *Reflective teacher education,* ed. L. Valli, pp. 147–60. Albany: State University of New York Press.

Stallings, J. A., and Kowalski, T. 1990. Research on professional development schools. In *Handbook of research on teacher education,* ed. W. R. Houston. pp. 251–63. New York: Macmillan.

Valli, L., ed. 1992. *Reflective teacher education.* Albany: State University of New York Press.

Wasley, P. A. 1991. The practical work of teacher leaders: Assumptions, attitudes and acrophobia. In *Staff development for education in the 90's,* ed. A. Lieberman and L. Miller, pp. 158–83. New York: Teachers College Press.

Winitzky, N., Stoddart, T., and O'Keefe, P. 1992. Great expectations: Emergent professional development schools. *Journal of Teacher Education* 43: 13–18.

The Staff Development Course Leader

A New Professional Role for the Classroom Teacher

Scott M. Mandel

I walked into the room on the first day of class. Already I could see that there could be trouble. It was only minutes before the class was to begin, and three-quarters of the class was missing. One student moved his chair to a remote corner of the room and was deep inside a paperback novel. Two other students were busy eating breakfast in the front row. Before I could even put my materials down, one person came up to me and asked if she could leave early because she had an early dinner date. A couple of other students immediately informed me that I should not call on them; they didn't plan on doing any major participation since they were being forced to take this class. At this point, I had only been in the room for five minutes! It was then and there that I began to question my decision—maybe it was a mistake to offer to teach this Saturday teacher in-service class!

A scenario from a horror novel? Not really. This is a true account of the beginning of an in-service class that I once taught. Granted, things eventually became better and we did have an excellent, successful class. However, as a fellow classroom teacher, this opening scenario of dealing with my peers in an atmosphere such as this was not an appealing thought. Luckily, I had learned how to teach colleagues in in-service classes through years of experience. But as I looked into the room across the hall at a teacher friend who was offering her first in-service class, I couldn't help but wonder: Is there a body of knowledge that she could have learned that would have assisted her in teaching colleagues? What are the significant issues an in-service leader must deal with when teaching one's peers?

> **Chapter 7 HIGHLIGHTS**
>
> - Teaching Adults, Not Children
> - Motivation for Professional Development
> - Professional Development: Teachers' Perspective
> - The Ideal Inservice Leader

THE TREND TODAY

In-service course requirements are regularly being added throughout the nation as new standards of teacher professionalism and competence are established. An example of this trend comes from the California legislature, who in their last credentialing overhaul, passed a requirement that teachers must spend 150 hours attending in-service programs in order to renew the California five-year standard teaching credential.[1]

Although credentialing and staffing requirements are continually being upgraded, this is not a boon to academicians and administrators who have regularly taught in-service courses. Quite the opposite. The trend today is for classroom teachers to share their expertise with their colleagues in offering courses and workshops.

Refer back to the vignette presented in Chapter 1 of this book concerning the new teacher (case study of a novice teacher). In only her third year of teaching, the teacher's principal acknowledged that she had a special expertise in social studies and asked her to teach an in-service class on social studies activities for primary grades.

This real-life situation is no longer the "exception to the rule." In the past, only "experienced" or mentor teachers would teach in-service classes and workshops. Today this opportunity is shared by all teachers who have knowledge that they are willing to share in a collaborative environment with their peers.

Even curriculum-producing institutions are using teachers in this role. An excellent example is the Center for Civic Education. This non-

---

[1]For the sake of brevity in this chapter, "in-service courses" will also include those described as "staff development," referring to any teacher education situation in which the teacher's professional development is being addressed, whether the length is a one-hour workshop or a year-long course of study. However, most of the examples are aimed at in-service courses of three to twenty-four hours in total length.

profit organization specializes in writing government- and civics-oriented curriculum. The center has received a number of government grants with the purpose of implementing programs for educating teachers in how to conduct their own in-service workshops using the center's curricula. The result is they have classroom teachers throughout the country, teaching others how to use the new curricula produced by the center, rather than out-of-classroom consultants.

Finally, this trend is also manifesting itself in school districts. Just recently, the Los Angeles Unified School District abolished their paid "professional" in-service course program. In its place, they established Learning Collaborative™ Networks. These "networks" are basically teacher-initiated, teacher-led, and teacher-directed in-service course offerings. These courses cover most of the same topics originally offered in previous years by paid professionals.

TEACHER EDUCATION AND ADULT LEARNING THEORY

Sharing one's teaching expertise has truly become another facet of today's teacher professionalism. However, until recently, this has not been a subject covered to any significant degree in university teacher education programs. Consider the vignette at the beginning of this chapter. Although we learn through our course work how to deal with situations when the "unruly" students are *children*, how does one handle situations involving adults? Are they similar, or totally different? Must one carefully plan out an entire learning environment, as would be the case when teaching children in the school classroom? Or can a teacher just go in and say, "Hello, I'm so-and-so—this is what I know about this subject," and expect the adults to politely listen and participate? (reasoning that they *are* adults). An even more basic question is: How do adults learn and is the process different from children?

Luckily, there has been a significant amount of research conducted concerning in-service teaching (usually referred to in the research as "staff development"). This area of teacher professional development is just beginning to be seen as an additional component of the move to change and improve schools. It is starting to join innovation, implementation, and institutional development as areas of concern for researchers and innovators (Fullan, 1990).

Showers, Joyce, and Bennett (1987) conducted a major synthesis of research on staff development in order to analyze what currently exists and to discover a framework for future programs. Many of their findings can be incorporated by the teacher who is about to teach an in-service course. For example, among the most important findings that these researchers culled from their meta-analysis of nearly two hundred research studies, was that:

> Almost all teachers can take useful information back to their classroom when training includes four parts: (1) presentation of theory, (2) demonstration of the new strategy, (3) initial practice in the workshop, and (4) prompt feedback about their efforts. (p. 79)

Upon careful examination of these findings, one sees that they are very similar to the normal "lesson plan" followed by the everyday teacher: (1) presentation of material, (2) demonstration of the material, (3) practice by the students, and (4) prompt feedback about and/or evaluation of the students' work and their understanding of the new material.

Other researchers have investigated the issue of whether or not teachers use a different teaching style when dealing with adults. These studies showed that the leaders who were in children-oriented classrooms during the day used more student-centered approaches when teaching adult classes than those leaders who were not. When questioned about the differences between teaching adults and children, the study's respondents stated that as a whole when teaching adults, they spend less time on discipline and giving directions, provide less emotional support, structure instructional activities less tightly, and vary teaching techniques more (Imel, 1989).

Does this mean that the in-service course leader should basically teach adults as he or she would teach students? Not entirely, according to the work of Malcolm Knowles (1984). Knowles is one of the recognized experts in the area of adult education and learning theory, which he calls *andragogy*. Andragogy is based on five fundamental assumptions about adult learning:

1. They have a deep psychological need to be self-directing.

2. Their past experiences are a rich resource for learning.

3. Their readiness to learn is connected to what they need to know in order to carry out successfully their roles and responsibilities in society.

4. Their learning orientation is problem-centered rather than subject-centered.

5. They are more motivated to learn by internal factors than external rewards.

Whereas those assumptions were at first postulated as pertaining only to adults, many experts now agree (including Knowles himself) that of these five assumptions of adult learning, all but the one concerning experience also apply to children (Feuer and Geber, 1988).

What do all of these research data mean to the future in-service teacher-leader? They mean that a *teacher can basically use the teaching skills that he or she has already acquired, adapt them to an adult level, take into account situational differences and problems, and become a successful in-service leader.*

Although many similarities exist between teaching teachers and teaching children, often special circumstances must be addressed when teaching teachers. In addition, the teacher in-service class experience is in many ways different from other adult continuing-education situations. Unlike normal adult courses, teacher in-service attendance in the past was often *not* a voluntary experience; the teacher may have been "forced" to attend by the school administrator, or attended in order to advance on the salary schedule or meet credentialing requirements. This phenomenon led to low motivation for the teacher, or, at best, extrinsic motivation—which does not lend itself to long-term adult learning (Knowles, 1984). Often the session was offered at the worse possible time—after school, after a long day of teaching, or on a Saturday, the teacher's much-cherished time off.

A great deal of the negative attitude toward in-service courses can be alleviated by dealing with teachers as the professionals we would like them to be. This would definitely affect the way in-service work is chosen. If teachers are professional, they will select in-service topics and opportunities that directly relate to and assist them in their everyday professional life—just as professionals in other fields choose *their* in-service-type areas of professional education.

This process has already been initiated in some districts. For instance, in the Los Angeles United School District, school leadership councils have been established to deal with this issue. These councils are comprised of 50 percent teachers and 50 percent administrators, classified school personnel, and parents. One of their contractual functions is to plan for all of the in-service activities for that school's staff. No longer are in-service decisions solely in the hands of an on-site administrator. Within the individual schools of this district, teachers are equal partners in their professional growth. Unfortunately, this professional partnership does not exist in most areas.

As a classroom teacher for many years who regularly teaches in-service courses, I have observed what "works" in the in-service arena and conversed with teachers about their in-service experiences. This chapter will now concentrate on these various areas with the hope that teacher-leaders planning to offer in-service workshops can use these ideas and suggestions to become successful, valued in-service instructors. But first, one needs to understand teachers' motivations in taking in-service offerings.

WHY DO TEACHERS ATTEND IN-SERVICE COURSES?

Most teacher in-service experiences happen within the individual school and are often called professional development. Through professional development on the university level and within the school, teachers are usually already familiar with a number of concepts and practices that promote professional inquiry. These include reflective practice, collaboration, action research, clinical supervision, and coaching (see Holland et al., 1992, for a detailed description of each). Whereas most of these areas deal with supervision and evaluation within the schools, these workable, positive programs often do not extend to in-service course work or workshops that classroom teachers regularly attend.

Promoting one's professional development is only one of three basic rationales for which a teacher enrolls in these courses:

1. The participant is interested in the topic and is there to improve his or her own personal knowledge and skills. This sort of participant is usually excited and ready to participate fully.

2. The participant wants to move up the salary scale and needs the salary level the course offers. This participant's enthusiasm is directly proportional to his or her interest in the topic, and the requirements of the course.

3. The participant is forced to attend because of an administrative directive or a credentialing requirement. Such a participant has the least enthusiasm about attending the course.

Too often the second and third rationales above are the reason a teacher attends an in-service class. In-service attendance, as the system is currently established, is an extension of the lack of control that teachers have over their own supervision. Traditionally, administrators have dictated the criteria for attendance and the makeup of teacher in-service sessions, with little input from the professionals for whom the in-service experience is meant to help. This policy is a continuation of the practice

of evaluation as a form of control over the teachers. The teacher empowerment movement that is slowly beginning to change supervision and
evaluation will hopefully begin to extend to teacher in-service requirements (Gitlin and Price, 1992).

In the meantime, teachers still are attending in-service sessions they
do not select, and classroom teachers are more and more beginning to
teach their colleagues in these situations. Principals are also using staff
members to provide in-service opportunities in their schools. However,
although principals work with teachers in a collegial relationship to
improve teaching students, they often have little experience in helping
prepare a teacher for leading an *adult* in-service session. It is to this practical, everyday circumstance that this chapter now turns.

WHAT DO TEACHERS WANT IN AN IN-SERVICE SESSION, AND HOW CAN AN IN-SERVICE LEADER PROVIDE IT?

Serving as an in-service leader, you are confronted with both motivated
and unmotivated colleagues—from those that want to and are excited to
attend, to those who are there under duress because of an administrative
directive. However, regardless of the original motivation for attending, I
have found that once they are there, teachers want to enjoy the session and
learn from the experience. Therefore, the easiest and most successful way
to provide for a positive in-service course is to give the participants, one's
teaching colleagues, what they want in a class. Using the earlier analogy of
the in-service leader as an entertainer and the participants as the audience,
if the entertainer does not provide the audience with the kind of experience that they want to receive, they will leave, or at least not fully attend to
the "performance." The same problems apply to the in-service leader who
is not cognizant of the attitudes and desires of the participants.

The balance of this chapter will address the issues that have arisen
during my years of working with, talking to, and observing teachers in
in-service sessions. These insights come from serving both as an in-service leader and from my own personal attendance as an in-service participant through my role as a classroom teacher.

Teachers Want to Be Treated as Professionals

I asked a doctor friend of mine if there was an in-service course requirement for continuing medical education. He said that in his state, he was
required to acquire 100 hours of in-service experience every two years;

he could pick any course, workshop, or lecture to attend. When I asked how the system was supervised, he told me that it was basically on an "honor system"; that he only had to provide proof if he was asked by some regulatory agency. In addition, up to 60 of those 100 hours could come from reading his medical journals.

I asked a lawyer friend of mine if there was an in-service course requirement for continuing law education. She said that in her state, she was required to acquire twenty-four hours of in-service experience every two years: one hour each in the areas of "ethics" and "substance abuse," the rest were her choice. When I asked how the system was supervised, she told me that she had to submit a course number and/or agenda to a state agency.

I asked a teacher friend of mine in another district if there was an in-service course requirement for continuing teacher education in her area. She said that there was a twofold requirement, both state and local. On the state level, she was required to attend 150 hours to renew her credentials every five years. When I asked who selected the courses, she stated that she did with the approval of her supervisor and that she had to submit proof to the state. On a local level, she estimated that she had to attend 45 to 50 hours of mandatory teacher in-service workshops through her school every year. Of these she had no choice in the selection of topics, found little applicable relevancy in three-quarters of them, and was basically marked "truant" if she missed any of the sessions.

Teachers want and need to be treated as professionals, similar to professionals in other fields. As you can see with the examples above, this does not often occur when one deals with in-service requirements.

Whereas the in-service leader does not have control over the "system," he or she does have control within the in-service course. Teachers want the course to be conducted in a professional manner. This is applicable to anything from leader-participant interaction, to course requirements, to classroom participation. Essentially, however, regarding one's teacher colleagues as professionals within the in-service session is a *state of mind*. If the in-service leader has this mind-set, it will permeate all other aspects of the in-service experience.

Teachers Want to Feel Comfortable and to Be Treated as Adults

The initial overall environment is an item that is rarely addressed when discussing the implementation of in-service courses. The in-service leader must remember that teachers often attend an in-service class after a long day of teaching or on the weekend, after a long week of teaching. Therefore, no matter how well thought out the course is, no matter how relevant the topic, without establishing a positive in-service environment, the leader runs the risk of having a less-than-successful experience.

Although this may sound simplistic, the easiest way to start your in-service session in a positive manner is to provide refreshments for your participants. More than just satisfying their hunger, one would be amazed at the psychological change in attitude that occurs when one's peers see that the in-service leader has gone out of his or her way to make them comfortable.

This is not a foreign concept in the professional business world. A great number of formal meetings begin with refreshments or they are served during a break time. Even on a TV show such as *L.A. Law* they start each staff meeting with doughnuts and pastry!

Even a small gesture such as this affects the attitudes of the participants. They personally feel more comfortable, and more important, they see the importance of their comfort acknowledged.

As the session begins, initial introductions should not be glossed over or turned into a childlike activity. Introductions are very important and should be taken seriously because they give valuable information to both the other participants and to the in-service leader. For this reason, in addition to name and school, it is important always to make sure that every participant verbalizes two pieces of information: (1) current teaching position and/or situation (this lets the participants know whether or not there are others in similar situations in the class), and (2) previous experience in the course subject matter, both resulting from previous in-service courses or from classroom experience involving the topic at hand (this information helps the leader in shaping the course to novices or experienced participants). Additionally, by treating the introductory period at an adult level (instead of incorporating a "getting to know you" childlike activity), the participants immediately feel that they will be treated as adults throughout the session.

Teachers Want an In-Service Leader Who Is Empathetic

After introductions and before the presentation of the material comes one of the most important elements of the in-service course: the in-service leader establishes credibility with the participants. It is here that collegial *empathy* is formed, as the in-service leader demonstrates innate understanding of his or her colleagues' teaching situation and regularly does, or has, experienced the same issues and problems each of them currently must deal with.

Establishing empathy with the teachers in the in-service class is not to be trivialized. Studies have shown that the selection of the in-service leader is a critical component in the implementation of any of the material presented in the course (Little, 1989). Unless the topic is a very specialized one that only a few people in the community can teach, teachers tend to give less credibility to in-service leaders who are not in the classroom or who have little connection with everyday classroom life, especially when the topic of the in-service class deals with classroom teaching methodologies. This phenomenon is the primary reason so many school districts are moving toward hiring teachers to teach in-service courses. Even when the in-service leader is a university professor or an outside consultant, unless that person has spent considerable time in the classroom as a teacher or is currently working with teachers in a classroom setting, he or she will suffer decreased credibility with the participants.

Teachers Want Their Professional Experience Considered

Throughout the years, I've noticed that teachers readily admit to areas of in-service work in which they have little experience. When sitting in the class, they want to learn and improve their skills. Likewise, one of the most frustrating experiences for teachers is to be subjected to basic professional or technical knowledge they already know and practice. The competency of an in-service leader is open to question if professional, pedagogic, and subject-field knowledge is not adjusted to class participants.

For example, when offering a course on cooperative learning, unless I have been informed otherwise, I normally plan for a mixture of novices and people with some experience using the methodology. However, on occasion, I've walked unaware into classes where the participants knew virtually nothing about cooperative learning. After receiving the introductory information discussed earlier, I had the opportunity to adapt my lesson plan immediately to give them some important basic material I originally had not expected to use. Conversely, I've walked into a couple of cooperative learning courses where all of the participants had previous, extensive use of the method and were knowledgeable of the related research. Upon acquiring this information, I found myself immediately discarding most of my introductory material and adapting the rest to a higher level, matching that of the participants.

Teachers Appreciate Good Teaching during the In-Service Course

The presentation of the curricular content is the primary area of the in-service course for which the participants come. It also is the primary area of the in-service class that is remembered over time—for better or worse.

Teachers want good teaching; they want the in-service leader to present the material in a variety of ways, using various models of teaching. Models such as the advance organizer, concept attainment, inductive thinking, and inquiry training, all are excellent ways of starting out and structuring one's presentation. Each is appropriate to various subject matters and leader goals. (For a detailed description of these and other models, see Joyce et al. 1992). Teachers in in-service classes want the teaching to be enjoyable and efficient—that is, they want to learn all of the material the leader has to offer without wasting time. The same curricular rules that one learns to use as a teacher are applicable when one is

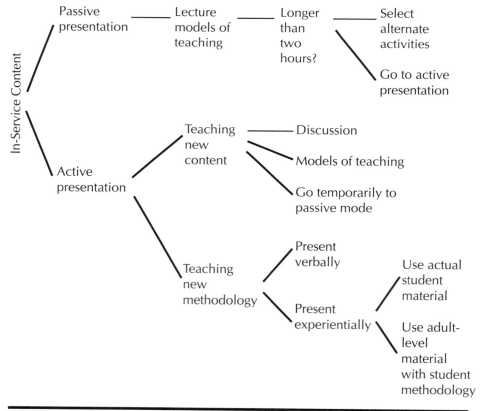

FIGURE 7.1   The decision-making process for presenting in-service curriculum.

teaching colleagues. As an in-service leader, one should generally follow the basic teaching pattern of presentation, demonstration, practice, and evaluation. Experiences should be varied to limit boredom and to present the material with a number of learning modes and patterns. Figure 7.1 gives an illustration of the possibilities for presenting in-service material.

Whereas teaching factual subject matter can easily be accomplished using the same skills as in effective classroom teaching, problems arise when the task is to present teaching methodologies that are curriculum-specific. Typically, in most courses, the in-service leader uses a lesson from the curriculum being presented, incorporating the actual printed children's text or the curricular supplemental material. This is how a method is illustrated.

By using this procedure, in-service leaders can show their colleagues how as classroom teachers they would present the material, and the participants internalize the information on an adult level, fitting it within its appropriate place in their cognitive framework for teaching. However, by simply role-playing the part of children, the participants feel no real empathy with the students who will be using the material, as they are not experiencing children-type reactions. That the teachers will not receive this important information until they actually implement the methodology in their individual classrooms may impede initial success with the new program.

A potentially worse drawback to using children's material at this point is that the easier the student material is, the more the activity may become a "fun and games" time for the participants. Ironically, the problem is that everyone is having such a good time, it limits their active cognitive analysis of the material!

A potential solution to this problem is for the in-service leader to present new teaching methodologies using adult-level rather than child-level material. Using adult material is not an option that has typically been implemented in many in-service courses. However, I have found over and over that teachers prefer methodological instruction at their cognitive level. By using professionally relevant material, teachers learn to use the methodology and then begin to internalize, empathize, and understand its effects on students before they even teach one lesson using the new pedagogy.

The following are three anecdotes of in-service sessions in which various new methodologies were presented using professionally relevant material instead of the actual child-level material. The examples move from the presentation of a very general methodology to a specific curricular-connected one.

Example 1: A General Methodology—Using Cooperative Learning

The goal for the in-service lesson was to teach the Jigsaw method of cooperative learning. In Jigsaw, curricular material is broken down into "sections," based on subject components. The students, one from each group, meet together to become "experts" in one section and then go back to teach their group their new expertise.

At the end of a session the participants were asked to bring in a copy of the local newspaper for that day, which they did. Before the session began, I had selected one of the international stories making headlines that day, one that had not been covered extensively in the media during the previous week. The teachers then proceeded through every step of the entire Jigsaw method using the newspaper story as the curricular material.

During a debriefing discussion at the end, the teachers determined that by actually experiencing new material as a student would, they understood and internalized the methodology at a significantly greater level. They also experienced many of the potential problems and shortcomings of the method through this process. Thus, they were better prepared for deviations when implementing the method in their individual classrooms.

Example 2: An Overview of A New Curricular Methodology—History

At the close of the adoption process for the last California History/Social Studies curricular framework, only one publishing house was approved to provide state-adopted textbooks and programs to the various school districts throughout the state. This severely limited the choice of textbooks but made it very easy to provide in-service classes in the new methodology on a massive scale.

The teachers with whom I was to be meeting were all experienced history teachers. As I was planning this in-service class, I recalled a previous experience leading a session using the new curriculum. During that session, every time we discussed a particular historical period, the teachers were preoccupied with sharing how they had been teaching specific curricular material. This preoccupation prevented them from fully attending to the new material that was being presented. They were too involved with how to teach particular *content,* rather than trying a new *methodology.*

Not wishing to duplicate this experience, I prepared for the current in-service session by studying an old textbook used in teaching Chinese history. Material was selected equivalent to that of a typical history lesson, as presented in the new curriculum. The Chinese history material was then adapted to fit into all of the components of the new methodology. Worksheets were created, a couple of pictures were enlarged into "poster" form, and some supplemental curricular activities were adapted. A test from the section on American government was also selected; names and ideas were simply substituted from the Chinese history material. Then the entire lesson was taught, using exactly the same methodology as promoted in the new curriculum.

The result was that although the teachers were experiencing the new history curriculum methodology, they were confronted with material they never saw previously. They became genuinely interested and excited—a tribute to, and an example of, the motivational activities of the new curriculum. Through experience, the teachers now understood how the curriculum worked, without being prejudiced by previous knowledge from their personal teaching. During debriefing, we then discussed changes to, questions about, and potential problems with the new method, all the while using the Chinese history material as our subject matter. We concentrated on *methodology* rather than on *material* and thus achieved the original goal.

Example 3: A Specific Teaching Methodology—A New ESL Program

A new ESL (English as a second language) program was being implemented in a particular school. This program had a specific methodology and lessons that were to be followed. It had been previously determined that one of the problems of the old program was limited teacher empathy with the experiences of the students. These particular teachers did not understand why the program was not working and blamed the students' work habits and lack of motivation for their inability to "catch on."

I decided to ask the in-service participants to play the role of the students. Then I taught one of the first basic lessons in the book. For the lesson I created my own "language," which came complete with symbols totally foreign to any known written language and unique grammatical rules totally different from those in English. The lesson was then taught using the process and materials in the target curriculum, but substituting the "foreign language" for the English words in the book. Flashcards and charts were made; a cassette tape was created to substitute for the "audio component" of the lesson.

The result was very interesting. The teachers all experienced serious levels of frustration—some even became resentful and angry during the activity! They went through the entire lesson, but it was extremely difficult, even at this basic level.

During the crucial debriefing session immediately following the lesson, the participants verbalized frustrations. By personally experiencing the curriculum on an adult level, they quickly realized, and acquired, empathy with their students. This led to a deeper understanding of the students' situation and why they possibly were not succeeding. The group then turned to a discussion on how to alleviate much of the students' frustrations, ultimately gaining a better grasp of the new ESL curriculum. By the end of the session, their frustrations had turned into appreciation—that of having a colleague helping them to acquire new insights into the teaching process.

Teachers Want the Opportunity to Debrief and Adapt Material

Too often during professional courses, we are so pressed for time (especially in two- to three-hour workshops) that a debriefing session is not incorporated. This often leaves teachers unresolved about the activity, with questions left unanswered about implementation of the material that was presented. It is especially important when the material is presented experientially, as in the earlier anecdotal examples, to enable teachers to think and talk about means to adapt new ideas.

A debriefing session is an important component of all in-service course activities. To illustrate, during each of the debriefing sessions above, we addressed five basic questions together as a group:

1. What did we *experience* during the activity?

2. What were some of the frustrations that we felt while doing the activity?

3. Putting ourselves in the place of our students, what concerns do we now have that we did not have previously?

4. As teachers, how can we address the concerns enumerated in the previous question?

5. What are some concerns pertaining to our unique teaching situations? Relate/discuss/brainstorm solutions and ideas.

During debriefing, the in-service leader can also review and strengthen points that need added attention, approaching areas that may have arisen that did not, or could not, be addressed during the actual activity. Either way, the debriefing session is a crucial part of the in-service class curricular presentation.

Teachers are individuals, each with his or her own unique personality, characteristics, teaching styles, and preferences. However, in-service leaders regularly present generic teaching material to teachers and have them work on personal adaptations on their own time. If the in-service material is quite new to the teachers, it is unrealistic to expect them to implement adaptations when they have yet to practice, let alone master, the original material. Therefore, regardless of the time allotted for the presentation of the material, the in-service leader must always save time for adaptation questions, which allow the participants to work with the leader to adapt the material to their individual teaching situations. Everyone in the group will talk about "what ifs"; everyone will talk about individual student "types." The group will also share ideas among themselves about things that have worked in roughly similar situations, or about new ideas generated by one of the participants. Although the participants may not have time to anticipate all of the adaptation problems that will arise, at least they will be given the opportunity to reflect, brainstorm, and problem-solve, enabling them to practice on their own.

Teachers Want the Information Presented to Be Practical and Relevant

Nothing seems to bother teachers more during an in-service session than listening to material that is mostly theoretical in nature and has little practical application to their everyday teaching situations. Although teachers do want theory, they expect technical information to have practical implications for teaching. The material presented needs to be relevant to current, or anticipated, future teaching situations.

Although the in-service leader is seen as a peer among the participants, his or her colleagues will have a somewhat egocentric approach toward what is presented. They will expect to see the personal practicality and relevancy from the start of the course. As the material is introduced, it should be phrased in such a way that participants perceive what *they* are going to get out of the course, rather than what the in-service leader is going to present. Therefore, in stating the session goals, one should (1) use terms that relate to a change in the participants' behavior and (2) tie the curriculum directly to a practical classroom example. Whether or not the initial example directly fits to each participant is not important here as long as the leader is showing *practicality.*

There is a basic difference between treating teachers as professionals and treating teachers as students. Professionals in all fields expect and demand that staff development sessions are relevant to their immediate professional life. Rarely are professionals in any field required to study material or perform specific functions simply on the basis of an outside authority's presentation. Yet personal relevancy is often not a concern to either in-service decision makers or in-service leaders.

Even within the course, many in-service leaders require culminating projects that have little relevance to the participants' everyday teaching lives. As a consequence, teachers create curricular projects that often are not used. As an in-service leader, whenever the supervising agency requires the participants to create a final project, I always insist on one stipulation at the very beginning of the course—that the project be relevant to the subject area that my colleague is teaching, or an area that he or she reasonable believes will be taught in the near future. I insist on a usable project, even if I need to make exemptions or alterations in the requirements for individuals. It is more important for the final project to be adapted to individual teaching environments than to adapt the teachers to the requirements of an arbitrary final project.

Teachers Want to Come Away from the Session with Reference Material

One of the components that make an in-service session significant is the use of reference materials. By these I am referring to the use of *informational handouts* to exemplify, explain, or supplement the material that is being presented. A constant complaint I hear from teachers is that very often, by the time they are ready to use some in-service material, so much time has passed that they have forgotten much valuable information. An important value of providing literature for teachers is that it serves as a long-term reminder of the material covered in the session. Too often in-service sessions that occur during the second semester of school are not applicable to the participants' classrooms until the following school year. Six to ten months is a long time to remember material, especially if the teachers have not been able to practice what they studied during that period. The situation becomes exasperating when the teacher attends an in-service class thinking that he or she will be teaching one grade the following year and, lo and behold, is transferred to a different grade—one where the material is no longer relevant. The teacher might have to wait a couple of years before being able to implement the in-service material. This problem can be alleviated through the use of resource literature. One's colleagues can review or remember much of the workshop, if they can read the major points from hand-outs they saved from the course.

It should also be noted that the lack of relevant professional literature may be interpreted by colleagues as a lack of respect on the part of the in-service leader toward the group.

Reference material need be no more than a rough outline, lists of key ideas, an advance organizer, or a graphic design representing primary elements of the course. Even newspaper comic strips can be incorporated to make a particular point. For instance, one of the best resources I have found is the daily comic strip *Calvin and Hobbes*. During discussions concerning the hidden curriculum that teachers often inadvertently use, I pull out a particular strip. In this scene, Calvin's first-grade teacher is tracking the students into reading groups. Her student teacher tries to get her to use animal names instead of labeling the groups "high" or "low," which, she points out, negatively impacts the child's self-esteem. The teacher agrees to try it the new way. The final panel shows the teacher grouping the students in this fashion: "Okay, Tommy, you're a 'lion'; Sally, you're a 'tiger'; Bobby, you're a 'lower crustacean.'" The humor in the strip and its relevance to the workshop material will be remembered by the course participants long after the course has ended.

Reference materials can also supplement information that one simply does not have the time to present or to discuss at great depth. Teachers often want to read the research behind the in-service material presented. However, long, multipage articles are often not read in their entirety and are costly to reproduce. Therefore, I regularly supply abstracts of important articles, or pertinent sections, summaries, and conclusions, along with bibliographies.

Teachers Want the In-Service Leader to Have Good Management Skills

One of the most frustrating experiences I have ever had as a teacher attending a session was when the in-service leader had poor management skills. The conversation "wandered" from topic to topic, individual participants were able to monopolize and redirect the conversation, and overall the experience was a waste of time.

Each in-service leader must find a comfortable, workable way to match his or her personal management style to the needs and functions of the group. Many management issues must be addressed. Figure 7.2 presents a number of these. The problem of management is compounded when one realizes that the participants are one's *peers*. Teaching one's peers is one of the hardest things to do. Being a successful group leader requires deep understanding of one's colleagues along with careful advance planning.

In teaching a class to peer teachers, it is important to remember that one's peers are expert too. Some teachers are expert at pedagogy, some are expert in subject matter, some are expert in organizational skills. We contribute to each other through our in-service course work.

The role of the in-service group leader should be one of "facilitator and resource person." By facilitating, one is *helping* and *sharing* with one's peers through one's teaching skills. As a resource person, one is there to

FIGURE 7.2   Management issues.

provide information *if they want it*—to offer it to them to use if they wish. In many ways, the leader serves as a "walking teacher resource room." Teachers see what the resource room has to offer and then use what they feel is most appropriate to their individual situation. Each participant is in turn encouraged to become a resource in his or her own area of expertise.

The key to this process is the feeling of empathy that was previously discussed. The in-service leader assumes a particular role, though the only difference between the leader and the teachers is that the leader has more experience and knowledge in a particular area. Thus the in-service information and skill is presented by a peer, a fellow educator, in a formalized peer coaching situation.

The in-service leader plays an important professional leadership role. As a group leader in the in-service process, one has an obligation to assist in the overall professional development of colleagues. In many ways, one becomes a "role model" for other teachers. Being a facilitator does not mean that one does not take important stands when cause arises. Often there are times when it is important to speak up on an important matter, even in direct opposition to the participants.

A case in point is a situation I encountered when teaching an in-service session concerning a new social studies curriculum. The discussion topic involved supplemental activities used to teach the unit on ancient Egypt. A participant was describing an activity she used in which she had the sixth-grade students write postcards "home" from ancient Egypt. She pointed out to the entire in-service group how she expected her gifted students to write long paragraphs, whereas she was satisfied if the ESL students could write a line or two in their native language. At that point it was necessary to take a professional stand on an issue not directly related to the material—that just because a student does not speak English, he or she is not dumb! As the in-service leader, I pointed out to the group that cognitive expectations should be just as high as those of English speakers; the students' problem is language, not intelligence!

Sessions that last over a few days or weeks serve an important function for teachers especially if well managed by the in-service leader. Since teachers have limited interaction time with other adults throughout the school day, the in-service class is often the only place where teachers can talk freely about professional issues with other teachers. During these extended in-service courses, it is important to encourage talk about professional issues—even if the issues are not related to the topic at hand! This opportunity acquires added importance if the local professional climate is volatile—such as when intense labor negotiations are being conducted, or other controversial community issues are prominent at the time.

To illustrate, at the start of one of my multiweek in-service courses, the local teachers' union was intensely involved in preparing for a probable strike. This strike was the primary item on the minds of all of the participants—much more so than the in-service topic that was about to be presented! Shortly after the introductory period, the conversation led to "strike talk." We began to talk as a group about our strike feelings and concerns. Over the next half-hour opinions were shared among group members. When a lull in the discussion was reached, I formally moved us into the topic of the course. After satisfying the need to discuss this important issue, we were ready to concentrate on the in-service topic for the rest of the course. In addition, an even more important goal was accomplished—the participants began to network with each other, to make connections that would last beyond the end of the in-service class.

Teachers Want to Network with Other Teachers

Networking is a natural process in which teachers in similar teaching situations gravitate to each other and form long-term, professional partnerships. They listen to each other, help each other, and share with each other.

In the in-service class, the introductions may begin the networking process. Stating the participant's current position tells others in the group whether or not there are teachers in similar teaching situations. The natural tendency of people with comparable positions is to begin to congregate, especially those in the more specialized areas, such as special education, kindergarten, and the arts.

As an in-service leader, one can assist in setting up the network during the sessions. At some point during the course, teachers with comparable teaching situations should be given an opportunity to work together in some form relevant to the material, be it a project, exercise, or discussion group.

For those who have not had an opportunity previously to network formally with other teachers, there needs to be discussion of the benefits of networking, which include

- Sharing ideas, and getting feedback about those ideas.

- Creating and sharing materials equally, thereby reducing the work load for all.

- Communicating day-to-day teaching frustrations with someone who understands.

- Having the opportunity to expand professional teaching horizons by gaining educational perspectives beyond their individual school.

It is networking that most effectively incorporates in-service material into the participants' classrooms. Networking also helps in the long-term professional development of the individual teachers. This is the ultimate goal of all in-service offerings.

CONCLUSION

As teacher in-service course requirements are being added throughout the nation, the new trend is for classroom teachers to serve as the in-service leader. This trend is apparent in both school districts and in curriculum-producing institutions.

The research indicates that teaching teachers in staff development situations is not identical in all respects to the teaching of children. Nor is it identical to other forms of adult education. Sometimes teachers' reluctance to attend in-service courses make it difficult for the staff development leader.

In the move toward professionalism and teacher autonomy, teachers will begin to control their own professional growth activities. This will lead to self-determination concerning personal needs. If teacher-leaders are to teach these courses, they too will need assistance. Until recently there was no university preparation for teachers to serve as in-service leaders. Though intuitively most teachers know what their colleagues want and expect in an in-service course, preparation for teaching it is difficult because the teacher-leader also is responsible for a normal teaching load.

In addition, most teachers have not had experience sharing their expertise with colleagues. Learning to do so requires a whole new set of interactive courses and a true sense of commitment, particularly when one considers the preparation time involved and the frequent lack of remuneration. I do it because there is nothing as invigorating as working with peers, sharing expertise, learning from each other, and helping to make everybody's students better off. This is an experience increasingly shared by many teachers across the country as they become the primary in-service leaders for their colleagues.

Recap Notes: Suggestions for Leading Staff Development Classes

- Treat teachers as professionals beginning with initial leader-participant interaction, course requirements, and classroom participation.

- Provide a comfortable environment.

- Be empathetic. Establish your credibility by demonstrating that you innately understand diverse teaching situations, experiences, and problems.

- Take into account the professional experience of your participants. Adjust professional, pedagogic, and subject field knowledge to participants' levels.

- Use everyday teaching strategies. Use a variety of teaching models. Present curriculum-specific material on an adult level, rather than the way it is presented in the student-oriented curriculum.

- Provide time to debrief material and adapt it to participants' personal teaching situations.

- Make sure information is practical and relevant to everyday classroom life.

- Provide reference material to serve two purposes: as a future reminder of major points of the session and to extend material in complexity and depth.

- Use good collegial management skills to help the group move efficiently. Be a resource and a role model for your peers.

- Help teachers begin to network with peers.

REFERENCES

Feuer, D, and Geber, B. 1988. Uh-oh . . . Second thoughts about learning theory. *Training* 25(12): 31–39.

Fullan, M. G. 1990. Staff development, innovation, and institutional development. In *Changing school culture through staff development,* ed. B. Joyce. Alexandria, Va.: Association for Supervision and Curriculum Development.

Gitlin, A., and Price, K. 1992. Teacher empowerment and the development of voice. In *Supervision in transition,* ed. C. D. Glickman. Alexandria, Va.: Association for Supervision and Curriculum Development.

Holland, P. E., Clift, R., and Veal, M. L. 1992. Linking preservice and in-service supervision through professional inquiry. In *Supervision in transition,* ed. C. D. Glickman. Alexandria, Va.: Association for Supervision and Curriculum Development.

Imel, S. 1989. Teaching adults: Is it different? *ERIC digest no. 82.* Columbus, Oh.: ERIC Clearinghouse on Adult, Career, and Vocational Education.

Joyce, B., Showers, B., and Rolheiser-Bennett, C. 1987. Staff development and student learning: A synthesis of research on models of teaching. *Educational Leadership* 45(2): 11–23.

Joyce, B., Weil, M., and Showers, B. 1992. *Models of teaching.* 4th ed. Boston: Allyn and Bacon.

Knowles, M. 1984. *Andragogy in action: Applying modern principles of adult learning.* San Francisco: Jossey-Bass.

Little, J. 1989. The 'mentor' phenomenon and the social organization of teaching. In *Review of research in education,* vol. 5, no. 6. Washington, D.C.: American Educational Research Association.

Building New Professional Roles

JOHANNA K. LEMLECH

Teachers, principals, and university-based educators are all working through new problems, defining new roles, and accepting new responsibilities. Areas of expertise differ, but most educators are engaged in making changes and in establishing an environment for professionalism. Professional development activities include designing new curriculum, engaging in study groups and staff development, participating in research projects, developing problem-based case studies, experimenting with new ideas, developing resource centers, and networking with other educators in cross-role teams. These are but a few of the ways that educators are involved in growth and development. This chapter will expand on some of these activities, offering a modest proposal for the preservice preparation of teacher professionals, and suggesting means to sustain the education of new teachers through the support they receive during their first two years of practice.

DEVELOPING EXPERTISE

Recently I visited my local shoe repair shop to consult with the owner about stretching a pair of shoes. While there I asked whether he would

Chapter 8 HIGHLIGHTS

- Expertise Defined
- Cross-Role Teams
- Education Networks
- Collegial Relationships
- Action Teams
- Peer Coaching
- Staff Development
- Changing Roles and Relationships
- New Teacher Preparation
- Reshaping the Apprenticeship Experience
- What New Teachers Need to Know
- Helping the New Teacher

consider starting from scratch to make personally designed shoes. He shook his head and stated, "I'm a cobbler, not a designer."

Unlike the cobbler who was proud of what he knew and could do, and recognized what he did not know, some educators (and some lay folk) seem to think that "anyone" can teach; anyone can be a teacher educator, and anyone can administer a school.

Not so. Specialized knowledge in subject matter, pedagogy, and curriculum is vital for teaching. In addition, the "expert" teacher recognizes what students know and do not know, and it is *this* knowledge that speaks to the teacher in planning lessons. The skillful teacher intertwines subject-matter content with pedagogical learning and knowledge about the learners. A Nobel Laureate in biology is an expert in that field, but that does not mean that the individual can teach biology to a class of fifth graders. Lee Shulman (1990) cites the case of a young secondary teacher who wanted his tenth graders to read and appreciate *Julius Caesar*. He began by creating a simulation using the television show *Star Trek* to acquaint the students with the problem of megalomaniacal behavior. Recognizing what would motivate the students, he transformed the content of the book into understandings the students would appreciate. Then he inspired the students to examine similar aspects of *Caesar*.

In a distance-learning mathematics project developed jointly by Los Angeles County Office of Education and leaders in the National Parents-

Teachers Association (PTA), math was to be taught to parents to enable them to extend math learning for their children to the home. The televised program was shown in 111 sites around the United States between 5:30 and 6:30 P.M. The original plan was to have a parent-leader at each site facilitate discussion of the program. However, at all 111 sites the parents asked a teacher to lead the sessions; they were uncomfortable with the facilitator role. The researcher concluded that the facilitator role required teacher expertise, and the parents recognized this (Lanich, 1993).

Though I was an elementary teacher for fifteen years, I am presently more adept at teaching at the college level than I would be if I attempted once again to teach elementary school. I have developed my expertise at transforming curriculum and instructional knowledge using teaching models to educate graduate students in educational leadership. Neither the principal of an elementary school nor a teacher at the high school nor an expert in education policy would fare as well as I do in this role. Teaching is complex. We need to know our subject field, we need to understand pedagogy, and we need to know how to connect the two for a specific audience.

Managing a school requires special knowledge as well. Resource management, interpersonal skills for coordinating the work and skills of others, technical skills for improving and supervising curriculum and instruction, and organizational skills to provide assistance to others and to plan for the total school community, are some of the tasks of a school principal. These tasks require knowledge of administration, supervision, the structure of the curriculum, understanding of instruction, common sense, and experience.

We can all be leaders and professionals, but we do not all have the same specialized skills and technical behaviors. Nor should we. Let us build appreciation of what our colleagues know and promote the sharing of expertise. Even experienced educators misunderstand the value of expertise when they advocate that classroom teachers teach methods classes and university-based educators teach third grade. Situational leadership and specialized knowledge need to be recognized; the third-grade teacher can share his or her expertise about third-grade subject matter and the management of third-grade students in multicultural settings.[1] College professors need to share their knowledge of how curriculum conceptions affect curriculum planning for whole-language instruc-

[1]See the appendix for a case study of an innovative secondary English as a Second Language teacher-leader.

tion. Each can connect with the other to expand knowledge and improve teaching (and schools). We do not need to prove we can do each other's job, because that makes "doing the job" insignificant and belies the wisdom of practice.

CROSS-ROLE TEAMS

Decision making in schools often can be enhanced by including in the decision-making process individuals who have different areas of expertise and who perform different roles. Because decisions affect members of the school community differently, it is important to recognize varied perspectives on school problems before decisions are made. For example, suppose some members of a school faculty want to consider changing to a performance-based system for recognizing and communicating students' learning. How would this system affect teachers in different disciplines or grade levels? What does the school counselor think of the idea? How would the system be perceived by parents? By the students themselves? If this occurred at the high school level, how would it affect admission to colleges?

Before this decision is made it would be wise to form a cross-role team or committee composed of teachers in different fields or grade levels, students, parents, the principal, the school counselor, the district representative, and university advisers. This group must be perceived by others as legitimate and clearly empowered to make a decision. The members could then consider how the change would affect each "stakeholder" by considering questions such as:

1. How would the change affect the immediate school community? How would it affect other district schools?

2. What would be the impact on teachers' roles and authority?

3. How would the decision affect parental knowledge of students' learning progress?

4. How would the change affect students transferring to another school? How would it affect incoming students?

5. At the high school level, what would be the impact on college admission?

6. How would standards be determined? Who should be involved in developing rubrics, standards, criteria?

If the members favored the change, then the cross-role team would have to consider the readiness of the school community, the resources (human and material) needed, and other external groups who would need to be informed. The cross-role team would then serve as the agents of change and begin the implementation process, or they might select a smaller group to manage such efforts.

The cross-role team is a leadership strategy that develops a collaborative culture by inviting individuals with differing interests and perspectives to participate in decision making that affects all members of the school community. It is a means to expand the school decision-making base, develop leadership, and build commitment to improve curriculum and instruction.

EDUCATIONAL NETWORKS

A variation of the cross-role team is an educational network of individuals from a variety of schools and/or organizations who come together for an unspecified period of time to consider joint or similar problems. The educational network is a means for school leaders to share ideas, knowledge, and resources. The network serves as a social support system, helping its members work through problems of change. The participants in school networks recognize the similarity of their problems and together seek real-world solutions.

Principals and teachers who have participated in networking comment that listening to others in similar situations helps them to recognize antecedent conceptions and practices that affect present relationships. For example, if principals have traditionally made decisions about which educational program for teaching math will be used in the schools, teachers (and parents) will hesitate to become involved in redefining who ought to make program decisions. Unfortunately, hesitance may be misinterpreted as unwillingness until the involved parties recognize the context of the problem.

The network may be composed of school leaders within a particular geographic region, or of leaders addressing specific problems. An example of a network created to focus on a specific concern was one initiated by teacher education program faculty to improve communication with the school leaders responsible for working with the institution's student teachers. Conversation among the participants led to the realization that both the schools and the university wanted recognition for "doing things right." Neither group wanted to feel threatened by the other. The school-based educators wanted information about what the students were learning in their methods class, and the university-based educators wanted to know that the student teachers would obtain the necessary reinforcement in the clinical classroom. Networking improved their communication and enabled each to support the other through a team approach.

COLLEGIAL RELATIONS

Working effectively and respectfully with others, as in cross-role teams and through the process of networking, requires that individuals respond in collegial ways. Collegiality, defined in Chapter 1, discriminates between "visceral" collegial relations and a "veneer" of collegiality; the key criteria for the formation of collegial relationships are (1) service and accommodation to another through (2) the mutual exchange of perceptions and expertise.

Collegial relationships do not develop because you teach next door to, or drive together, or share books, or supervise each other's students, or even share information about the last principal's meeting. *Collegial relations require the sharing of interest, concern, commitment, and critical judgment.*

In Los Angeles, Project LEARN (Los Angeles Educational Alliance for Restructuring Now) held intensive management training sessions at the University of California, Los Angeles. The *Los Angeles Times* (August 27, 1993) described the first session as follows:

> To foster a sense of collegiality, they had the group perform ice-breaker activities, such as standing in a circle and keeping a balloon in the air without using their hands.

Items such as the above do not gain respect for the teaching profession. It makes participating teachers and principals look like buffoons. Instead of fostering commitment, mutual respect, the assumption of responsibility, and utilizing each other's expertise to develop reform plans, the activity embarrassed and ridiculed adults who needed to be engaged in very significant tasks. (Does anyone really believe that attorneys attending continuing education of the bar classes, balance balloons to develop collegial relationships? Do medical doctors use "ice-breakers" during a medical conference to develop collegial relations?) Nevertheless, the participants then used the same activity in their own schools.

We will not succeed in teacher development or in the improvement of schools until we accept adult status and engage in appropriate professional tasks. Principals must stop treating teachers as children and as technicians to be trained; instead collegial judgment and expertise must be cultivated through opportunities to reflect together. The use of action teams provide an interesting way to expand professional study.

ACTION TEAMS

The Glendale Unified School District in California instituted a variation of the cross-role teams to implement their six strategic planning goals. With teachers directing the teams and accounting for at least 50 percent of the membership, teams of teachers, student teachers, classified personnel, and parents serve together to develop implementation strategies for components of the school mission.

With fifteen minutes added on four days per week, the school day begins one hour later on the fifth day. The action teams meet on Wednesdays at 8:00 A.M. and school begins at 9:30 A.M. (Teachers are required by state law to arrive thirty minutes before the beginning of school.) Using school time for the meetings rather than extending teachers' hours for school-related business improved teacher morale at a time when their salaries had not been increased substantially.

An example of an action team problem was the school goal to use technology across the curriculum on a daily basis. An action team gathered information by looking at available research, interviewing experts, and studying school and classroom resources. The team depended on the teachers to answer such questions as "What do we need to carry out a plan for . . ." and "How will the plan affect curriculum and instruction?" The teachers needed to consider their own knowledge and expertise. Staff development would need to be a component of the action plan.

The action teams in Glendale provide an example of teacher involvement in significant decision making that in past years was considered the domain of administrators. The inclusion of parents and staff in the structure of the teams guarantees that all affected by a change are involved in the process and will be committed to the plan. The ultimate plan will be *owned* by all the groups. The inclusion of all the "power" groups ensures that consideration is given to negative aspects, limited resources, and recognition of realities.

PEER COACHING

Joyce and Showers (1982) introduced the concept of the coaching of teaching by drawing parallels between it and athletic coaching. The process was introduced as a means to help teachers develop executive control in the use of teaching models. "Like athletes, teachers will put newly learned skills to use—if they are coached (p. 5)." Joyce and Showers recognized how difficult it is for teachers to learn a new pedagogical model in one environment and then transfer the model to another environment using their own content with a specific group of learners.

The coaching process currently advocated by Joyce, Weil, and Showers (1992) includes three steps:

1. Companionship.

2. Analysis of application.

3. Adaptation to the students.

The early work by Joyce and Showers suggested that teams of teachers and/or others, such as administrators, should engage in coaching.

Research at the University of Southern California (USC) in the Collegial Preparation Program indicates that coaching should be performed by a "peer." It is important that the individual to be coached feels comfortable during the process, and it is equally important that the peers exchange roles. After observing the application of coaching by partner student teachers, my colleagues and I advocate that the individuals who have an established relationship follow a prescribed procedure:

a. The *individual to be coached* identifies the focus of the observation.

b. The tools for the observation are selected by the coach, if they are needed, and *the coach attends to the requested area of concern.*

c. Both individuals engage in the analysis of the data, using the observation notes and/or observation instruments; *feedback is given only on the requested area of concern.* If the individual requesting the coaching asks about other events, then the coach may volunteer additional insight.

The actual process may occur as follows:

Jerry and Jean agree to coach each other. Jerry intends to use the concept attainment model of teaching to introduce the concept of life cycle to his fourth graders. In the past when he has used the model he has had the feeling that he "cuts off" the students' opportunity to hypothesize too soon. He asks Jean to check him out on this.

Jean observes the lesson and tells Jerry that he needs to "wait longer" between students' responses in order to elicit additional ideas. She suggests, in addition, that Jerry look at different students, "perhaps gesture to them" to encourage more discussion. "You might even wait at the board with your chalk poised, to clue them that additional ideas are okay." "Also, it may be that your positive exemplars were too difficult for some of the students."

Then Jerry asked Jean, "Is there anything else you noticed as you observed?" Jean reconsidered her notes and responded: "the students closest to the chalkboard tended to respond, is this typical? Why would that be?"

One can assume that the closing dialogue took the teachers to another round of coaching and discussion. Perhaps they would look again at the exemplars used in the lesson, and they might consider using a seating-chart observation form to record who responds during lessons in order to determine the cause.

The USC research emphasizes that the coach is performing a collegial service for a peer. That service is performed between and among individuals who have an established collegial relationship. The service is linked to professional ethics; as such, the consultation is restricted to the requested service.

Teachers and principals both need to learn instructional leadership roles in order to engage in peer coaching and facilitate instructional improvement and professional growth. It should not be assumed that because an individual is an administrator these skills are already in the leader's repertoire.

Another form of peer coaching exists outside the classroom. Principals need to coach their peers—other principals. The need for this type of coaching relates to a variety of leadership tasks. Principals may need help working with community groups, dealing with group behavior in conflict situations, preparing for faculty meetings, delegating decision-making responsibilities, working with staff members, and supervising curriculum and instruction.

Principal-to-principal peer coaching may include visiting each other's school site to "shadow" work behavior, sitting in on conferences, helping to plan for group discussion, observing ways to develop group consensus, recognizing when and how to delegate responsibility for decision making, changing leadership style from "push-pull" to collaborative-facilitative, and distinguishing between dysfunctional and responsible task roles.

BROADENING STAFF DEVELOPMENT

In the past staff development was used as a vehicle to deliver training to teachers. Typically it was planned by administrators or central office supervisors to communicate new programs, hand out district plans, and train teachers to use specific materials. The concept of staff development changes when you contemplate new professional roles and leadership responsibilities for teachers and principals.

For example, in California new curriculum frameworks are produced every seven years. During the planning stages, committees of teachers, academic disciplinarians, and specialists work together to conceive the new framework. Once produced, implementation becomes the responsibility of the State Department of Education and the school districts. In an environment where teachers are considered responsible decision makers, both teachers and principals and subject-field specialists will sit down together to study the framework to decide:

■ Who needs to learn what? What explicit goals, themes, and content in the new framework will affect what students are to learn? (To what extent is this different from what has been taught in the past?)

■ What do we (teachers) need to learn in order to implement the new framework? (To what extent is this different from what we have taught in the past?)

■ Who else needs to learn what? Do principals, mentors, consultants, and others need to learn what is new in order to assist and support the process of implementation?

■ Are there support services and resources affected by the new framework?

Once these questions have been considered by teachers, principals, and others, then decisions need to be made about how learning will be accomplished. Suppose teachers decide they need conceptual learning and pedagogic assistance to teach in new ways. They might decide to form a professional study group to learn about the new concepts required to implement the framework. They may want to use the process discussed by Lewison in Chapter 4, in which they ask an outside consultant to help them locate appropriate professional reading materials for study.

To accomplish learning pedagogic alternatives they may decide to ask one of their peers to act as the staff development leader to assist them with new teaching models. To locate and decide on new instructional materials, they may want to form districtwide committees.

As teachers assume more responsibility for their own professional growth, the roles of principals and district-level administrators and supervisors change. At the district level, leaders assume new assistance and facilitation roles. Instead of monitoring and evaluating compliance, leaders will study school needs and provide support services. Both principals and district-level leaders will focus on how to improve the likelihood of successful change efforts. Facilitation may take the form of creatively designing new resources, arranging time, accommodating space needs, and providing school-site control over resources.

In addition, teachers and principals may need to consider how to involve the community in the change process. They will need to decide what the community knows about—and what the community needs to know—in order to appreciate the new curriculum and instructional changes. How the community will learn about and be engaged in the process will be another area of decision making.

Perhaps the most important point concerning new professional roles and the broadening of staff development is that unless teachers and principals work together to create new professional environments, bureaucratic impediments will continue and reform efforts will fail. Teachers, counselors, consultants, and mentors all need to be involved in constructing new forms of education, leadership, and professionalism.

CHANGING ROLES AND RELATIONSHIPS

Trapped by the roles we enact, we become prisoners of tradition. For example:

■ Highly skilled teachers are recognized by all the students of a school. When a "recognized" teacher enters the classroom of a not-so-skilled beginning teacher, the students become quiet and "behaved."

■ Though school faculties have faculty chairs, most meetings do not begin until the principal is present.

■ Principals cite how difficult it is to get teachers to come to a decision; at decision time, the group awaits the principal's word.

■ The tone of a school reflects the leadership of the principal. New teachers are "taught" to adhere to the rules by experienced teachers who enact the roles set by the environment of the school.

These examples are similar to the old democratic leadership studies of Lewin, Lippitt, and White (1939), who found that only in democratic environments was work sustained when the teacher left the classroom. In part, because of habit (tradition) and "rules" we tend to function in accustomed ways. Building a team approach whereby roles overlap and decisions are made collaboratively is difficult because the culture of the school has not traditionally been democratic.

Flat Schools and the Assumption of Competence

To change the hierarchical pattern prevalent in most schools, one must change underlying assumptions about competence. If one assumes that both teachers and principals are *competent* to perform their jobs then *trust* and *collaborative work patterns* can be developed.

The diverse population of the modern school coupled with the problems of a global society can no longer be managed by a single person. It is imperative that the school become a learning community and that decisions be made by teams of concerned professionals sharing a common purpose. Writing about the governance of organizations, Handy (1993) states that "imposed authority no longer works." Instead, organizations must develop a theory of learning. For some years now the school as a learning community has been recognized as essential to student achievement.

Handy describes learning in organizations as a wheel of learning in which participants are prompted to pose questions, generate ideas, test their ideas, and then reflect on the outcomes. The process is similar in effective schools. The "good" school of the future will be a place where powerful teaching and learning go hand in hand.

Everyone in the school is a learner. As a consequence, relationships change. Learners depend on each other to raise questions and to respond in divergent ways. Because authority is shared and competence is assumed, any member of the community can take the initiative in trying out ideas.

With initiative comes risk taking and the responsibility to communicate with other members of the learning community. Together the learning community shares problems and insights about what works. The learning community meets together on a regular basis to share knowledge.

Who is the learning community? The school may be structured into many learning communities as well as a community of the whole. Schlechty (1993) sees teachers as leaders and the principal as a leader of leaders. Handy (1993) says the modern organization is "flat" because the pyramid has collapsed. He sees the flat organization as more responsive, efficient, and cost effective. Restructured schools may be viewed similarly, requiring less supervision and demonstrating more leadership within the learning community.

The Principal's Role

For teachers' roles to change, there must be administrative support; therefore, the role of the principal must change first. To be a leader of leaders, principals will need to reject the status quo and begin to redirect their energies in the following ways:

■ Work collaboratively with teachers, staff, and parents to define success so that everyone shares a common vision.

■ Coordinate the work tasks and responsibilities of teachers, staff, and parents. Expand the involvement of all participants and maintain good communication channels.

■ Foster teamwork skills and demonstrate linkages among people, tasks, and problems. For example, help specialist teachers and regular teachers work together to improve the learning for children with special needs.

■ Encourage teachers to "take charge" of as much as they reasonably can. Eliminate the boundaries inherent in teachers' work so they can exert power in the workplace. For example, teachers can participate in budget decisions affecting the school, in the hiring of curriculum specialists, and in consulting with other specialists.

■ Encourage initiative by teachers and staff so that individuals assume responsibility.

■ Provide time and space for teachers to meet together and perform new collaborative responsibilities by eliminating nonessential meetings. If communication can be handled by memoranda, use them. Enable teachers and staff to use work time more efficiently for small group meetings.

■ Encourage the sharing of knowledge, thereby beginning a self-perpetuating process. Provide time and opportunity for the sharing of expertise.

■ Encourage postmortem examination of work accomplished and work *not yet* accomplished so that reflection yields learning.

■ Develop partnerships with other social agencies; help to integrate the work of other professionals to ensure support for children and their families.

■ Dream about what ought to be; think divergently. Knowing "what is" is not as significant as considering new horizons. Demonstrate that you value divergent thinking.

Remember that none of the above is possible in a hierarchical environment. Relationships and roles only change through trust, respect, and common purpose.

The Teacher's Role

New expectations for teachers' participation in restructured schools can be bewildering and overwhelming. Not only must teachers be outstanding educators in the classroom, but they are now expected to perform leadership roles in helping to run the school enterprise, help to coordinate community services, and work interdependently with other teachers, administrators, and parents. The array of role expectations and tasks include the following:

■ Work collaboratively with administrators, staff, and parents to define a vision of school success.

■ Help to create a professional culture in the school by accepting responsibility to work (and interact) in new ways.

■ Develop collegial relationships, share expertise, and serve as a consultant for colleagues.

■ Develop group process skills for participating in groups and leading teams of educators.

■ Help to develop action plans for accomplishing school goals.

■ Create new curriculum and instructional approaches utilizing interdisciplinary connections.

■ Lead staff development classes that help colleagues expand teaching repertoires.

■ Peer-coach colleagues; mentor beginning teachers. Thoughtfully dialogue with colleagues about curriculum and instructional approaches.

■ Think divergently and reflectively; be willing to speak out concerning organizational and management structures in the school and in the classroom.

■ Help colleagues and students be autonomous learners and workers.

■ Initiate alternative practices. Raise questions about "what has always been"; experiment; engage in research. Be bold in thinking and actions and accept the challenge of leadership roles.

There are no neat and explicit words to define the leadership roles teachers must enact to create learning communities and professional environments. Each setting is unique and depends on people, place, and circumstance.

NEW TEACHER PREPARATION: DEVELOPING PROFESSIONALISM

New teacher preparation must begin with the ideas, skills, and knowledge that future teachers are expected to need in professional practice. Traditionally, however, this has not happened. Historically, after fulfilling liberal arts requirements, the preservice teacher was placed with a master teacher for apprenticeship training. The clinical experience of the novice in a conservative and traditional environment served to strengthen and reinforce existing practices. When university programs conflict with traditional apprenticeship training, the novice experiences conflict and is overwhelmed by the need to survive in both the university and school environments. The consequence of this is that most novice teachers mollify the university teacher educator(s) and attempt to model the master teacher. The cloning of the master teacher reinforces preexisting practices.

Katz and Raths (1992) very aptly identified the dilemmas confronting teacher educators in the preparation of teachers. From my perspective the major dilemma affecting preparation in California institutions (and across the United States) has been whether to prepare new teachers to adapt to existing conditions in schools and prepare those new teachers for a policy-driven state evaluation system that validates only one instructional model (direct instruction) *or* develop a constructivist professional program that encompasses the knowledge teachers need, forces commitment to a repertoire of teaching strategies, is sensitive to children with diverse cultures and needs, and promotes collegial relationships.

Institutions choosing to adapt are often characterized by the use of part-time instructors from the public schools to teach the methods class and supervise the student teachers. In contrast, when program goals drive the program, it is more likely that a coherent pattern of instruction by university and clinical faculty will characterize the preparation program.

To address the decisions affecting professional preparation of new teachers, I will use examples from the program I direct. These decisions include how to:

Connect methods instruction and subject-matter knowledge with clinical practice in schools.

Provide opportunity for preservice teachers to gain understanding of the teacher's professional role in a flat organization.

Provide opportunity to develop collegial relations with peers.

Provide opportunity to work collaboratively with experienced teachers.

Reshaping the Apprenticeship Experience

If new conditions for professional practice are to come about, novice teachers must be caringly placed in appropriate work environments that yield opportunities for learning and practicing teaching tasks and forming professional relationships. Thoughtful, reflective professionals cannot be developed by chance, or by placing student teachers in the rigid, traditional environments that need to be transformed.[1] Teacher educators must seek school environments that "fit" their program aims and philosophy. For example, if collaborative behaviors, a repertoire of teaching strategies, flexibility, and decision making are program goals, the student teaching experience must support and provide opportunity to achieve these goals.

Choosing the place for professional practice requires significant decision making, including:

■ Selecting an appropriate school site for the clinical experience.

■ Selecting experienced teachers to supervise the student teachers.

■ Orienting school-site and university-based educators to goals and resources that *each* contribute to the student teaching experience—this includes explaining the professional education program.

■ Provision for experienced-teacher and university faculty development and student teacher involvement.

■ Clarifying how the program will be monitored.

Each of these points will be briefly described:

1. Select an appropriate school environment in which the achievement of program goals is feasible. The school setting should provide

---

[1] I am well aware that most school environments need to be transformed; however, student teacher(s) must be placed with master teachers who share the institution's philosophic and pedagogic goals.

opportunities for student teachers to observe a variety of programs, teachers working in concert and thoughtfully considering teaching and learning problems, and an administrator who welcomes the opportunity to interact with novice teachers.

The apprenticeship environment at a selected school site should include at least three to four experienced teachers who work together as a collegial team. The school itself must provide a social setting in which professional values prevail and the student teachers will be accepted as faculty members. The administrator conveys caring, sensitivity, and commitment and works collaboratively with teachers, staff, and parents to achieve community-defined goals.

2. Select experienced teachers who either model the behaviors consonant with the university teacher education program or who are considered "flexible" in their teaching style so that student teachers can practice what they are learning. Verify that the experienced teacher is professionally oriented (wants to grow professionally by learning and experimenting with new methodology, studies new research, and has developed professional relations with peers). Verify that the room environment arranged by the teacher and the teacher's classroom management skills are appropriate for new teachers to experience. The master teacher should *never* be selected without a previsit to validate the aforementioned and to confirm the teacher's interest in preservice education. University-based educators should not rely on school district placement of student teachers; teacher education and the student teachers are the university's responsibility (see following discussion).

3. An orientation meeting should be planned for the individuals who will be involved at the school site: the experienced (master) teachers, the school administrator, and the university coordinator. At the orientation meeting university personnel should learn about the resources and programs at the school site and about the overall mission of the school. School-site educators should learn about the goals of the teacher education program, specific methodology to be taught to student teachers, the sequence of the methodology, university expectations, and how linkage and communication will be maintained throughout the student teaching period.

An underlying concept often forgotten during the student teaching period is that school-site educators are responsible for the education and well-being of the children who attend the school; the university is responsible for the education and well-being of the student teachers. Sometimes these responsibilities tend to be forgotten when (a) student teachers are not allowed to practice what they need to learn to be successful from the university's perspective and (b) when student teachers are unsuccessful in student teaching yet permitted to continue miseducating children.

4. At the orientation meeting of all the involved parties it is important to clarify not only what each expects of the other but how the programs contribute to each other. For example, how will the two institutions share knowledge? What are the teachers' interests in professional and research studies, and how can the university contribute? It may be very significant to plan future meetings to demonstrate methodologies taught to the student teachers in which the experienced teachers may lack knowledge or competence (for example, models of teaching).

New programs and resources in use at the school site may need to be shared with the university educators. For example, suppose the master teachers engage in a televised science program with their students. Learning to use the science kits in conjunction with the program and working collaboratively with a distance education teacher requires skills not normally taught in preparation programs.

Scholarly coupling through research activities by school-site and university educators to gain insight on school problems is a real benefit of the association. Teacher participation in the development of case study problems for student teachers will help to reinforce the connections between theory and practice.

Also, it is important to determine what structures exist for involving the student teachers at the school site. For example, the inclusion of student teachers in action teams to develop plans and make decisions concerning school goals is a significant learning activity for student teachers. In addition, are there staff development programs at the school site or in the school district that student teachers may attend?

Similarly, are there university programs that experienced teachers may attend without cost? If there are intellectual discussions at the university by teacher educators (and I assume there must be) about reforming schools and teaching, are experienced teachers and mentors encouraged to join in the conversation?

5. From time to time, school-site educators may need to inform the university educators about what the student teachers may be missing in subject-field knowledge, pedagogy, and understandings of cultural diversity. When novice teachers confront the pluralism of the classroom, do they understand our expanding community? The experienced teachers at the school site should be relied on to help fill this void.

How often will student teachers be observed by university personnel? What procedures exist to help student teachers who have problems? How will the master teachers "know" what is being taught in the methods class so they can reinforce and validate the practice? How does each communicate with the other on a consistent basis and for emergencies?

The Methods Class: What Should New Teachers Learn?

There has always been a debate about whether the methods class should be taught during the semester before student teaching or in conjunction with student teaching. I believe it is most productive when it is taught during the same time period. At USC we teach the methods class at the beginning of the week, and the student teachers practice what they have been taught the other four days.

The methods class for elementary and secondary preservice teachers communicates three structures of knowledge:

Concepts for Teaching   Concepts for teaching encompass the melding of subject-matter knowledge into appropriate concepts for teaching, understanding curriculum, how to link conceptual knowledge across subject fields, decision making about breadth versus depth, sequence, continuity, and state and district requirements. Clear content goals need to be articulated to the student teachers.

Pedagogical Knowledge   The new teacher must learn about instructional processes and the concept of consonance—matching pedagogical choices to instructional goals. The matching process requires that teachers learn specific teaching models (rejecting the one-best-model approach) to accomplish the range of teaching and learning options.[2] The teacher needs to use knowledge about content and instructional strategies to teach the content. Instructional process choices need to integrate instruction in the subject areas. Pedagogical decisions must include understanding how to help children with cultural and language differences.

Professional Knowledge   It is in the professional arena that many programs fail the new teacher. Five areas of professional knowledge are essential for teacher-leaders:

1. Cultural understandings related to the specific community and the community at-large, including understanding cultural differences, identity issues, and their effect on school learning.

---

[2]At USC we teach preservice teachers four teaching models: concept attainment, advance organizer, group investigation, and direct instruction.

2. Understandings about what students know—and don't know—help the teacher adapt instruction to students' needs, interests, and abilities.

3. Cultivation of relationships among teachers and administrators and exchange of professional feedback among peers: these endeavors must be practiced.

4. School and organizational knowledge: understanding the flat organization and understanding other relevant social institutions (how can a teacher help "broker" care for their clients?).

5. Relationships with parents and the public at large (how can teachers improve their public image?).

These areas of knowledge are extremely significant in the professional development of teachers. The choice of the instructor who will teach these structures to new teachers is critical, yet too often it is considered lightly. In many schools of education the social and psychological dimensions of teaching are taught by "real" professors, and the methods class is sloughed off as insignificant.

Linking Theory and Practice

Student teaching initiates the intern period during which the novice should practice what is taught in the methods class, in a safe environment, with mutual support from university- and school-site educators. A safe environment is defined as a classroom that is distinctive because the students and teacher work purposefully and constructively together, recognizing the significance of learning. Experiences are planned to enable all students to be participating members of the learning community. The master teacher recognizes his or her role as guide and coach for the student teachers.

The university coordinator recognizes the importance of a coherent program of study and practice for new teachers (Skyes, Judge, and Devaney, 1992). Concepts and theories taught in the methods class are reinforced in practice under the guidance of the master teacher and the university coordinator. The university coordinator must help to interpret not only program purposes, values, and theories for the master teachers but the sequence and pacing of the practice experience.

Continuity and integration of experiences are achieved through communication of the methods professor, coordinator, and master teacher. Each must know what is valued, what should be elaborated upon, and what needs to be reinforced. To achieve coherence, continuity, and integration of experiences, the methods instructor and coordinators must meet and share observations frequently. In the program I direct, this occurs twice monthly, and coordinators frequently sit in on the methods class. To monitor practice, student teachers should be visited weekly by a university coordinator, and the master teacher and coordinator should communicate during each visit. The coordinator serves as the eyes and ears of the methods instructor responsible for communicating how the students' practice is progressing.[3]

Collegial preparation is the theme of the program I direct. By pairing student teachers for practice, the professional agenda can be emphasized. Peer coaching begins from "day one." The feedback and reflection of the partner student teachers are evaluated by the coordinators and master teacher. The partners observe each other, write feedback notes, and discuss lessons together. Professional conversation is practiced during these feedback/coaching sessions. The partner student teachers may plan together; they are required to support, assist, share, reflect, and analyze each other's performance. (See Table 1.1, Chapter 1, for collegial development stages.)

It is expected that the master teacher will lead the team of student teachers and facilitate the study of teaching through guidance and collaborative arrangements. Sometimes the master teacher will sit with the non-teaching partner to focus observation and share insights. Sometimes the master teacher will need to demonstrate how subject-matter knowledge can be managed through pedagogical metamorphosis. Throughout the experience the master teacher must exhibit sensitivity to the needs of beginning teachers for the practice of technical skills, yet not compromise the education of the children.

The role and responsibilities of the master teacher are vastly expanded in the collegial preparation program. Still serving as a model and observer, the master teacher also must coach, facilitate thinking, focus, support, critique, confer, and assess. Conferences are usually held with both student teachers together. Notes for the conference may be based on the observations of the partners as well as the master teacher.

To establish a cohort group, student teachers at a school site are brought together to talk about their experiences and share reflections and concerns. Coordinators in our program do this weekly in a seminar that addresses the needs of the particular group of student teachers assigned to the school. This seminar is in addition to the methods class. It is designed to focus not only on the needs of the student teacher but on the social and cultural needs of the community of learners at the

---

[3]At some institutions the methods instructor and the coordinator are one and the same. It is my view that this puts the student in double jeopardy when one individual assesses the student's readiness for credentialing.

school. Master teachers are frequently invited to join these sessions to share expertise and contribute clinical problems for study and reflection.

Assessing Student Teacher Competence

The connecting of pedagogy and subject-matter knowledge is assessed through daily lesson plans, long-term planning of curriculum, actual teaching, the room environment, and the products of the children. The master teacher, university coordinator, and the methods instructor are able to assess this program objective.

Understanding of the teacher's professional role in a flat organization is assessed through participation in school-site activities, such as the action team, participation at seminars, and school-based problem solving. The master teacher and university coordinator assess this dimension.

Collegial relations are assessed by the individual student teacher (self), partner, coordinator, and master teacher. Evidence includes feedback notes, analysis of lessons, team conferences, co-teaching and planning, and children's reactions.

Collaboration with experienced teachers depends on the student teacher's ability to work as a team member with both the master teacher and the partner. Student teacher involvement in site-based activities also is used to assess this dimension.

Through the study of student teachers at practice and analysis of coordinators' feedback notes, it is possible to plot a learning-to-teach cycle and juxtapose it with the feedback needed by the novice teacher. The first column in Table 8.1 represents practice and the second, feedback.

Building new professional roles and responsibilities must begin in preservice education. The appetite must be whetted. Some examples of how this can occur follow.

Collegial Consultant   Instead of isolating student teachers from each other, encourage them to share the planning process using their own knowledge of subject matter and ideas for motivation. Encourage every elementary candidate to become an expert in one of the disciplines. Encourage elementary school and secondary school teacher candidates to work together to share subject-matter expertise.

Staff Development Leader   Culminate the student teaching period with a teacher conference put on by the new teachers for graduate and experienced teachers. Encourage the novice teachers to lead some sessions. As staff development leader, encourage graduates to share children's products and the lessons that produced them.

TABLE 8.1   Learning-to-Teach and Feedback Cycle

Attention to self (How do I look?)	Personal feedback
Awareness of total class	Classroom management
Attention to students' needs and abilities	Classroom management and instructional feedback
Attention to motivation and other lesson components	Coherence, sequence, logic of instruction
Attention to significance of content and match of instructional models	Subject-field expertise, technical knowledge
Attention to consonance of instructional goals and teaching model; self-talk	Knowledge base, reflection, professional values

Reflective Practitioner   Reflection can be encouraged by asking teachers to select the lesson they are most proud of and talk about how else they might have taught it. How many alternatives did they consider and how many can they design? Why was their choice sensitive to children's needs and backgrounds? How did the lesson reflect their own experiences and expertise?

Researcher   To encourage research as a professional goal novice teachers can be asked to select a theory taught in the methods class to test in the classroom. Under what circumstances does it work? fail? How can practice inform the teacher's knowledge base? How does theory need to be transformed for practice?

Sustaining the Beginning Teacher

During the first two years of practice the beginning teacher needs help to sustain what was learned during the student teaching period. Making context-driven decisions concerning room standards, instructional strategies, choice of content, resources, time, and professional relationships, the beginning teacher is often overwhelmed. The reflective conversation valued and nurtured during student teaching may be lost during the development years if the new teacher is forced to go it alone. I believe that new teachers can be helped through the following means:

1. Provide opportunity for *tacit learning*. New teachers do not want to ask about everything they need to know. Give them opportunity to engage in conversation and work with experienced teachers as members of a team so they will gain situation-specific information.

2. Provide opportunity for new teachers to observe and coach each other. Let them begin to establish a collegial relationship with other new teachers. Our research on collegiality has pointed out that new teachers establish collegial relations with peers, not individuals who are much more experienced than they perceive themselves to be.

3. Provide opportunity for the new teacher to engage in small talk with community members so that they do not fear parent-teacher conferences.

4. Furnish the new teacher with sample letters to be used as examples when they need to write notes to parents. Should these notes need to be translated, provide this service in the office.

5. If their university provides a telecommunications network to assist new teachers, see that the teacher is connected and has opportunity to participate.

6. Contact the university teacher-education program director if the teacher needs classroom management and instructional help. It is the responsibility of teacher-education institutions to assist their graduates and help to facilitate a successful transition to professional life.

In the collegial preparation program, we have found that colleague partners from the student-teaching experience are often able to help each other through a difficult transition time. (Many of our graduates teach in year-round schools. As a consequence colleague partners may be teaching during different calendar schedules and/or for different school districts. Thus they have time available to visit their colleagues and analyze what is happening.)

7. Mentor programs can be of great help to the novice teacher, if the assistance is provided in a nonevaluative way. If novice teachers feel that their needs are reported to the administrator, they are less likely to be receptive of assistance proffered by a mentor teacher.

Since mentor teachers have rarely been responsible for adult learning, they too need preparation and support. Both the university and the school district need to develop programs jointly for mentor teachers to help them learn about teaching adults and combining theory and practice.

To help a struggling teacher with a problem, it is important to (a) understand his or her perception of it, (b) observe its incidence and dimension, and (c) provide very specific feedback. It is a good idea to follow the peer-coaching guidelines suggested in this chapter.

For the nonstruggling beginning teacher, it is just as important to provide support in various forms: time to reflect, opportunity to share ideas and dialogue with others, and encouragement to practice what has been learned in teacher education—even if that means upsetting their more traditional school-site associates. The novice teacher needs to be fortified with courage to "teach against the grain" (Sykes, Judge, and Devaney, 1992).

8. Enable novice teachers to assume leadership positions by teaming them with experienced teachers who are reform-minded. Encourage theory-practice reflective conversations applied to teaching and school problems.

9. Novice teachers have been educated in the language of teaching; many experienced teachers are not aware of its specificity. Seek ways to involve new teachers in sharing their own skills and expertise. For example, some highly skilled novice teachers can demonstrate teaching models.

CONCLUSION: TOMORROW'S PROFESSIONAL LEADERS

What is it that we expect of leaders in the teaching profession? Several powerful concepts come to mind: democratization and the development of a professional culture in the schools, thoughtfulness, problem solving versus problem hiding, autonomy, dignity, respectfulness, and responsibility. These are easy to identify but hard to achieve in the workplace.

Problem solving and risk taking do not occur in a culture in which group members claim, "I can't do it; *they* won't let me." In recent years researchers have been studying the social nature of learning—how students grow through the sharing of experience and knowledge and how this can lead to active processing of knowledge and to awareness and understanding through dialogue, shared problem solving, and group projects. What we are learning to do in classrooms with children should help us develop thoughtful communities of teachers who collaborate with each other in support of problem solving and research.

We need to value the study of teaching and learning environments. In many schools punitive and divisive patterns of discipline, reminiscent of early American schooling, prevail, influencing students' motivation and school success. I believe the reenforcement of these patterns also affects teachers and administrators' leadership roles. When students are not respected, neither are teachers and administrators.

To improve schools, we need to change their organization. We must look at teachers' responsibilities, the rules that govern the structure of schools and the ways that people behave in them, and the values we sustain, champion, or attack. When teachers recognize their own leadership potential, administrators can be treated as leaders of leaders. Teaching professionalism demands rational, purposeful, and visionary behaviors. These are the goals for which we must strive.

> **Recap Notes: Building Professional Roles**
>
> • Teaching is complex, and learning to teach is a developmental process.
>
> • Preparation programs for teachers are responsible for educating and assessing the competence of the new teacher prior to licensure.
>
> • Schools of education help to prepare teachers for professionalism and leadership roles through rigorous professional course work that (1) develops understanding of curriculum content, (2) builds sensitivity to culture and learner development, and (3) teaches a variety of instructional approaches based on goals and contexts. Teachers need to be educated to be professionals, not trained as technicians.
>
> • Extended practice, opportunity to develop and share expertise, and reflection with peers builds efficacy, responsibility, and commitment into the teaching profession.
>
> • Meaningful professional decision making occurs in collaborative work environments to which all individuals contribute.

REFERENCES

Handy, C. 1993. Managing the dream: The learning organization. *Benchmark* 10(1): 13–16. Gardena, Calif.: Xerox Corporation.

Joyce, B., and Showers, B. 1982. The coaching of teaching. *Educational Leadership* 40(1): 4–10.

Joyce, B., Weil, M., and Showers, B. 1992. *Models of Teaching.* 4th ed. Boston: Allyn and Bacon.

Katz, L., and Raths, J. 1992. Six dilemmas in teacher education. *Journal of Teacher Education* 43(5): 376–85.

Lanich, J. 1993. Impact and effectiveness issues related to mathematics distance education for parents, children, and teachers. Unpublished dissertation, University of Southern California, Los Angeles.

Lewin, K., Lippitt, R., and White, R. 1939. Patterns of aggressive behavior in experimentally created "social climates." *Journal of Social Psychology* 10: 271–99.

Schlechty, P. 1993. On restructuring roles and relationships: A conversation with Phil Schlechty. *Educational Leadership* 51(2): 8–11.

Shulman, L. 1990. Aristotle had it right: On knowledge and pedagogy. East Lansing, Mich.: The Holmes Group.

Sykes, G., Judge, H., and Devaney, K. 1992. The needs of children and the education of educators: A background paper for *Tomorrow's Schools of Education.* East Lansing, Mich.: Holmes Group.

Appendix

T his text is for, about, and by teacher-leaders. "Say Yes to Teacher Innovation and Leadership" is about a secondary ESL teacher who dares to be unusual and inspires other teachers to innovate. The author of the piece is another teacher-leader. Not only does she teach five periods a day from 7:30 A.M. to 12:30 P.M., but in the afternoons she visits other teachers and conducts workshops in several school districts to encourage the teaching of writing and networking among teachers.

This case study was excerpted from a longer version of the study. As you read it, consider the following questions:

- What do you think of the ESL teacher's learning activities?

- In what ways do these two teachers (Sabrina and Jane) demonstrate leadership and professionalism?

SAY YES TO TEACHER INNOVATION AND LEADERSHIP: A CASE STUDY OF A SUCCESSFUL ESL TEACHER-LEADER

JANE S. HANCOCK, Hoover High School, Glendale, CA.

INTRODUCTION: THE PROBLEM

I am a product of two years of Latin and six years of Spanish, two in high school and four in college. I never learned to speak either language. Not speaking Latin has not hindered me in any way. I benefited greatly from taking the language because so many words from other languages come from Latin and because English grammar is Latin based. I resent that I was not taught to speak Spanish in my classes. I learned the grammar and forgot most of it. I have never forgotten *"Maria tiene un lapiz,"* a sentence I have never had to use. I have always thought that there was a better way to learn a language.

In southern California we have students coming to our schools from all over the world, and they are all taking a foreign language—English. How is that language being taught? As far as I can tell as I visit schools, conduct workshops, and talk to teachers, it is being taught the same way I was taught Spanish—through an intensive study of grammar. Where is the conversation? Where are the stories, the legends, the fairy tales? Where is the dialogue with the teacher, both written and oral?

What does it take to move from ESL 1 to ESL 2? Students have to pass a test—a grammar test, a Scantron-corrected grammar test. Where is the authentic assessment? How about a conversation with the student, in English, about his portfolio? There has to be a better way.

AN ALTERNATIVE

Sabrina Lee has the right idea. I met her almost two years ago when we became quad-mates at Hoover High School in Glendale, California. She teaches ESL to language minority students. Just from talking with her I felt she had an approach to language development that was educationally sound, that she had high expectations for her students, and that she was willing to try new strategies to achieve her goals.

Sabrina has her ESL 1 students write on the first day of school. She came into my classroom and showed me their work. Some was in their original language; some was a mixture of English; some included creative spelling; most were short pieces, but it was writing. Sabrina has a poster of Betty Grable, a pin-up poster from World War II. Probably not even English-speaking students could have named her, but the students in Sabrina's class described her and named her, whatever they wanted. They noted her long legs, her blonde hair piled high on her head, her red lips. They wrote.

Sabrina shares literature with her students, not the literature that was on Glendale's approved list for ESL but chapters from *The Joy Luck Club* by Amy Tan and portions of *House on Mango Street* by Sandra Cisneros. It seemed to me that this teacher was doing all the things I thought ought to be done and succeeding. She even was trying portfolio assessment.

I talked about Sabrina in a workshop I was conducting with other teachers. The workshop participants wanted to see the work that Sabrina's students do and asked to visit her classes. What follows is the observation of one of those class sessions.

THE OBSERVATION

The Level 1 class was making calendars. It sounds simple on the surface, but in doing so the students were finding out about other countries, were becoming familiar with U.S. holidays, were learning to work in groups and communicate with each other in English, were developing an awareness and acceptance of other cultures, were learning how their culture was different from and like other cultures.

The students had formed their own groups; however, each group had to be multicultural. Each student was to make a calendar page featuring his or her own country that related to a theme chosen by the group. Then each student had to pick another country represented by someone in another group and interview him or her in order to make a calendar page for that culture. Resource books were also available for student use.

What I saw was a rehearsal for talking to other students to find out about their countries. Sabrina modeled the language, emphasizing asking nicely and saying, "Thank you for helping me with my calendar." Then students volunteered to try it. When I left they were ready to work in their groups and go seek information on their own.

Later, I went back to see the finished products, which they proudly showed off. We talked about the calendar lessons that I had observed. "It felt great," said Sabrina. "They were really nice to each other." This is very important—that along with the learning of the language the students also became aware of other cultures and accepting of them.

On still another visit to the class I found the students involved in role playing the part of Antonio Sabato, the soap opera idol of *General Hospital.* As I joined the class they were taking turns reading aloud an article about Antonio, one of the question and answer pieces that appear in magazines. As they read, Sabrina explained vocabulary when they requested it—words such as *wisdom, admire, folks, pedestal.* Sabato is an Italian immigrant and was an ESL student himself at one time. As I watched and listened to the students talk about this Italian heartthrob who *admires* older women and puts them on a *pedestal,* I couldn't help but remember my Spanish class and Maria and her pencil.

On my third visit to the class I found Sabrina wearing a shirt with

Peace written on it in many languages. On the board was a Maya Angelou quote: "Life doesn't frighten me." The students were finishing individual letters to Antonio that Sabrina was going to mail. Then came a vocabulary lesson. Everyone copied down the words and their definitions as she explained them, sometimes using body language or pointing to pictures. The words were all from a series of two-minute segments of *General Hospital,* which she had taped and was going to show. There were words and idioms like *care for, dump* (a boyfriend or girlfriend), *loser* (he's a loser), *reservation* (for a table at a restaurant), *all out of* (food at the restaurant), *bummed* (not happy). The vocabulary lesson over, I could see the excitement mount as Sabrina walked to the television monitor.

The two-minute segment took place at a high school dance—a typical love triangle situation between Jagger (Antonio) and Karen and Jason. The conversation used the vocabulary words. The girl has to make up her mind between these two boys. Is one a *loser?* Which one does she really *care for?* Will she *dump* one of them?

I reverted back to my Spanish class. I don't think I was ever asked a thought question in all six years. After viewing the *General Hospital* segment Sabrina asked, "Would you really want someone to stay with you if she really doesn't love you?" Garnick answered, "I'd be so mad I'd have to hit someone." "That's scary," replied Sabrina—and they started talking about self-control.

INTERVIEWS WITH SABRINA LEE AND STUDENTS

Sabrina speaks four languages—English, Dutch, French, and German. None of these is spoken by the students in her classes. They come from eight different countries and speak Armenian, Russian, Spanish, Farsi, and Korean. I was curious how she communicated with them on the first day of school. She told me she uses many gestures, body language, objects, and pictures. She smiles and looks them in the eye. "I know what it's like not to fit in," she said. Although she was born in the United States, she spoke Dutch at home before she learned English.

The 33 students in her ESL 1 class have been in the United States from one month to just under a year. The majority were literate in their own languages before coming to the United States. However, almost one-fourth of the students were not literate in their own languages.

Students receive no high school credit for ESL 1 and 2. They must demonstrate Level 4 proficiency in order to graduate. There is an exit test for each level. Exit criteria include listening (understanding directions, asking and answering questions necessary for survival), reading readiness and speaking, vocabulary development, writing, and standard English grammar and usage. Sabrina does not teach grammar-based lessons. The grammar comes from the reading and writing. The students begin to write on the first day of class. She feels they can do it, and they do.

Sabrina's students answered my questions with much animation, and I understood them! Two of the students came from Armenia. When I asked them what Ms. Lee did to help them learn English, they practically answered in unison. "We write more—a lot." "We read and watch movies." "We read a lot." "We read library books and the books Ms. Lee gives us." "We write in our reading journals and in our commonplace books." (Commonplace books are similar to scrapbooks; the students use them to write about anything they want.)

"We do group work." "Ms. Lee mixes us up." "We learn other languages." "In this class we are all friends." "We watch movies on television and write about them." "We talk in English."

I asked Sabrina how she checks to make sure everyone is contributing to the oral conversations taking place in class or if that is important at this time. She told me about the silent time, a time when students would rather listen than speak but they soon work themselves out of it. Then when a new concept is taught, they might return to their silent period for a short time. Because Sabrina was like these students once, she understands the "silent" time and respects it. She feels it takes guts, bravery, to speak out in class in a foreign language before you are ready.

CONCLUSION

On April 26, 1994, Sabrina and I spent a complete day with sixteen teachers from four different schools in Glendale, and I think we made a difference. The general comments from the sixteen participants were they were going to try the new strategies and hoped we could meet again next year for support. Sparks (1993) says that change doesn't happen over night, that the teachers involved need lots of training and staff development over a period of time. In addition, teachers need:

1. An intellectual understanding of the new practices.

2. Support from administrators.

3. Time to experiment—free from immediate evaluation.

Perhaps sections of this case study could be reproduced for people who want to change, to see on paper a *connoisseur* at work. Sabrina chooses her own textbooks, instructional materials, and strategies for teaching. A look at the Course of Study for Glendale ESL classes shows *Modern American English, Textbook Three,* and *New Horizon Workbook* as the choices for Level 1 classes. *The Joy Luck Club* and *House on Mango Street* and two-minute segments of *General Hospital* sound much more interesting to me.

REFERENCE

Sparks, D. 1993. Thirteen tips for managing change in schools. *Education Digest,* 58(6):13.

ABOUT THE AUTHORS

Hillary S. Hertzog is Clinical Professor at the University of Southern California. She has had many years of experience as a classroom teacher in the Los Angeles Unified School District. Dr. Hertzog once served as the university liaison in a university-school professional development project. She has authored articles on the role of the supervising teacher working with preservice teachers.

Peter Hodges serves as a school principal in the Central Valley of California. For Dr. Hodges, who runs a year-round-education school in a multicultural and multilingual environment, the challenges of education in an era of diversity are daily realities. Dr. Hodges is also an education professor and consultant, working with teachers in the humanities curriculum and organizational development.

Johanna K. Lemlech is Professor of Education and Director of Student Teaching at the University of Southern California. She has written numerous articles but is best recognized as author of *Curriculum and Instructional Methods for the Elementary and Middle School,* third edition (1994), *Classroom Management,* second edition (1988), and *Handbook for Successful Urban Teaching* 1977).

Mitzi Lewison is the Language Arts Content Director for the GALAXY Classroom, a nationwide interactive telecommunications program for elementary school students and teachers. Dr. Lewison has held positions as a classroom teacher in the Montebello Unified School District in California, as a reading and language specialist, an assistant principal of instruction, and a district language arts consultant.

Laurie MacGillivray is an Assistant Professor of Literacy in the School of Education at the University of Southern California. She received her doctorate from the University of Houston in 1992. Currently, her research interests include teacher research, critical literacy, and reading and writing as social processes.

Scott M. Mandel is a middle-school teacher in the Los Angeles Unified School District. He has served as principal for a parochial school. He is a frequent (and popular) in-service class leader. Dr. Mandel's research interests include cooperative learning and the uses of qualitative research methodology for studying classroom processes.

Author Index

Abbott, J., 10
Acheson, K. A., 63
Anders, P. L., 79
Atwell, N., 121, 136, 138

Bacharach, S. B., 23, 38, 44
Barnes, D., 78
Barnes, V., 36
Bates, M., 69
Bishop, W., 78
Bolin, F. S., 78
Buddy, C., 127, 132, 133
Burke, C. L., 76, 79
Burton, F., 138

California State Department of Education, 66
Calkins, L., 95, 120
Canter, L., 55
Canter, M., 55
Carnegie Forum, 8, 141
Carter, K., 148
Center for Civic Education, 173
Clark, C., 76, 78
Clay, M., 66
Cohen, M. D., 65
Colbert, J. A., 162
Colton, A., 77, 78
Cook, P. E., 78, 79, 85
Cuban, L., 43
Cutler, B. R., 78, 79, 85

Darling-Hammond, L., 13, 44, 144, 145, 146, 150
Dawe, R., 30
Devaney, K., 214, 218
Dewey, J., 77, 78
Driekurs, R., 56

Edmonds, R. R., 63
Eisner, E., 12, 78, 82

Fenstermacher, G., 44
Feuer, D., 176
Fullan, M., 79, 159, 174

Gall, M. D., 63
Geber, B., 176
Gebhard, J. G., 78, 79
Gitlin, A., 178
Glickman, C., 72
Goldhammer, R., 63
Goodlad, J., 79
Goodwin, A. L., 13, 44
Goswami, D., 120, 123
Graves, D., 95, 120, 123, 125, 136
Griffin, G., 141, 166
Guyton, E., 156

Hackl, A., 35
Hall, G. E., 47
Handy, C., 206, 207
Hargreaves, A., 30

Henson, K., 162
Hertzog, H., 35, 151, 152
Holland, P. E., 177
Holly, P., 160
Holmes Group, 9, 141, 142, 143, 144
Hord, S. M., 47
Houston, H., 144
Howey, K. R., 11
Hubbard, R. S., 120
Huling-Austin, L., 47
Hunter, M., 63

Imel, S., 175

Johnson, C., 10
Joyce, B. R., 11, 164, 165, 174, 182, 201, 202
Judge, H., 214, 218
Jumpp, D., 130

Kaplan, S. N., 27, 83, 105, 151, 152
Katz, L., 209
Keirsey, D., 69
Knowles, M., 175, 176
Kottkamp, R. B., 78
Kowalski, T., 162
Kucer, S., 86
Kuhn, T. S., 104

Lanich, J., 197
Lanier, J., 143
Lemlech, J. K., 27, 35, 83, 105, 151, 152
Lester, N. B., 76, 77, 78, 79
Lieberman, A., 54, 63, 148, 151, 159, 166
Liston, D. P., 77, 78
Little, J., 143, 151
Lortie, D. C., 14
Lyon, S., 162
Lytle, S. L., 119, 129, 135, 136, 138

McIntyre, D. J., 156
McLaughlin, M. W., 22, 83, 105, 153
Macrorie, K., 123
March, J. G., 65
Martin, N., 120
Mayher, J. S., 76, 78
Miles, M. B., 79

Miller, L., 54, 63, 148, 151, 159, 160, 161, 166

National Commission on Excellence in Education, 141
Nelson, J., 56
Newmann, F., 77, 78, 153, 154, 156, 158

O'Keefe, P., 143
Olsen, J. P., 65
Onore, N. B., 76, 77, 78, 79
Oprandy, R., 78, 79

Page, D., 10
Pajak, E., 8
Paterson, B., 37
Patterson, J. L., 14, 150
Peterson, P. L., 76
Pinnell, G. S., 66
Power, B. M., 120
Price, K., 178
Purkey, S. C., 63

Raths, J., 209
Richardson, V., 79
Richert, A., 163
Rolheiser-Bennett, C. 174
Rosenholtz, S. J., 27
Ross, D.D., 78
Routman, R., 158
Russell, D., 63
Rutherford, W. L., 47

Sarason, S., 54, 62, 72
Schlecty, P., 206
Schon, D. A., 76, 143, 147
Schwartz, J., 160, 165
Shedd, J. B., 23, 38, 44
Short, K. G., 76, 79
Showers, B., 164, 165, 174, 201, 202
Shulman, J., 162, 163
Shulman, L., 196
Silverman, R., 162
Sirotnik, K., 145
Smith-Cochran, M., 119, 129, 135, 136, 138
Smith, F., 78

Smith, H., 160, 161
Smith, M. S., 63
Smyth, J., 76, 78
Sowers, S., 120
Sparks, D., 225
Sparks-Langer, G. M., 77, 78, 147
Spradley, J., 134
Stillman, P., 120, 123
Stoddart, T., 143
Strieb, L. Y., 130
Sykes, G., 214, 218

Valli, L., 141
Vygotsky, L., 79

Wasley, P. A., 7, 164, 165

Weaver, R., 162
Wehlage, G. G., 78, 79, 153, 154, 156, 158
Weick, K. E., 65
Weil, M., 202
Welty, W. M., 162
Wigginton, E., 161
Wiles, K., 43
Winitzky, N., 143

Yarger, S. J., 11
Yee, S. M., 22
Yinger, R. J., 78
Young, J. R., 78, 79, 85

Zeichner, K., 77, 78, 79

Subject Index

A Nation at Risk, 141
A Nation Prepared: Teachers for the 21st Century, 8, 22
Action teams, 201
Adult learning, 174–176, 179–180
Apprenticeship, model, 31, 143; reshaping of, 210–213

Case studies, 147–148, 163–164; and reflective activity, 162–164
Collaborative relationships, 21–22, 54–57; and collegial relations, 26–28; and decision making, 23–27; in professional development schools, 146; models of, 63; principal's role in, 62–65
Collegial Preparation Program, 202
Collegiality, and expertise, 165–166; in school-university partnerships, 150–151; relationships, 200–201; stages of, 28–31; study groups, 103–104; support system, 137; and supervision, 152–153
Community building, 68–71
Consultants, role of, 107
Cross-role teams, 197–198
Curriculum, adapting materials, 186–187; development of, 60–62; inquiry about, 148; leadership teams, 57–58; teacher-proof, 11–12

Edison Project, 11
Education Week, 11

Flat schools, organization, management, 206–207

Glendale Unified School District, 201

Journal writing, 84–85, 118, 129. *See also* Teacher research.

Learning Collaborative Networks, 174
Los Angeles County Office of Education, 196
Los Angeles Times, 200
Los Angeles Unified School District, 174, 176

Master teachers, collegial conferences, 153; roles and responsibilities, 152–153, 214–216; traditional supervision versus collegial, 152
Mentoring, 151–152, 218–219
Methods class, 213–214. *See also* Teachers, Teacher-leaders, Teacher professionalism.

Networking, 199–200; and study groups, 160–162; with other teachers, 191–192

Parent-Teachers Association, 196
Peer coaching, 164–165; coaching process, 201–203; principal-to-principal, 203
Principals, changing roles and relationships, 205; community building, 72–73; leadership styles, 47–50; perception of change,

102–103; role, 62–65, 67–68, 106–107, 207–208; study groups and, 91

Professional Development Schools, 142–143; characteristics of, 144–146; purpose of, 9

Project LEARN (Los Angeles Education Alliance for Restructuring Now), 200

Reflection, and case study, 162–164; and classroom change, 80; critical approach to, 147; inhibitors to, 77–78; and journal writing, 84; and professional reading, 85, 93–96; and teacher education, 141; about teaching, 147

Restructuring movement, 153–159. *See also* School.

School, bureaucratic, 38–40; improvement, 65–67; management of, 12–13, 206–207; organizational problems, 24; reform, 80; restructuring, 35–40

School-university partnerships, 143; teacher decision making, 150; teacher-leader in, 146. *See also* Collegiality.

Staff development, defined, 173; 204–205

Study groups, and classroom practice, 97–98; group sessions, 84, 160–162; participation in, 86–87; and problems, 92–93; professional reading, 85; and staff development, 108–109; and students, 99–100

Teacher, accountability of, 45–46; as inservice leader, 183; as technician, 78; autonomy, 14; changing roles and relationships, 205, 208; credentialing, 13; decision making, 40–43; evaluation of, 43–44; historical perceptions of, 11; inservice of, 177–188; knowledge base,

213–214; learning from others, 87–88; new teacher preparation, 209–210; professional development, 177–178; social norms, 88–90; support systems, 137; sustaining beginning teachers, 217–219

Teacher center, 165–166

Teacher-leaders, defined, 7; habits and styles, 47–50; inservice and, 176, 183; roles, 7–8, 205–206, 208, 214–216

Teacher professionalism, autonomy, 14; inhibitors of, 10–14, 42; knowledge, 213–214; learning from other teachers, 87–88; new teachers, 209–210; process of, 18–22, 209–210; reading and, 85, 93–96, 105; signs of, 22; traditional models, 79–80

Teaching, change in beliefs, 101; change in classroom practice, 97–99; critiquing practice, 92–93, 216–217; exemplary practice, 154–159; expertise in, 195–198; inquiry and reflection, 159–160; learning and, 217; networking and, 160–162, 191–192; research on, 12; study groups about, 160–162

Teacher research, 119, anecdotal records, 126; children's work, 123–126; defined, 119–120; descriptive/interpretive, 133–134; designing study, 131–135; dissemination of, 135, 137; generating questions, 131; informal assessment, 128; interviews and questionnaires, 121–122; journals, 84–85, 118, 129–131

Time, 41, 56, 120, 136, 166–168

Tomorrow's Schools, 8, 9, 22

University of California at Los Angeles, 200

University of Southern California, 202, 203, 213